Excursions and Recursions Through Power, Privilege, and Praxis

A Volume in
The Curriculum and Pedagogy Series

Series Editors:
The Curriculum and Pedagogy Group

The Curriculum and Pedagogy Series

The Curriculum and Pedagogy Group, Editors

*Surveying Borders, Boundaries, and Contested Spaces
in Curriculum and Pedagogy* (2011)
edited by Cole Reilly, Victoria Russell,
Laurel K. Chehayl, and Morna M. McDermott

Excursions and Recursions Through Power, Privilege, and Praxis (2012)
edited by Brandon Sams, Jennifer Job, and James C. Jupp

Excursions and Recursions Through Power, Privilege, and Praxis

Edited by

Brandon Sams
Auburn University

Jennifer Job
The University of North Carolina at Chapel Hill

and

James C. Jupp
Georgia Southern University

Information Age Publishing, Inc.
Charlotte, North Carolina • www.infoagepub.com

Library of Congress Cataloging-in-Publication Data

Excursions and recursions through power, privilege, and praxis / edited by

Brandon Sams, Jennifer Job, and James C. Jupp.
    p. cm. — (The curriculum and pedagogy series)
    Includes bibliographical references.
    ISBN 978-1-61735-980-4 (paperback) — ISBN 978-1-61735-981-1 (hardcover) —
ISBN 978-1-61735-982-8 (e-book) 1. Education—Curricula—Social
aspects—United States. 2. Curriculum change—United States. 3. Critical
pedagogy—United States. I. Sams, Brandon. II. Job, Jennifer. III. Jupp,
James C.
    LC191.4.E93 2012
    370.11'5—dc23

                                                            2012027935

Printed in the United States of America

CONTENTS

Acknowledgments . . . . *ix*

The James T. Sears Award . . . . *xiii*

Foreword: Fast Swirling in the Middle Within
a Culture of Cruelty
  William M. Reynolds . . . . *xv*

Introduction: Traveling Together
  Brandon Sams . . . . *xxi*

EXCURSIONS

Introduction by Jennifer Job *1*

1. Learning in Discomfort
   Polly F. Attwood *5*

2. Browning Beyond Debate: Mapping an Excursion
   Through Power, Privilege, and Praxis
   Cole Reilly and Zahra Murad *9*

3. Perdida/Lost: Self-Reflections in Nepantla as Voice Emerges
   Elva Reza-López *27*

4. Getting Lost in Life/Death Disruptions:
   Reclaiming the Right of a Legal Space
   Miryam Espinosa-Dulanto *35*

5. Becoming ELL Teachers: The Learning Trajectory of Two
Preservice Teachers and Their Implications for Teacher
Education Curriculum
Bridget A. Bunten 47

6. Restless and Lost in Curriculum and Pedagogy:
Excursions and Interventions
Jennifer L. Milam 65

RECURSIONS

Introduction by James C. Jupp 73

PART I:
RE/TURNING TO HISTORY

7. "Hopefully They Will See You in a Different Light":
A Critical Race Analysis of Double Consciousness
Raygine DiAquoi 81

8. The Nested Nature of M/Othering:
Complicating Curriculum Conversations
Boni Wozolek 97

9. (Re)Righting the Script: Speaking Back to Public
Curriculum to Secure a More Humanizing Citizenship for
African American Women and Girls
Monique Cherry-McDaniel 115

10. Vision, Practice, Reflection: The Influence of Four Women
on Progressive Education
Elinor A. Scheirer 131

PART II:
RE/TURNING TO PRAXIS

11. Purple Crayons, Wild Things, and Dots: Getting Lost
in Children's Literature and Curriculum
Chris Loeffler 145

12. Troubling Teaching: Learning From Social Media
Susan L. M. Bartow 163

13. Receptive Praxis
Laura Rychly 179

14. Agency and Choice in Two Second-Grade Classrooms
   Katrina F. Cook *191*

About the Editors *209*

About the Contributors *211*

ACKNOWLEDGMENTS

> On this road
> on which I do not know how to ask for bread,
> on which I do not know how to ask for water,
> ...
> I long for the mantle
> of the great wanderers, who lighted
> their steps by the lamp
> of pure hunger and pure thirst,
>
> and whichever way they lurched was the way.
>
> —Galway Kinnell, "The Shoes of Wandering"
> (1971, lines 95-97, 103-107)

Compiling and shaping this volume would not have been possible without the generosity and guidance of others—without them we might have been permanently and irrevocably lost. First, we would like to thank the Curriculum and Pedagogy (C&P) Governing Council for giving us the opportunity to do this work. The annual C&P conference is a remarkable gathering of passionate, diverse, and committed educators, activists, and scholars, and we have been honored to gather a moment of this work in one volume. We are especially indebted to the inspirational call of "getting lost in curriculum studies" and the exceptional work produced from the Browning Caucus; many of these papers would not have been possible without you. Every present also has a history that makes it possible, so we want to thank C&P founders Jim Sears, Kathleen Kesson, Jim Henderson, Louise Allen, Patrick Slattery, Susan Edgerton, Kris Sloan, and Tom Kelly. Your vision of creative, compassionate, critical, reflective work has made possible this present and, we hope, many possible, unanticipated futures.

Excursions and Recursions Through Power, Privilege, and Praxis
pp. ix–xi
Copyright © 2012 by Information Age Publishing
All rights of reproduction in any form reserved.

We were able, through the C&P community and our various networks, to gather generous and insightful reviewers—including teachers, graduate students, faculty, and community activists—to contribute their diverse perspectives on curriculum and pedagogy to the authors of this volume. We owe a special thanks to Polly Attwood, Corliss Brown, Colleen Patton, Boni Wozolek, Zahra Murad, Jessica Powell, Jim Kilbane, Allison Kootsikas, Kris Sloan, Scott Morrison, Erik Malewski, Beth Bilek-Golias, Virginia Taylor, David Brooks, Jason Wallin, Jennie Stearns, Jake Burdick, Laura Jewett, Betsy Reyes, Rob Helfenbein, Kirsten Edwards, Bill Reynolds, Sean Fretwell, Philip Bernhardt, Laura Rychly, Jennifer Snow, Bev Schieman, Teresa Young, Melissa Rivers, Antonio Garcia, Jamie Lathan, Kelly Waldrop, Julie Garlen Maudlin, Beth Pollock, Miryam Espinosa-Dulanto, Morna McDermott, Deb Freedman, Jennifer Milam, Jeremy Hilburn, Liz Hallmark, Meredith Sinclair, Karla Martin, Kevin Talbert, Cole Reilly, Cary Gillenwater, Zan Crowder, Bridget Bunten, Jenny Sandlin, Debbie Randolph, Robert Lake, Gabe Huddleston, Sharon Peck, Kelly Vaughan, Chris Osmond, Billye Rhodes, Ben Blaisedell, Ana Luisa Munoz Garcia, Chandi Desai, Lara Willox, and Julie Keane. We hope you have benefited half as much from your involvement in this project as we have from yours.

We owe particular gratitude to Morna McDermott and Jim Kilbane, chairs of the publications committee, for Skype conversations and your (always generous) response to our emails about the logistics of putting this book together. Thank you. George Johnson at Information Age Publishing was also endlessly helpful. He and his team graciously answered our questions about copyright permissions, book cover design, and other logistics of book production. George ensured that every piece was as the authors envisioned it. Finally, a special thanks goes to Cole Reilly who, along with Victoria Russell, Laurel Chehayl, and Morna McDermott, edited the first volume in *The Curriculum and Pedagogy Series* with Information Age Publishing. Via email, phone, and Skype, he has mentored our team throughout the moments of book production.

To our authors, you have taken up the theme of "getting lost" in wonderfully rich and surprising ways. Thank you for being flexible with revisions, formatting, and paperwork. Most of all, your work and vision has allowed us, as editors and readers, to "get lost" with you and, in the journey of losing and finding our way, locate new questions for ourselves to pursue and live through. We also owe a special debt of gratitude to the author of our Foreword, William Reynolds, whose work considers the current culture of cruelty and ressentiment in education and public life. Getting lost in the overrun of cruelty demands that we read and live tactically, in the "in-between," and pursue "lines of flight" that might invite a different, more just and loving, future. Reynolds asks that, in such a moment of "fast swirling," of being overrun with antiintellectualism, hate, racism, and bottom-lines, that we live, read, think, and write against the grain, with courage, creativity, and solidarity. We are excited to see all of these pieces in print so that others may read their way into the questions, possibilities, and complicated conversations you present in the coming pages.

Finally, as editors we want to acknowledge each other. This was a collaborative—even col*labor*ative—project that required generosity and demanded sustained attention to both broad visions and the smallest details. We have leaned on each other, sometimes lightly, other times heavily, for this work to become.

—Brandon, Jennifer, and Jim

REFERENCES

Kinnell, G. (1971). *The book of nightmares*. Boston, MA: Houghton Mifflin.

THE JAMES T. SEARS AWARD

The annual James T. Sears Award began with papers submitted for the 2004 Curriculum and Pedagogy Conference. Now in its eighth year, the award is presented to the author(s) of an outstanding paper or multimedia presentation presented for the first time at the conference and selected for inclusion in this edited collection. The primary author of the winning paper or presentation must be a graduate student in the field of education or a school or community-based practitioner/scholar. The award consists of three features: inclusion, with recognition, in the edited collection, a plaque recognizing the recipient(s), and a small cash award. Additionally, a paper judged to be of outstanding quality and contribution will also be recognized with a distinction of "honorable mention" in the edited collection and again at the Curriculum and Pedagogy Conference the following year.

The selected work will reflect the spirit of "soulful" curriculum scholarship, as evidenced in James T. Sears' lifelong commitments to curriculum scholarship and engaged action embodied in his valuing multiple, diverse communities, his cogent critique of dominant norms, and his pursuit of social justice for all. Each year, the award winner is selected by the fellowship and awards committee of the Curriculum and Pedagogy Governing Council upon recommendation by the editing team of this collection.

We are honored to present the 2012 James T. Sears award to Boni Wozolek, a doctoral student at Kent State University. Boni's essay, "The Nested Nature of M/Othering: Complicating Curriculum Conversations," is a sophisticated answer to the conference call, both in creating an excursive path to follow in understanding the problematic tensions of holding the positions of both mother and academic, but also in expressing the powers and shackles of navigating both positions as a woman of color. Her paper frames the nurturing act of breastfeeding as a subversive curriculum, challenging the preconceptions of others in her community of how she is supposed to respond to her child's needs. Boni's essay echoes with the voices of those women who have complicated such conversations before—Grumet, Noddings, Miller—while still striking out new territory with a strong and artful voice of her own. The story she weaves into her theory is singularly her own, and yet we find ourselves forming community within it.

We are also pleased to distinguish with honorable mention the work of Raygine DiAquoi, a doctoral student at Harvard University. Her essay, "'Hopefully they will see you in a Different Light': A Critical Race Analysis of Double Consciousness," uses generational counterstorytelling, critical race theory, and W.E.B Du Bois's concept of double consciousness to critique notions of a postracial society. Her mother's wise counsel and stories about the past help Raygine and the reader understand the harm caused by colorblind, postracial ideologies that are still too much with us. In returning to the through-line of history, Raygine's work shows how stories that move from body to body, that carry the past forward, can help us understand the present and imagine a line of flight for a different future.

We congratulate Boni and Raygine for their contribution to the work and vision of the Curriculum and Pedagogy Group.

—Brandon, Jennifer, and Jim

FOREWORD

Fast Swirling in the Middle
Within a Culture of Cruelty

William M. Reynolds
Georgia Southern University

What's going on in education around the world is part of what I often times called a recovery movement. A recovery of dominant power; whether it be colonial power with new forms of colonialism; whether it be gendered power with new forms of patriarchy; racial power with new forms of the recovery of White supremacy; whether it be class power with new forms of class elitism and of global Empire that exist and unfortunately no matter where go now, Education plays the role of helping to support that empirical behemoth. (Kincheloe, 2007)

What I mean is that every form of repression today, and there are multiple, is easily totalized, systematized from the point of view of power: the racist repression against immigrants, the repression in factories, the repression in schools and teaching, and the repression of youth in general. (Deleuze, de Lapouja, & Taormina, 2004, p. 210)

FAST SPINNING AND THE IN-BETWEEN

I will admit it. I am a political junkie, constantly reading political postings on *Truthout, Salon.com, The Huffington Post, In These Times, The Nation, MSNBC, NPR* and of course *Facebook*. These readings are not comforting. Many times I wonder which problem needs immediate contemplation

Excursions and Recursions Through Power, Privilege, and Praxis
pp. xv–xx
Copyright © 2012 by Information Age Publishing

and action, and then that dilemma leads me off on another path attempting to read as much as I can about those issues, and then another problem
arises, and I run to that issue and start the process all over again (many
times never getting back to the original issue I was thinking about in the
first place). There it is—swirling in the middle or as many write about in
this volume, a sense of being lost. As Julie Webber and I claimed, working
from one of Jacques Daignault essays (Reynolds & Webber, 2004), this is
fast swirling[1] in the middle, or as Deleuze discussed it, the "in-between."
Working from the in-between as we claimed can be productive of positive
"lines of flight." Perhaps, these middle or lost places can provide us with a
creative potential (lines of flight) to imagine differently, write tactically,
strategically and act. I do not want to suggest what curriculum studies,
educational research, cultural studies, critical pedagogy should be. Those
debates will, no doubt, continue. As Webber and I discussed, there needs
to be a multiplicity of lines of flight research (recursions and excursions).
"The 'struggle' is to keep on finding lines of flight that disrupt, overturn
and tactically weave through the global corporate order" (Reynolds &
Webber, in press).[2] We suggested then that the work was tactical, but as
the times and circumstances have become more cruel and constraining,
there is a necessity for tactical and strategic struggle as well. Of course, we
have witnessed this strategic struggle globally not only with the Occupy
movement but the global protests of students from Montreal to Paris.

EDUCATION AND THE BOTTOM LINE

Oftentimes at this historical moment, I believe, I am witnessing this cruelty in the dismantling of the thing I love—education. I dwell these days
in disbelief and anger. As Peter McLaren's (2006) book title so aptly states,
I am filled with rage and hope. The United States is engaging successfully
in moving public education with standardized curriculum, standardized
tests, standardized lesson plans, and standardized objectives to a place in
which the schools develop at best into heartless training camps for the
global corporate economy and at their worst training camps for incarcera-
tion, particularly for youth of color. "Conservative policies have systematically disinvested in public schools, turning them largely into dull testing
centers for middle-class students and warehousing units and surveillance
centers for working-class and poor youth of color" (Giroux, 2009, p. 14).
This is done all in the name of some type of continual monitoring in the
name of accountability that wallows in its praise of high scores on high
stakes tests of which schools and teachers can be judged as being successes
or failures. "Accountability is the face of fascism in America today" (Pinar,
2004, p. 163). Schools and universities have become insidious corpora-

tions whose grandiose goal is to make a profit—whether that profit manifests itself in public schools with increased funding because of high test scores or in the universities in increasing the number of student credit hours. Universities have shinning buildings, beautiful lawns and a soulless organization (Reynolds, in press). Deleuze warned us about the businessification of education.

> Even the state education system has been looking at the principle of "getting paid for results": in fact, just as businesses are replacing factories, *school* is being replaced by *continuing education* and exams by continuous assessment. It is the surest way of turning education into a business (Deleuze, 1995, p. 179, emphasis added).

American schooling dwells with apparent stubborn steadfastness to the bottom line business mentality. Of course, this is antiintellectual and dangerous. William Watkins discusses this bottom line.

> The testing movement, first embraced by behavioral psychologists around the time of World War I, has now become the tail that wags the dog. Bestowing life or death entitlement, the standardized test has become an instrument of social engineering. It is a killer of dreams for some and a ticket to the promised land for others. No civilized society should exclude and distribute people on the basis of tests. (Watkins, 2012, p. 190)

Deleuze in an interview with Michel Foucault discussed the devaluing of education, schools and intense surveillance and monitoring:

> It's not only prisoners who are treated like children, but children who are treated like prisoners. Children are subjected to an infantilization which is not their own. In this sense schools are a little like prisons, and factories are very much like them. All you have to do is look at Renault's entrance. Or anywhere: you need three vouchers to go to make pee-pee during the day. (Deleuze et al., 2004, p. 209)

THE CULTURE OF CRUELTY

The current historical conjuncture is a time of exceptional cruelty conjoined with a politics of ressentiment[3] and antiintellectualism (Pinar, 2012) within the United States and globally. Schell in *Cruel America* (2011) discusses the nature of this cruelty:

> There have been many signs recently that the United States has been traveling down a steepening path of cruelty. It's hard to say why such a thing is occurring, but it seems to have to do with a steadily growing faith in force as

the solution to almost any problem, whether at home or abroad. (Schell, 2011)

This "culture of cruelty" (Giroux, 2012) surrounds us not only in educational contexts, but in our daily lives as well. In schools cruelty and force predominate as children are regulated to marching in line, having silent lunch, participating in reduced recess time, being overprescribed medications, enduring zero tolerance policies, being put in handcuffs, and even shackled in courtrooms. In our daily lives we witness a politics of control and containment (which is part of cruelty and ressentiment) that punishes and controls difference and portrays the poor as lazy and as the cause of many of the economic problems that plague the global economy and particularly the economy of the United States. Not only the poor, but lesbian, gay, bisexual, and transgender populations, immigrants, women, and "liberals" are vilified as causes for all the problematic issues that we face. We witness this culture of cruelty daily. On November 9, 2011, at the University of California-Davis, students who were participating as part of the Occupy Wall Street protest were met with cruel and immediate punishment. The students were sitting on the ground in peaceful protest when they were confronted with police in riot gear. After not responding to a request to move, they were sprayed with extrastrength pepper spray. So, nonviolent resistance is met with force and cruelty. In the case of immigration, the state of Georgia's governor signed into law in May of 2011 one of the most restrictive pieces of legislation concerning immigration. Among other provisions "the law allows state and local police officers to request immigration documentation from criminal suspects and, if they do not receive it, to take the suspects to jail, where federal officials could begin the deportation process" (Brown, 2011, p. A12).

Profiling is also an example of cruelty and punishment. Recently, it was discovered that in 1965, Mitt Romney, the presumptive Republican candidate for President of the United States, hazed a student (John Lauber) whom he assumed was homosexual. The incidents, as reported by fellow students, started out by Romney's taunting of Lauber and his bleached blond hair that hung over one eye. It progressed until Romney had his fellow students hold Lauber down while Romney snipped at Lauber's hair with scissors. Ironically this story surfaced the same day that President Obama stated that he supported gay marriage. Despite the fact that the Romney incident happened in 1965, it is indicative of the attitudes in our society. Another in the continuing cases of cruelty and force is the now infamous case of the murder in Florida of 17-year-old Trayvon Martin. The shooting was justified by the legislation of "Stand Your Ground," which allows people who feel threatened to stand their ground and not retreat. Of course, this can be used to defend the use of guns for self-defense. It is legislation which falls in line with the culture of cruelty and punishment and in this case can be used in an attempt to justify shooting an unarmed 17-year-old.

So, not only are we swirling fast in the middle of our own conceptualizations and theoretical conundrums, but the world around us is swirling in cruelty and punishment.

RUNNING

I have raised all of these issues not as words wrapped in hopelessness, but as necessary considerations for all of us concerned with curriculum studies, the state not only of our schools, but the fate of democracy, dissent and the progress toward social justice. As I sit here in my study writing this on my fairly new laptop in comfortable air conditioning, listening to music from the stereo, I am constantly aware of my privileged position as a White, male academic. I can comfortably write of these things because I do not have to struggle for my next meal or for the basic necessities of survival. Nor am I faced with restrictive legislation, whether it restricts marriage or enforces cruel immigration policies or allows for a violent response to perceived threats (and on and on).

> Thus, a life of dissent requires us to expel the success myths of capital that pollute the ivy-covered halls of academia and to reject the warped and distorted privileges of power, preserved and doled out to the obedient servants of the empire. And as such, dissident voices reject the incarcerations of our minds and bodies, by the neat and orderly colonizing rationale that conserves the hegemonic order. True to this commitment, radical dissidents rail against the most underhanded crime against humanity—namely, sentencing the majority of the world's population to a life of wretched poverty and dependence and then blaming them collectively for the "moral ineptitude" or "cultural deficiency." (Darder, 2011, p. 5)

As curriculum scholars, educators, and activists, we are, indeed, living a life of dissent. And, at times we are fast swirling in our individual middles, as we run out, on, back and again, and we remember that these in-betweens can be productive of positive lines of flight. But, let us not forget that at some points we must also learn to run together.

NOTES

1. This is a concept originally discussed by Jacques Diagnault (1992, p. 204).

2.   See Jason Wallin's text *A Deleuzian Approach to Curriculum: Essay on Pedagogical Life* (2010) for an excellent and multifaceted discussion of lines of flight.
3.   See Reynolds and Webber (2009, pp. 19-21).

REFERENCES

Brown, R. (2011, May 13). Georgia gives police added power to seek out illegal immigrants. *The New York Times*. p. A12.

Daignault, J. (1992). Traces at work from different places. In W. F. Pinar & W. M. Reynolds (Eds.), *Understanding curriculum as a phenomenological and deconstructed text* (pp. 195-215). New York, NY: Teacher College Press.

Darder, A. (2011). *A dissident voice: Essays on culture, pedagogy, and power.* New York, NY: Peter Lang.

Deleuze, G. (1995). *Negotiations 1972-1990* (M. Joughin, Trans.). New York, NY: Columbia University Press.

Deleuze, G., de Lapouja, D., & Taormina, M. (2004). *Desert islands.* Los Angeles, CA: Semiotext(e).

Giroux, H. A. (2009). *Youth in a suspect society: Democracy or disposability?* New York, NY: Palgrave Macmillan.

Giroux, H. A. (2012, April). *Youth in revolt: Coming of age in an era of savage inequality.* Keynote presentation at the inaugural International Youth Studies Congress, The University of Calgary, Calgary, Alberta, CA.

Kincheloe, J. (2007). *Address for the Paulo Freire and Nita Freire International Project for Critical Pedagogy.* Address presented at the 150th Anniversary of the Faculty of Education at McGill University, Montreal, Quebec, Canada.

McLaren, P. (Ed.) (2006). *Rage and hope: Interviews with Peter McLaren on war, imperialism and critical pedagogy.* New York, NY: Peter Lang.

Pinar, W. F. (2004). *What is curriculum theory?* New York, NY: Erlbaum.

Pinar, W. F. (2012). *What is curriculum theory?* (2nd ed.). New York, NY: Routledge.

Reynolds, W. M. (in press). Iron man nation: Militainment and democratic possibilities. In A. Abdi & P. R. Carr (Eds.), *Educating for democratic consciousness: Counter-hegemonic possibilities.* New York, NY: Peter Lang.

Reynolds, W. M., & Webber, J. A. (Eds.). (2004). *Expanding curriculum theory: Dis/positions and lines of flight.* New York, NY: Erlbaum.

Reynolds, W. M., & Webber, J. A. (2009). *The civic gospel: A political cartography of Christianity.* New York, NY: Sense.

Reynolds, W. M., & Webber, J. A. (Eds.). (in press). *Expanding curriculum theory: Dis/positions and lines of flight* (2nd ed.). New York: Routledge.

Schell, J. (2011, September). Cruel America. Retrieved from http://www.thenation/print/article/163690/cruel-america.

Wallin, J. J. (2010). *A Deleuzian approach to curriculum: Essays on a pedagogical life.* New York, NY: Palgrave.

Watkins, W. H. (2012). *The assault on public education: Confronting the politics of corporate school reform.* New York: Teachers College Press.

INTRODUCTION

Traveling Together

Brandon Sams
Auburn University

And I walk out now,
in dead shoes, in the new light,
on the steppingstones
of someone else's wandering,
a twinge
in this foot or that saying
turn or *stay* or *take*
forty-three giant steps
backwards, frightened
I may already have lost
the way: *the first step*, the Crone
who scried the crystal said, *shall be*
to lose the way.

—Galway Kinnell, "The Shoes of Wandering"
(1971, lines 9-21)

Journeying.

Wandering.

Losing and finding one's way.

Excursions and Recursions Through Power, Privilege, and Praxis
pp. xxi–xxvi

Other editing teams can probably attest to the journey that is making a conference collection. Ours has been at various times rewarding, arduous, satisfying, and surprising. At the time of this writing (and nearing the end of one milestone of this journey), I write through profound thankfulness. The editors have indeed "traveled together" to make this volume possible, contributing equally our various interests and talents to this project. The contributors have, I imagine, experienced a sense of journey as well, writing (their texts), responding (to the requests of reviewers and editors), reading (more texts to write), writing. We imagine, too, that readers of this volume will have opportunity to journey into and with the texts gathered here; the creative process, thus, does not end with the author's pen, but is re/engaged with each reading.

> I want the forest before the book, the abundance of leaves before the pages, I love the creation as much as the created, no, more.... Acts of birth, potency, and impotency mingled are what I'm passionate about. The to-be-in-the-process of writing or drawing. (Cixous, 1993, p. 91)

The 2011 Curriculum and Pedagogy (C&P) conference, following the work of Patti Lather (2007), invited participants to get lost in the limits, refuse a desire to know in favor of finding "what goes beyond what we know" about curriculum and pedagogy (p. 13). Getting lost, Lather argues, is a way of living with/in risk, anxiety, and tension. C&P hoped that such an invitation to be with and write through risk, anxiety, and tension would offer us, as a group and individually, an opportunity to challenge "entrenched" beliefs about education, social justice, what it means to theorize about and/or practice curriculum and pedagogy.

Following the conference our editing team wondered how to invite the lost; the wanderer; the unexpected, im/possible questions about education and curriculum studies. In our wondering, we asked, "what are the productive possibilities of lostness, risk and tension in the curriculum field and in sites of curriculum, schools, and, more largely, public life?" In reading and wandering through different texts, we stumbled upon interesting etymological ties between excursion (which, to us, connoted adventure, lostness, journeying, risk, possibility) and *currere*, the running of the course, a keystone method of the reconceptualist curriculum tradition (Pinar & Grumet, 1976).

Echoing the method of *currere* and in trying to invite work taking up the theme of wandering, risky, restless curriculum and pedagogy, we envisioned a book representing two intertwining themes: Excursions and Recursions.

Excursions (ex-*currere*)—to run out

With the theme of excursions, we wanted to collect creative scholarship and conference reflections dwelling with/in the difficult and promising spaces of getting lost in curriculum theory. We recognized that "getting lost" was not "starting over"—as there are purposes and values that the C&P community remained committed to, including democracy and social justice. The recent C&P town hall meetings and the recommendations of the Browning Caucus had foregrounded social justice, structural and racial inequalities, and political activism as focal sites for the C&P community. At the 2011 meeting, members of the Browning Caucus raised concerns about C&P's commitment to challenging (white) privilege and power within its own organizational structures and, more largely, within curriculum studies. Two papers in this section (Attwood; Reilly & Murad) reflect on how C&P needs to respond to these challenges. As a group, excursions offer readers an opportunity to "get lost" in complex and contested conversations along the lines of structural and racial inequalities, identity, mothering, and epistemology as these topics relate to society, schools, and curriculum. As Jennifer Job suggests in her introduction to Excursions, these complex, uneasy and contested conversations create important illuminations, "paths of light," for others to recognize (even confront), learn from and build upon. The papers in this section offer various openings into these areas of curricular and pedagogical life, with the hope that, in time, these passages of rupture and discomfort might renew and re/focus our individual and collective commitments to democracy, education and social justice.

Recursions (re-*currere*)—to return, to run back, to run again

With the theme of recursions, we envisioned creative scholarship and conference reflections re/turning the field and readers to our practices of working with administrators, professionals, preservice teachers, students in schools, and public pedagogy. By returning to teaching practices, we hoped to engage dispositions that revitalized public focus on teaching and learning in and outside of all types of classrooms.

As we imagined might happen, the response to the idea of recursions was in excess of the call. The authors in this section have "turned"—focused—their attention on curriculum and pedagogy through two through-lines, *history* and *praxis*, the latter focused especially on K-16 schooling. As James Jupp explains in his introduction to Recursions, these through-lines are often neglected in reconceptualized curriculum studies. The papers in this section, perhaps appropriately, find and reengage modes of thinking and action lost or underemphasized in the field. They also trouble any easy distinction one might make between getting lost (excursions) and *returning home* as a certain, safe, always predictable arrival. *Currere*, as described by Pinar and Grumet (1976) and as taken up by the authors in this volume, is a never-ending journey/story of understanding self, world and their interrelation. *Currere* is performative, open-ended, taking up the past (remembering through regression) and present (through analysis) to imagine a not-yet future. In keeping with the performative spirit of *currere*, recursion carries with it a double movement of arrival (running back) and going out again (running again). The collected papers in this section, through re/turning to, focusing our attention on, history and praxis making in classrooms, invite us to be, think and do (go out again) otherwise.

> Is it the foot,
> which rubs the cobblestones
> and snakestones all its days, this lowliest
> of tongues, whose lick-tracks tell
> our history of errors to the dust behind,
> which is the last trace in us
> of wings?
>
> And is it
> the hen's nightmare, or her secret dream,
> to scratch the ground forever
> eating the minutes out of the grains of sand?
>
> —Galway Kinnell, "The Shoes of Wandering"
> (1971, lines 84-94)

As I write, I keep thinking about Kinnell, the hen, and the foot. Part of "getting lost" is being immersed in the territory; lacking a transcendent optic, perhaps, yet working through the abundance of presence demands from the walker, the wandering, an improvisational pedagogy. Our presence on the ground, our immersion in the territory, and the creative potential it offers—for theorizing and for praxis—stands in stark contrast to what Jardine (1992) 20 years ago identified as the technical-rational-scientific approach to inquiry in education and curriculum making. In this scheme, truth is method and knowledge the bits of information, sequenced objectives, the regurgitated facts of history, literature, and science. In a drive for mastery, everything is turned "inside-out" until it delivers its secret (p. 118). Such an approach (to research, curriculum development, and teaching) suppresses the fecundity and mystery of classrooms, pedagogical moments, even life. These methods, for Jardine, are "essentially *informative* … designed to pass on information that is already understood" (p. 117). Such a reproduction renders invisible the particularities of the places, times and bodies that (per)form every curriculum encounter. Who could say that things have gotten better?

Ironically, the climax of this tale, Jardine argues (and this perspective is now prescient), is the end of inquiry, a kind of twisted perfection that "[pins] down the life of the developing child in such a way that, in the end, nothing more will need to be said" (p. 117). Against this tale of "foreclosure," where the wor(l)d "no longer lives," the task for curriculum workers is to return to the "original difficulty" of life concealed by technical-scientific discourse (pp. 118-119). In many ways, the papers of this collection keep teaching, learning, curriculum an open question that invites a future.

My friend Andrew is writing a novel. One of his characters is charged by his father to write an Aesop's fable, which slowly becomes an existential, in addition to a literary, task. When he finally gets his fable right, he refuses to put the moral in—he refuses to close the task with a perfect ending. If he puts the moral in, he's afraid of never acting on it in real life. The story becomes too perfect, too closed, to leak. I find in this personal example a heartening notion of ending without closure—especially timely given the "nightmare that is the present" as Pinar (2004) describes it, part of which we should read as the closure of curriculum spaces that are overwritten by (common) standards, more frequent testing, less trust in teachers as public intellectuals (p. 4). What if curriculum writers/workers envisioned curriculum texts—theoretical and practical—that were open enough to invite re/reading, surprise, the unexpected guest of meaning. What does it mean to leave a hole in writing, in teaching? What does it mean to write, read or teach through such openings? Is this, are these, the *passages* through which ones loses and finds? The spirit of this collection takes up this question by writing through invitation—inviting the gifts that reading, the unknown, otherness might bring—by not closing down meaning through textual form or through advocating best, perfect, practices. In our journeying, our wondering/wandering in their texts, we can hopefully find the openings to read ourselves and so think, be, write and teach differently. These pages, I think, provide passages for us to enter and travel together.

REFERENCES

Cixous, H. (1993). Without end no state of drawingness no, rather: The executioner's taking off. *New Literary History, 24*(1), 91-103.

Jardine, D. (1992). Reflections on education, hermeneutics, and ambiguity: Hermeneutics as a restoring of life to its original difficulty. In W. F. Pinar &

W. M. Reynolds (Eds.), *Understanding curriculum and phenomenological and deconstructed text* (pp. 116-127). New York, NY: Teachers College Press.

Kinnell, G. (1971). *The book of nightmares* (pp. 17-24). New York, NY: Houghton Mifflin.

Lather, P. (2007). *Getting lost: Feminist efforts toward a double(d) science.* Albany, NY: SUNY Press.

Pinar, W. (2004). *What is curriculum theory?* Mahwah, NJ: Erlbaum.

Pinar, W., & Grumet, M. (1976). *Toward a poor curriculum.* Dubuque, IA: Kendall Hunt.

EXCURSIONS

Introduction

Jennifer Job
University of North Carolina at Chapel Hill

The desire to "get lost" can offer an enticing pull away from our lives, especially when faced with ongoing difficulties, day-to-day distractions, and the contradictions that make up our world. Who among us has not felt the desire to wander away with no destination in mind? And yet, it would be too simple to describe what has been done in this section as just "getting lost." The original 2011 conference call, drawn from Patti Lather's (2007) description in *Getting Lost: Feminist Efforts Toward a Double(d) Science*, asked us to "get lost in the limits, refuse a desire to know in favor of finding what goes beyond what we know." The Curriculum and Pedagogy Group did not just offer us an opening, but rather gave us a charge—that of finding "alternate possibilities, new understandings, and a rethinking of entrenched beliefs concerning social justice, curricular theorizing and practices, and pedagogical practices." Such a charge should not be reduced in metaphor to merely wandering off into the woods (the vision that first came to mind when I thought of "getting lost"), but rather a purposeful expedition, charting into the unknown.

The word "charting" is one that I return to often in my consideration of this expedition. To begin a journey, even one with no known destination (as *getting lost* implies), a charted point of beginning must exist. However, the chapters within this section reject the idea that the beginning

Excursions and Recursions Through Power, Privilege, and Praxis
pp. 1–4

point is the same for any of us. How can we envision such trajectories with so many different points of entry? To help answer that question, I look to William Pinar's (2007) exploration of the notions of verticality and horizontality in the discipline of curriculum studies. Verticality to Pinar expresses the intellectual history of the discipline—how ideas were formed and threaded throughout the study of curriculum. Horizontality refers to the context of the discipline as it stands at this moment—the culture, the politics, the standards, the influences surrounding the matter of schooling in today's world. Where we enter this work, our point of striking out, is somewhere in the spaces of both verticality and horizontality. But what connects us to such ends?

I imagine the work that has been previously done in curriculum and pedagogy mapped as filling spaces in the sphere of all such studies past and future. The x axis represents horizontality, the y axis verticality. The z axis is the necessary creation of the three-dimensionality of our imaginative world, that of all possibility of all intellectual work. There are spaces that are enlightened, and those that are dark—Lather's "unknown" and the unstressed boundaries. The work that curriculum and pedagogy scholars do, the work that is within these pages, spreads to enlighten those darkened spaces, reaching into the crevices and corners that were before ignored, misunderstood, avoided. As the spaces are filled, the trajectories of these scholars' works form paths of light that chart the ways for others to follow and jump off in their own right. These overlaps and fractals (which inspired our image choice for the cover of the book) create what Pinar (2007) refers to as planetarity, our work, constantly growing and illuminating and changing shape to redefine our discipline and how we view education.

However, we can never escape our histories as these trajectories of light are charted. Often the work we do is the work of identifying those histories, of not staying on the vertical axis as it is written but recharting its path as we incorporate the knowledges of others who had before been kept silent. Mary Hanley (2011) warns us against the dangers of resisting *sankofa* (learning from the past), of becoming "those who resist acknowledging how the past lives in the present, and who are arrogant enough to think that their answers respond to all questions" (p. 7). As we do the work of getting lost, remembering our starting point, those who came before, the platform from which we stood—all offer us a place to return and thus give meaning in a context larger than ourselves. This is our charge as curriculum and pedagogy cartographers, providing charts to those who will look to *our work* as their histories soon enough.

Often (but not always!), trajectories into new dark spaces begin as resistance to the trajectories of light by those who came before. Much of the work of excursion in this section springs forth from such resistance. This

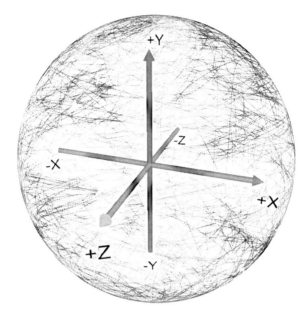

Figure 1.   Sphere of curriculum work.

work is uncomfortable, often painful, and thrusts us against the dark spaces—there is no time for timidly stepping onto the path, but rather, we are shoved into the unknown. This is the work represented in Polly Attwood's "Learning in Discomfort," which connects insights on discomfort, learning and power that emerged during a conference workshop to Curriculum and Pedagogy Group's commitment and struggle to challenge practices of privilege and power within its own conference and organization. Cole Reilly and Zahra Murad's "Browning Beyond Debate: Mapping an Excursion Through Power, Privilege, and Praxis" tackles a similar problem with methods that are purposely porous, investigating their own feelings upon leaving a contentious conference meeting to see what illuminations they may bring as well as inviting us into the conversation.

In reading the essays of this section as a group, where the excursions reach into the nether areas of what we thought we had known about curriculum and pedagogy, I am struck by a jolting juxtaposition of the term "charting" with another interpretation of the term "getting lost." I am reminded of days on the elementary school playground when I tried to join a group of girls playing kickball. The tallest of the group turned to me and said, "Get lost." Those two words, said with such animosity, expressed so much: "You're not welcome here." "You are different from us." "We don't understand you." And in many ways, the chapters of this section express their own stories of being told to "get lost." Elva Reza-López, in "Perdida/Lost: Self-Reflections in Nepantla as Voice Emerges," recounts the difficulties of being thought ignorant due to being Latina. Through poetry and currere, she constructs a voice that talks back and temporarily cuts through the confusion. In "Getting Lost in Life/Death Disruptions: Reclaiming the Right of a Legal Space," Miryam Espinosa-Dulanto expresses through poetry the legal invisibility of Maria as she travels, border crossing, from Mexico into the United States. Miryam's work raises questions about (be)longing, living on borderlines, and the potential of creative research to help outside readers (dis)connect to the lives and circumstances of others. Bridget Bunten's "Becoming ELL Teachers: The Learning Trajectory of Two Preservice Teachers and Their Implications for Teacher Education Curriculum" describes the learning journeys of two ELL teachers. Her work helps us see these journeys as replete with rupture, confusion, and the complex negotiation of what Bakhtin refers to as authoritative discourse and internally persuasive discourse. Jennifer Milam, in "Restless and Lost in Curriculum and Pedagogy: Excursions and Interventions," tries to find a place within the academy as she asks questions that continually remove her from it. She explores the fruitful connections between feminist mothering and reconceptualized curriculum work, framing wandering/wondering as a tactical site of resistance to reductive, patriarchal curriculum and pedagogical practice.

Yet in being told to "get lost" and then in following through with "getting lost" in charting their own paths, each of these authors leaves a trajectory, a blazing trail, that has left us more illuminated than before. These particular forms of "lost" bring forth awareness of many issues of social justice that were previously subsumed in the discussions of curriculum and pedagogy. They force us to face our own preconceived notions and perhaps lead us into our own wanderings to discover new purposes in our work. It is fitting that Jennifer Milam's chapter ends this section with an invitation to make our own excursions, as it gives us an opening to create our own trajectories of light now that we've read the work of others.

REFERENCES

Hanley, M. (2011). Resisting sankofa: Art-based educational research as counter-narrative. *Journal of Curriculum and Pedagogy, 8*(1), 4-13.

Lather, P. (2007). *Getting lost: Feminist efforts toward a double(d) science.* Albany, NY: SUNY Press.

Pinar, W. F. (2007). *Intellectual advancement through disciplinarity: Verticality and horizontality in curriculum studies.* Rotterdam, The Netherlands: Sense.

CHAPTER 1

LEARNING IN DISCOMFORT

Polly F. Attwood
Northeastern University

At the 2011 Curriculum and Pedagogy (C&P) conference, I facilitated a workshop that invited participants to explore challenges and possibilities for teaching in "pedagogies of discomfort" (Boler, 1999). Together we examined places in our teaching where we found ourselves lost in questions of whether, when and how discomfort, including emotions and moments of conflict, can be fruitful for learning. Early in the workshop, participants identified instances of discomfort that surfaced in their classrooms where students were examining questions of race, culture, power, and privilege.

One person spoke of a student's anger in an introductory curriculum theory course that examined questions of knowledge and power. An ensuing e-mail copied to an administrator called the course and this teacher "doctrinaire." The student protested that the teacher included mostly "left" voices in the syllabus and was not open to conservative views. The following semester another student confronted this teacher with a similar critique, though this time the student was more willing to engage in dialogue. The teacher found himself wrestling with a dismissive anger that seemed to mirror the students' "defensive anger" (Boler, 1999) that enabled them to delegitimize the course content. He also expressed feeling an initial powerlessness over the e-mail that positioned him as institutionally vulnerable.

Excursions and Recursions Through Power, Privilege, and Praxis
pp. 5–8

Another workshop participant spoke of preservice teachers' "nonreaction" to studying texts that presented alternatives to the traditional Columbus "discovering America" narrative. This teacher found it deeply unsettling when the students collectively agreed that such texts simply reflect another equally valid interpretation of a historical event, thus stopping all further inquiry. Frustrated by these students seeming nonreaction, or what James Baldwin calls "willful ignorance," she was at a loss with how to invite them into deeper examination of the social construction of historical knowledge.

Such learning asks students to examine fundamental assumptions not only about what they know but also how they know. Indeed, teaching "contested content" (Attwood, 2011) can "shatter students' worldviews" (Boler, 2004), if not their very sense of self. When values and identities are at stake, emotions arise (Jaggar, 1989) as an inevitable and necessary part of the intellectual work. These emotions can include defensive anger, fear of change, anxiety of losing personal and cultural identities; just as joy, passion, new hopes, and a sense of possibility may be part of this learning, too. Moreover, such emotions are more than personal responses. Their patterning points to a "politics of emotion" (Boler, 1999; Hochschild, 1983; Mohanty, 2004) in which emotions are understood to be socially, culturally, and historically constructed.

We explored the politics of emotion present in these incidents, especially in light of a teacher of color raising questions about the differing, and shifting, "vulnerable positions" (Acosta, Moore, Perry, & Edwards, 2005) for those teaching about questions of privilege and power. How does a teacher's social location at the intersections of race, class, gender, nation, sexuality, and ability/disability inform and shape that vulnerability? In the e-mail incident, the teacher experienced institutional vulnerability due to his graduate student status. How did being White and male factor into his ability to weather this protest? How would a teacher of color have chosen or needed to navigate this same terrain? Indeed, learning to navigate students' various responses to content that troubles their worldviews is both personal and political for students and teachers.

Learning to theorize discomfort, including the place of emotions and conflict, in learning and teaching is not new in the field of critical pedagogy (Boler, 1999; Fisher, 1987). Participants in the workshop found it useful to learn more about past and current practitioner scholars who have theorized the "emotional labor" (Jaggar, 1989), for students and teachers, that is inherent to intellectual inquiry that interrogates power and privilege. Often this terrain of "emotional investments by and large remain unexamined during our lifetimes, because they have been insidiously woven into the everyday fabric of common sense" (Boler, 1999, p. 181). Yet, when we do take up this "emotional labor," we explore for ways to invite students, and ourselves, to learn from interrogating various responses, rather than backing away from them. Such learning asks teachers to grapple with tensions between comfort and discomfort, risk and safety, and how not to confuse comfort with safety.

Moreover, when we find, and lose, ourselves in this terrain, we must keep in mind that the discomfort we may be feeling as teachers or students stems from the very issues of structural injustice and relations of power about which we are teaching or being asked to examine. Such discomfort is at once personal and political as it reflects our differing, and at times shifting, locations in larger systems of social power. And, thus, given the dynamic nature of relations of power, who is at risk in educational spaces that take up questions of power and privilege also can shift in/across different contexts of time and place. Both the teaching and the learning here is deeply challenging and invites us all to be compassionate with each other and ourselves. At the same time, we need to find ways to stay with the discomfort rather than invoke questions of safety in order to escape the discomfort that may in fact signal we are learning, or even moving toward some kind of change. When we confuse comfort and safety, our concern for others' discomfort and our own becomes little more than another way to protect privilege.

This is the very same work C&P has been trying to do in the last few years in town hall meetings focused on "Browning" and interrogating power and privilege at play within C&P's community structures, in its conference practices and in its efforts to challenge the field of curriculum theory and K-16 education. In the Friday town hall at this year's conference, our efforts to risk more truth telling about dynamics of race, privilege, and power within C&P surfaced stirring questions and strong feelings that pointed toward our own politics of emotion and put us in a "crisis" (Kumashiro, 2000), facing a juncture of danger and opportunity. On the closing Saturday morning, some of us sat in a circle and responded to two questions: What gifts do you bring to the work of interrogating and challenging privilege and power? How do you understand your commitment to this work? Speaking and listening around the circle, we leaned a little further into "pedagogies of dissent" (Mohanty, 2004), pedagogies in which trust arises from shared risk-taking in the work instead of demanding safety at its outset. Such a process invites everyone to embrace discomfort, even conflict, as inherent to learning that has the possibility of being transformative.

We will not meet again as a full community until November 2012. Inevitably, when we gather some of what we will do is become lost again as we try to find where we are, individually and collectively, in this work within and beyond C&P. I share the following questions I find myself living into as I look toward meeting again, and as I continue to understand, challenge, and even transform the emotional investments I bring to this work and how that learning can change how I learn, teach, and live:

- When does focusing on my discomfort take me to valuable insight and when is it a distraction that leads me astray?
- When, and why, do I insist on "being safe" as a White person?
- When am I actually unsafe vs. deeply discomforted?
- Who gets to be comfortable or safe in these conversations?
- What helps me sustain the discomfort long enough to learn from it?
- What forms, and patterns, do our individual and collective resistances, confusions, and times of feeling lost take?
- How can I stay curious, open to learning, and compassionate, rather than shut down, when faced with familiar patterns such as people of color are angry/White people are hurt or guilty?
- When is safety created together by staying with, and learning from, discomfort, as we take the risk of telling each other more truths?

REFERENCES

Acosta, K. M., Moore, H. A., Perry, G. K., & Edwards, C. (2005). Dialogue on diversity in teaching: Reflections on research, pedagogy, and passion for social justice. In N. Peters-Davis & J. Shultz (Eds.), *Challenges of multicultural education: Teaching and taking courses* (pp. 20-37). Boulder, CO: Paradigm.

Attwood, P. F. (2011) The power of collaboration: Learning to teach antiracist content. *Multicultural Perspectives, 13*(3), 122-129.

Boler, M. (1999). *Feeling power: Emotions and education*. New York, NY: Routledge.

Boler, M. (2004). Teaching for hope: The ethics of shattering world views. In D. Liston & J. Garrison (Eds.), *Teaching, learning, loving: Reclaiming passion in educational practice* (pp. 117-131). New York, NY: Routledge.

Fisher, B. (1987). The heart has its reasons: Feeling, thinking, and community-building in feminist education. *Women's Studies Quarterly, 15*(3-4), 47-58.

Hochschild, A. R. (1983). *The managed heart: The commercialization of human feeling*. Berkeley, CA: University of California Press.

Jaggar, A. M. (1989). Love and knowledge: Emotion in feminist epistemology. In A. M. Jaggar & S. R. Bordo (Eds.), *Gender/body/knowledge: Feminist reconstructions of being and knowing* (pp. 145-171). New Brunswick, NJ: Rutgers University Press.

Kumashiro, K. (2000). Teaching and learning through desire, crisis and difference: Perverted reflections on anti-oppressive education. *The Radical Teacher, 58*, 6-11.

Mohanty, C. T. (Ed.). (2004). Race, multiculturalism and pedagogies of dissent. In *Feminism without borders: Decolonizing theory, practicing solidarity* (pp. 190-217). Durham, NC: Duke University Press.

CHAPTER 2

BROWNING BEYOND DEBATE

Mapping an Excursion Through Power, Privilege, and Praxis

Cole Reilly
Towson University

Zahra Murad
University of Toronto

Many of us left Akron last October uneasy with concerns for the Curriculum and Pedagogy (C&P) Group regarding what had happened at the annual conference, wondering how we, as an organization, will choose to respond. Particularly in light of how Browning efforts at and within C&P played out just a year earlier there—when Browning/Coloring Curriculum and Pedagogy was first recognized as a 2010 conference theme.

The Browning Caucus (BC) officially came into being at C&P in 2009, emerging from an ad hoc committee's efforts in the months prior to that (as well as less formal efforts and discussions toward these ends in the preceding years). In the aftermath of heated debates around race and the role of antiracism in curriculum, a number of scholars committed to critical inquiry and generative resistance to systems based around and intersecting with race came together as the first body of the Browning Caucus. The Browning Caucus's goals were and are diverse, but include making shifts in the culture of race and the ways in which it is included or erased from curriculum theorizing at the conference and in the field in general. The caucus' existence rests on the implicit acknowledgement that we are

Excursions and Recursions Through Power, Privilege, and Praxis
pp. 9–25
Copyright © 2012 by Information Age Publishing

9

living in a White supremacist, heteropatriarchal, settler society—or, in other words, that we live in nations whose wealth and privilege have and do depend on the appropriation of Indigenous land and resources as well as the exploitation of bodies and communities of color while those bodies and communities are pushed to the margins or outside of the nation. As teachers, we might see this reality at play when we wonder why our Black students are so much more likely to be targeted by police or suspended for minor or subjective infractions than our White students (Romero, 2011; Skiba, Michael, Nardo, & Peterson, 2002). As scholars we might notice these issues when we investigate the social conditions behind low rates of academic success correlating with high rates of poverty, criminalization and illness in minoritized communities (Akbar, 2011; Kivel, 2011; Razack, 2006; Wuerth, 2011).

What happened at C&P's 2011 conference in Akron did not start and must not stay there; given that so much took place in Rubber City, we need to bounce back. Each as active and invested members of both the C&P Council and the Browning Caucus, two scholars begin a process of riddling through this turmoil to consider its larger significance. What follows is a fusion of their contrasting perspectives and insights—a collaborative effort to correspond with one another, as well as an invitation for others to continue this necessary, albeit complicated conversation.

*   *   *

CR: As I try to take stock of what played out at this year's conference, I find myself tumbling down a rabbit hole of confusion, disappointment, and frustration. Several months have passed and I continue to be haunted by the ghosts of apparent issues with Browning (quite literally) that surfaced in Akron this year. Moving beyond dumbfounded shock, I feel called to respond—to somehow, *anyhow* do better. All the same, I fear my words could betray me if I were unable to ground them in communion with someone else's who was there—to verify my recollection of events and help inform their interpretations.

As such, I thought it'd be productive for you and I to process this together, from our distinct lenses of experiencing these phenomena, having both witnessed (and even engaged in) the same incidents. As a pair of council and caucus members, each committed to work we define as antiracist, anticolonial, feminist, and ever conscious of class and sexuality, et cetera, I sense that we perhaps feel a shared sense of responsibility for unravelling much of what went down in October and what moving forward from that might mean.

Yet, as contrasting individuals who come to the conversation from contrasting countries, cultures, races, genders, sexual orientations, religions, careers, and class experiences, et cetera, perhaps we offer a foil to one another, ever conscious of our investments and perspectives, without serving as merely the sum of our presumed representations—too readily dismissed or cavalierly cast in the light of a singular agenda (Tatum, 2011).

ZM: I appreciate this opportunity to sort through the events and implications of this year's conference with you. The space offered here for self-reflexivity and a continuation of the challenging conversations we started at the conference is representative of the parts of the culture and commitment to social justice that I appreciate about C&P. I see what we are putting together here as a contribution to that commitment.

My responses to the experience of C&P are couched in a theoretical framework that understands certain problems as manifestations of larger systems of domination and oppression. They also spring from my lived experiences and social positioning. While it's clear that our views are colored by our divergent social locations, it's also clear that we can dialogue with one another in challenging but not antagonistic ways because of our shared commitments to social justice. It's important to the theory and process of conversations like these to challenge the pervasive notion that engaging in identity politics and acknowledging social location stifles conversation; we can and must remain aware of the ways that dynamics of structural power mediate our personal relationships.

The material realities of racism and ongoing colonization make it imperative to understand the very physical impact of identity and its politics. These ideas were taken up in diverse and nuanced ways in the "Perspectives" section of last year's *Journal of Curriculum and Pedagogy*. Sandy Grande (2011) articulated some of the well-established historical and contemporary need for social and cultural protectionism in her piece. She argued that Indigenous peoples have not yet had the healing time and space to recover those elements of culture and community taken from them by colonialism. Because of this, she posited, the demands that Indigenous peoples make their bodies, communities and knowledges available to academia are harmful and inappropriate.

Andrea Smith's (2006) article "Heteropatriarchy and the Three Pillars of White Supremacy" lends some context to the political landscape of Grande's arguments and to the arguments you and I are making here more broadly. Smith's article points out that the basis of critical race activism and theorizing in settler-colonies has been built along the Black/White binary. While the color line which characterizes this binary is undoubtedly foundational to the construction of race in colonial nations, Smith points out that the uncritical reification of this foundation has done a disservice to our understandings of the disparate challenges facing Black, Asian, and Indigenous peoples. Colonization has placed Asian peoples outside of the west, but within the parameters of civilization, making Asians both a constant foreign threat and potential model minorities. Black and Indigenous peoples meanwhile have been interpolated by White supremacist colonization based on what their lands or bodies can offer. The understanding is that Black and Indigenous peoples exist outside of civilization. Black people are constituted as perpetually enslavable, which their worth residing in their physical rather than mental abilities; hence the idea that one drop makes a person Black, which stems from a need to increase the labor pool. Indigenous peoples meanwhile are characterized by the notion that they are always disappearing, thereby legitimating settler claims to the land; hence the colonial notion that any amount of non-Indigenous blood makes a person non-Indigenous.

Given the divergent needs of colonization which racialized people are socially and politically groomed to fill, Grande's argument is doubly important. Without engaging in self-questioning as non-Indigenous people on the basis that Grande and other Indigenous people might know better than we do what is required in at least some Indigenous communities, we risk causing further hurt in our good-faith attempts to do good.

In the same edition of the *Journal of Curriculum and Pedagogy*, Jin Haritaworn (2011) and Nirmala Erevelles (2011) addressed other facets of the materiality of race and colonization. Haritaworn discussed some of the complicated negotiations that multiply minoritized faculty are forced to make in order to survive in classrooms. His piece provides an important glance at some of the ways that the realities of trans, queer and/or of color practitioners and scholars are organized differently from those who are or can pass as dominant. Erevelles' article, meanwhile, briefly details the routinely high and often fatal costs of the dehumanization inherent in systems of Othering.

Importantly, none of the scholars I have mentioned address race in isolation; the papers deal with race, rather, as it is coconstructed by frameworks of dis/ability, gender, class and colonization. Engaging in the work of acknowledging our social locations and their impacts can in fact ensure that our conversations around race do not collapse the tensions of the intersectional, simultaneous (Bannerji, 1995) or interlocking (Razack, 2006) nature of oppression. Rather, this approach can enrich our conversations about race and allow us to see is the important point is that racialization does not happen homogenously across the board (A. Smith, 2006). Instead, it is deeply affected by both the simultaneous nature of privilege and oppression and the agenda that White supremacy has for different Others.

As racialized people, our identities are always grounded in very material lived experiences of violence, displacement and domination. This means that while I appreciate well-intentioned attempts to move beyond "us" and "them" categories, the reality is that, though fluid, there *is* an "us" and a "them." And, as Grande argued, sometimes the boundaries around "us" that are erected by oppressed peoples are put there for good reason.

I want to highlight these material foundations especially because as we expand to discuss race at C&P it's too easy to ignore the most material foundation of oppression in North America: theft of the land from Indigenous peoples. As our dialogue continues, it's important to remember that the racializations we speak about and experience are predicated on—and are emphatically not separate from—the colonization of Indigenous lands (Razack, 2008; A. Smith, 2006; L. T. Smith, 1999; Stoler, 1995, Zinn, 1990).

CR: Your sentiments here speak to a number of my own (Reilly, 2011)—particularly that we need to acknowledge and address the shadowy operationalism of supremacy culture within the field of curriculum as well as to challenge structural hegemonies of power, privilege, prejudice, and [indeed] pedagogy, even at C&P. For as progressive and self-critical as the organization sets out to be—and I don't question the sincerity of that intent—from its onset, not everyone has found certain theoretical sentiments of critical pedagogy empowering (Ellsworth, 1989) in terms of *how* they are operationalized in practice. [Of note, as I wove in a handful of additional references to add to the connections you had already made above, I could not help but notice how neither of us is attempting to simply perpetuate or further privilege some of the more canonical voices and works that often dominate mainstream multicultural literature in this regard.] Likewise, I worry that pseudointellectual musings that may pass for theoretical with certain audiences (i.e., postracial, postfeminist discourses, and the like) are shortsighted and destructive—offensively presuming to further discredit and dismiss marginalized voices and perspectives. These aren't minor issues that might be eradicated with simplistic solutions, no matter how well intended; as you've pointed out, such concerns are systemic.

ZM: This reality is reflected at the conference; as much as there are aspects of C&P that I appreciate, I'm unable to leave the conference without deep reservations about the state of curriculum studies in this colonial present. I think it's clear that the problems that manifest at C&P are symptomatic of broader problems in the field of curriculum studies, in the institution of schooling and in the structure of our society. It is frustrating at C&P because it's a space that strives to challenge and subvert systems of oppression but remains oblivious to its own perpetuations of these systems.

The problem isn't, of course, that the folks who come to the conference aren't intelligent or committed to change. It's that change cannot happen without an overall shift in culture. The insistence I hear frequently that we not tell people how to feel about race or that we not make it mandatory to talk about race and colonization stifles potential shifts in culture. It's also demoralizing, and contributes to an atmosphere of exclusion at the conference. How can I feel included or that my work is appreciated in a space where the processes of social domination, which circumscribe who I am, and which result in the deaths of countless people everyday from my communities, are considered subjects for debate?

CR: That's a powerful point, Zahra—one I hope will be earnestly considered by others in the C&P community. As we know, privilege affords those unaware to continue to turn a blind eye to what others experience (Freire, 1970, 1973; Hilfiker, 2002; McIntosh, 1990). However, when and if we are able to wake people from their respective slumbers of ignorance (and we might all suffer from these in different ways—I like to think of these as circumstantial "blind spots" because they're so dangerous), the baton of responsibility is passed and ignorance is no longer an excuse for inaction.

Each year I attend the conference I leave with a great deal on my mind and heart—carrying with me the precious cargo of renewed awareness and responsibilities, but also the inspiration and enthusiasm to move forward with and unpack such luggage afterward. As I set out for the long drive home from Akron, the expected spring in my step was gone this year. My weary body and spirit carried parasites of near defeat, disappointment, and exhaustion.

By my count, there were at least two, increasingly perplexing, troubling, and/or otherwise noteworthy key events with regard to Browning C&P at the 2011 conference:

(a) Without a featured town hall dedicated to Browning at this year's conference (unlike the 2010 conference), the "business meeting" structure of the second town hall gave way to a discussion-cum-debate questioning C&P's commitment to holding itself and its membership accountable for meaningfully responding to certain Browning concerns. Few would dispute these discussions became rather tense at times with latent pockets of apparent unrest, resistance, or disregard surfacing discursively in ways, I for one, had not previously imagined.

(b) Presumably in response to the prior evening's tumultuous town hall, an early AM session dedicated to a number of the Browning-inspired perspective pieces featured recently in the *Journal of Curriculum and Pedagogy* garnered a large audience. Despite this occurring on a Saturday morning—a time-slot historically plagued with low attendance at conferences—it was seemingly the most well-attended session at the conference. Given the unexpected (albeit welcome) turnout, the presenters opted to facilitate something of a hybrid between a workshop and a de facto town hall continuation.

In the aftermath of these developments, both the council and broader membership of C&P have raised questions about the nature of inclusivity, the kinds of theoretical and pedagogical approaches we would like to promote at C&P, and the social/political implications of how we approach these questions.

Through our conversation here [in this paper], with the luxury of time and emotional space at our disposal, perhaps we ought to strive to provide a partial theoretical framing for these questions. Not so that we necessarily answer them all outright, but so that we may be more aware of the contexts in which we explore them. With that in mind, it is important to make some connections between C&P and broader contexts of curriculum and education to better situate the critique that the Browning Caucus is trying to make.

For some time now, I've found myself toying with a pair of budding connections to make to remarkable events in Akron's history that may inform C&P. Zahra, I wonder if you might humor me in considering these to see if there's anything we stand to garner from them. In no particularly order, they are as follows:

(a) Little more than 20 years have passed since the National Women Studies Association's (NWSA) Board made the controversial "sister segregation" decision to dismiss Black feminist, Ruby Sales, from her position on the organization's national staff, when she bravely gave voice to cite instances of systemic racism in the organization that had gone unchecked for far too long. By the time the 1990 conference for NWSA was held in Akron, the stage was set for backlash—political eruption and unrest among many feminist scholars in attendance who cried fowl, demanding "Where is Ruby Sales?" (Gonzalez, 2002; Van Dyke, 2002).

(b) Sojourner Truth delivered her impassioned "Ain't I a Woman?" speech not more than a handful of blocks from where we held the conference in 2010 and 2011. Nearly 160 years earlier, she earnestly wrestled with the inevitable complexity of intersecting identity politics—herself an undereducated woman of color, poverty, and faith—at a time when such circumstances stood to stifle her voice and deny her access to basic human dignities.

I feel like both events may prove more than coincidental in our understanding of and response to what went down at C&P's 2011 conference in Akron.

ZM: Those are powerful reference points to connect our experiences at C&P to broader social and political contexts. And, of course, whatever place the conference may be in, we would find similar reference points cropping up, because the systems which frame C&P also frame and govern space and place throughout North America. We need to ask ourselves, whose treaty lands do we hold C&P on, every year, and what are our treaty responsibilities? Whose were the bodies cleared from the land to allow our presence, and whose are the bodies imported to serve us our lunches and breakfasts? These important contexts actively frame rather than passively background the events at C&P every year and the work we all do as educators and scholars.

I'd like to pick up on your example of Ruby Sales. How many Ruby Sales do I know? Her story is so hauntingly familiar that it took me a moment to realize that this is an issue rather than a fact of life. At C&P, I fear, we are in danger of making what happened to Ruby Sales and what is happening to countless other Indigenous scholars and scholars of color a familiar progression in an organization's life:

- the organization is perceived as all White;
- the organization invites or is breached by Indigenous and of color folks;
- the organization realizes that the work of antiracism and decolonization is much more complicated, difficult, and personal than they bargained for; and
- the organization pushes out said Indigenous and of color people or tolerates our continued presence with an expectation of quiet gratitude and deference.

This cycle is so dangerous; it seems to just confirm the racist notion that the problem is uncooperative or "lazy" racialized people rather than White supremacy.

CR: I think you offer a valid and crucial reading of some troubling blueprints, particularly in light of how this seems to be a perpetual and dysfunctional cycle that we need to actively work to disrupt—both at C&P and beyond. I initially bristled at your choice of words with the organization being *breached* by certain groups of people. For me, the term "breach" calls up a pair of difficult images: an army brigade being broken through by an attacking rival or the levies of NOLA (New Orleans, Louisiana) toppling to Hurricane Katrina. In either analogy, the one doing the "breaching" is seen as an unwelcome enemy or disastrous intruder—something I would hope no one feels at C&P. I concede, of course, I simply may not be privy to some conversations where people voice this.

ZM: I used this wording intentionally because of its confrontational imagery, because what I'm referring to are situations in which people of color *are* forced into the role of villains and represented as storming the borders, boundaries, or walls of civilization to come and mess things up. I understand why you would cringe at those implications and at the idea that people experience this sense at C&P—but imagine for a minute how much more uncomfortable it is to be the person at whom that feeling is aimed. While I appreciate that this may not be the intent, it remains a reality—one not easily countered by a change in the attitudes of a few individuals. Several White allies at C&P have welcomed me but these acts of kindness don't erase the structural racism present in the field and at the conference; in fact, the need for these acts of kindness *as kindness* highlights the existence of boundaries that I must force my way past.

CR: Fair enough—that helps to clarify the intention behind such wording and imagery.

ZM: Going back to my points on Ruby Sales, I was talking about the treacherous grounds on which White supremacy allows the inclusion of racialized peoples into its structures. Inclusion can be destructive when organizations manage to retain a few people of color or Indigenous people who can fit the organization's frameworks and requirements. Because, as the Browning Caucus keeps trying to point out, the problem isn't reducible to representation. Of course, representation is part of the issue, as the root of supremacy and its systems is couched in a fear of the Other (Ahmed, 2000). But that problem isn't solved when we cherry-pick safe Others to join our organizations and come to our conferences. The problem isn't just that Ruby Sales is Black; the problem is that Ruby Sales won't be quiet, and that the things she says threatens the status quo. The problem, in other words, isn't just inclusion (or exclusion) of racialized peoples: it's the entirety of the system.

As I thought about Ruby Sales, I remembered all the Indigenous scholars and scholars of color I have seen make one trip to C&P and decide never to return. Just in the 3 years that I have been attending I have met enough brilliant, racialized academics who have come to the conclusion that C&P, as a space, offers them nothing, that I recognize a pattern. And I don't think that racialized scholars are wary of C&P because they are unfair or oversensitive or mean. There are deep issues of color blindness and racism in Curriculum Studies generally and they manifest at C&P.

CR: It's deeply unfortunate that C&P could have made such a poor impression on anyone (much less many ones, as you suggest), yet it's better to recognize this and begin responding to these concerns than to remain ignorant of such matters. I imagine this would come as news to many C&P members, but I suspect some of the remarks made at the

Friday evening town hall this past year have made it impossible to ignore such color blindness any longer. As disappointing as some of this news is to hear, it stands to help us progress, if we learn from it.

Having attended the NWSA conference a handful of times in the 2000s, I cannot help but draw comparisons between my experience of it as an organization and C&P. To be sure, some of the most intellectually stimulating presentations I've yet attended (or facilitated) have taken place at C&P or NWSA, so I think highly of each. It's noteworthy, however, that the membership of each consists predominantly of progressive-minded White people who likely consider themselves (and their organization), socially liberal, antiracist, feminist/profeminist, queer/queer-friendly, and ever conscious of any myriad of social justice and equity issues relating to class, creed, culture, and the like. Such people take pride in the warm and safe space they feel the conference affords them and their work, juxtaposing their appreciation of this with how comparatively starchy, standoffish, conservative, or patriarchal other professional conferences or communities in their field seem by comparison.

Unfortunately, what neither group has yet found a way to fully do in praxis is to (success)fully integrate—not just the bodies, but voices, ideas, insights, perspectives, and critiques—of Indigenous and of color scholars, etc. Each organization proclaims to want to challenge hegemonies of supremacist thought and marginalization, yet attempts made in this direction have been rather measured, proceeding with undue caution. This suggests some level of trepidation about fully relinquishing the familiar processes and privileges afforded to certain foundational constructs, which inherently cater only to the dynamics of the group's most archetypal culture: White people—White women, more specifically, at National Women's Studies Association. [As a White man, I see some value in the *Other*ness I experience attending NWSA, because it serves as an appropriate reminder of the patriarchal privileges afforded to me in most professional spheres or circles. I don't feel unwelcome, but my presence there seems reminiscent of being on the "visiting team" for a sporting event. By contrast, it seems there is neither reason nor necessity for people of color to come to C&P if they are to be treated as though they were merely guests at an existing [White] dinner party.]

In the case of Ruby Sales, it seems NWSA felt ready to have a woman of color in a *visible position* of leadership within the organization [tokenized, consciously or otherwise]. However, it was the fact that Ruby actually assumed the post for what it was, speaking up accordingly—that made people uncomfortable. Twenty plus years ago, Ruby's physical representation was certainly welcome, but her Black voice and critical observations apparently weren't. So as to complicate any readings of this matter as purely black and white <pun intended>, it's worth acknowledging that the "Where is Ruby Sales?" campaign in response to Ruby's dismissal was led by the Lesbian Caucus as well as the African-American and Women of Color Caucuses (Van Dyke, 2002).

The Browning Caucus at C&P is one promising initiative for which I'm not aware of any NWSA equivalent just yet. Town halls offer still another built-in structure unique to C&P (and, as such, absent from NWSA) that intends to let every voice be heard. Granted they're imperfect and no one envies the person tasked with facilitating these, but I'm grateful for the forum to have complicated conversations at C&P—not just in stolen asides or individual presentations, but with and among the entire membership.

ZM: It's a positive sign that folks at C&P seem open to having public discussions on the issue, but I find these conversations frustrating because there is so much resistance to talking about racism as an institutional as well as an interpersonal issue. As Sarita Srivastava (2006) noted in her article, "Tears, Fears and Careers: Anti-Racism and Emotion in Social Movement Organizations," emotions and a consistent return to the interpersonal in dealing with issues of systemic injustice only serves to occlude and perpetuate the problem. When we reduce fighting inequity to a ritualized acknowledgement of the pain and guilt our complacency and power cause us, we detract from material work that needs to be done. Certainly the emotional work of antiracism is important, legitimate work; but it is not the extent of the work.

Because of this, I find it problematic that our conversations move from a statement that there is a problem into an immediate attempt to diagnose that problem by operationalizing the interpersonal dynamics at the conference with very little reflection in between. While I believe these are all in good faith, and are sometimes very useful efforts, we cannot afford to tackle social injustice in such a reductionist manner (sometimes rife with deflection, derailment, and more racism); as scholars and educators we really should know better. And until we can do better, C&P will continue to produce its own Ruby Sales, again and again.

CR: Agreed; one of the shortcomings of coming together just once yearly is that I think people are inclined to feel as though we need to address a year's worth of challenges in just a few days. For some things, perhaps we can, but this was a matter that seemed far too entrenched in the C&P fabric to imagine we could fix it all at once, crossing it off the to-do list prematurely. Similarly, the idea of setting out to craft and fund one or more activist/actionist project was taken up at this year's conference, with nearly two full town halls dedicated to it. Though I don't doubt the intention behind such an idea, it didn't seem we were able to fully incubate or develop these fledgling operations in our rushed time at the conference, despite some sincere efforts.

In the spirit of the brainstorming process, I think the pair of ideas put forward, if refined and crafted a bit, could evolve into some potentially positive steps worth exploring. Surely requiring a few more sentences in each proposal drawing connections to Browning may initially be superficial for many, but it could also serve as a form of data collection for making us more aware of what C&P members do and do not understand about Browning. And the suggestion that Browning Caucus members and other Browning scholars volunteer to act as mentors to those seeking an introduction to critical race theory also has promise. As a member of the Browning Caucus, I for one *would* be willing to serve as a mentor of sorts to someone who is genuinely interested in bringing the spirit of Browning to their work, but perhaps is having trouble imagining how that might begin for him/her. I've already had countless conversations with individual members of C&P who have approached me to help them begin to better understand what Browning is and how it might relate to them and their work. Admittedly, it's a baby step, but a step nonetheless. What would be dismissive, in my eyes, would be for C&P to ever imagine a few short strides alone could ever serve as an end or solution in and of itself. As Sojourner would assure us, it surely *ain't*.

ZM: Sojourner Truth is definitely important to contexts of race at 2011's C&P conference. Thinking through the implications of her work in light of other work ongoing in critical race might help us understand the strengths and limitations of the suggestions you just mentioned.

Although conference planners allocated time to honor her famous speech (Gaztambide-Fernández, 2011), the spirit of her words seems to have been lost at C&P. As I reflect on the conversations we [as a membership, not specifically you and I] have had at the conference, and on the resistance to addressing race as an institutional issue—and sometimes as an issue at all—I'm also thinking of the insistence upon thinking and speaking about race as an isolated issue.

I feel that the Browning Caucus has been very clear and deliberate about our commitment not only to address race as a phenomenon that is coconstructed with class, gender, sexuality, age, ability and more but as an issue that is meaningless outside of these other paradigms. And so it is difficult to interpret the insistence that we revert to discussing race within a context of oppression Olympics games, pitting race against other manifestations of structural power, as anything more than a deflection of the issue at hand. I know some folks might make the point that if we truly don't mean people to think about race simply as race we should change our language (i.e., Browning). Perhaps I'm being stubborn, but although that may be easier, I feel very strongly that part of the work of the Browning Caucus and our allies is to shift the way we think about amalgams of race and oppression in curriculum studies.

While instituting a mentorship program focused on race and understanding antiracism has promise, I worry that it functions to turn criticality into a transportable set of "skills" rather than situating it as a contextual mode of being in the world. Even with some reservations, however, an institutional commitment to speaking about race openly and pervasively as a multifaceted and intersectional/interlocking issue at C&P would create cultural shifts. The reality remains, however, that simply instituting a process will not rid us of the issue; we must also consistently engage with the process in honest and challenging ways, or the same problems will reassert themselves in different guises.

CR: Absolutely. Since its inception, the work of the Browning Caucus has been mindful of the innate intersections and intersectionalities that characterize all manner of identity politics (Collins, 1986, Reilly, 2011, Spelman, 1988). Granted, I was ill at ease with the term *Browning* at first—perhaps foreseeing the predictable snags of conflating "Browning" with something done only by "Brown people"—but it's grown on me with time and resolve. In that regard, it's not unlike how I've grown to embrace *queer* as preferable to *LGB2TI/QQ*, depending upon the circumstances. I can see how the term "Browning" may serve strategic purposes that I failed to recognize at first (Colón, 2007; Delpit, 2007; Delpit & Dowdy, 2002). More importantly, our efforts need to move beyond the limitations of searching for the perfect word or term, if doing so stands in the way of action and progress.

Having said all that, I contend that none-too-subtle sabotage may be afoot. As of yet, not everyone at C&P has been equally invested in the success of our Browning efforts; some may even be so wary of the changes/challenges true Browning might expect of them, that they act to stall or obstruct its forward motion. Not unlike setting up excessive speed bumps or felling trees in our path so that the vehicle must repeatedly stop for the tracks to be cleared. I can think of little other motive for putting forward the sham argument that Browning is preoccupied with race alone—particularly when all we've written, said, or done as a Caucus runs contrary to this.

Beyond C&P, I experienced something akin to this, years ago, with a particularly counterproductive discussion of diversity and matters of multiculturalism at a series of departmental meetings. A small committee focused upon helping the department clarify, coordinate, and improve its approach to multiculturalism, social justice, and matters of diversity in general asked to be afforded time at a faculty meeting to facilitate what ought to be a rather straightforward exercise. Their constructivist plan was to define some of the most relevant terms (e.g., diversity, multiculturalism, culturally responsive pedagogy) collectively, as a department. I, of course, anticipated a range of experiences and levels of training or comfort in this regard; what I hadn't foreseen was how some of the people who were clearly less enthusiastic—resistant even—to such efforts could effectively drag their feet in the conversation to the point of exercising a de facto filibuster. These resistors' strategies of distraction and deflection effectively held the conversation hostage with absurd roadblocks and flares—anything to stall progress that might expect our faculty to indeed refine our praxis. This experience was disheartening to say the least, but it's opened my eyes to be more conscious of how similar sabotage can play out in academic circles.

I draw much inspiration from Sojourner Truth's impassioned determination to be heard in spite of the socially constructed obstacles in her path at the time—presuming to stifle her voice or value. As such, her "Ain't I a woman?" speech serves as one of the most historically recognizable and significant efforts in North American history to plainly grapple with intersectionality within identity politics (Gaztambide-Fernández, 2011). The fact that she delivered it not ten blocks from our conference site, and more than 160 years earlier, is a testament to how such concepts are anything but new—neither to Akron nor C&P.

ZM: How can we think about race outside of other social processes? European colonization developed race, capitalism and heteropatriarchy with and through each other as they rebuilt the world within imperialist legislative, academic, and economic practices (L. T. Smith, 1999; Stoler, 1995). In the making of oppression in the modern era, one of these processes cannot be separated from the other. If we do separate them, we run the risk of missing great swathes of the picture we're looking at. We run the risk of imagining that queer rights started in and are particular to western nations and cultures. We run the risk of imagining that White women are the most empowered, and that Western cultural forms of gender empowerment must be inflicted on everyone everywhere. We run the risk of believing that the conditions that govern the lives of poor White people exist outside of racialization. And, as educators, we risk missing some of the challenges that our poor and White students will face because we see some problems as "Black" problems and others as "class" problems. We risk gaping holes in our knowledge that will prevent us from assuring our young, queer, Muslim students that queerness is not anti-Islamic, no matter what anyone says. It is important to insist on understanding race as a plural issue, as a lens through which all issues can be viewed (although one that might not always be productive to employ or to employ solely) because if we don't, we fail our students and our work as scholars.

CR: I champion the connections you make here (and have made repeatedly) to unsurprising pitfalls. We must never conceptualize race, class, or gender as *ever* functioning in isolation of one another, and much less are these frameworks unshaped by nation, language, body, sexuality, age, or health.

I suspect some of the turbulent exchanges and tensions that surfaced at this year's conference—particularly during the second town hall—may have startled a number of people awake. As a professional organization and scholarly community teetering on the precipice of something steep and scary, might we also collectively realize this as perhaps both a necessary setback (to take stock of troublesome pockets of offense that may be worse than many imagined) and yet also an opportunity to radically shift gears?

I'd like to think we're ready, but that's not a determination for any one or pair of us to make alone. We're neither Atlas nor Sisyphus and the burden of shouldering such mighty boulders of responsibility upward and onward lies not with any of us alone but with the C&P collective—Council, Caucus, and our community at large.

*   *   *

As an organization the work of Browning C&P has barely just begun—early steps among a journey of surely many if we hope to realize what the organization and field *can* indeed be. Let's hope we continue to revisit these tricky conversations.

REFERENCES

Ahmed, S. (2000). *Strange encounters: Embodies others in post-coloniality.* London, England: Routledge.

Akbar, N. (2011). Privilege in black and white. In K. L. Koppelman (Ed.), *Perspectives on human difference: Selected readings on diversity in America* (1st ed., pp. 43-49). Boston, MA: Allyn & Bacon.

Bannerji, H. (1995). *Thinking through: Essays on feminism, marxism and anti-racism.* Toronto, Ontario, Canada: Women's Press.

Colón, J. (2007). Little things are big. In W. Au, B. Bigelow, & S. Karp (Eds.), *Rethinking our classrooms* (p. 113). Milwaukee, WI: Rethinking Schools.

Collins, P. H. (1986). Learning from the outsider within: The sociological significance of black feminist thought. *Social Problems, 33*(6), S14-S32.

Delpit, L. (2007). Seeing color. In W. Au, B. Bigelow, & S. Karp (Eds.), *Rethinking our classrooms* (pp. 158-160). Milwaukee, WI: Rethinking Schools.

Delpit, L. & Dowdy, J. K. (Eds.). (2002). *The skin that we speak: Thoughts on language and culture in the classroom.* New York, NY: The New Press.

Ellsworth, E. (1989). Why doesn't this feel empowering? Working through the repressive myths of critical pedagogy. *Harvard Educational Review, 59*(3), 297-324.

Erevelles, N. (2011). Crippin' the curriculum at the intersections. *Journal of Curriculum and Pedagogy, 8*(1), 31-34.

Freire, P. (1970). *Pedagogy of the oppressed.* New York, NY: Seabury.

Freire, P. (1973). *Education for critical consciousness.* New York, NY: Seabury.

Gonzalez, M. C. (2002). The bridge called NWSA ["25 Years of NWSA: Vision Controversy, Transformation" issue]. *NWSA Journal, 14*(1), 71-81.

Grande, S. (2011). Confessions of a full-time Indian. *Journal of Curriculum and Pedagogy, 8*(1), 40-43.

Gaztambide-Fernandez, R. (2011, October). Field trip—Presentation at the site of Sojourner Truth's 'Ain't I a Woman' Speech. The 12th annual Curriculum and Pedagogy Conference, Akron, OH.

Haritaworn, J. (2011). Perverse reproductions: Notes from the wrong side of the classroom. *Journal of Curriculum and Pedagogy, 8*(1), 31-34.

Hilfiker, D. (2002). *Urban injustice: How ghettos happen.* New York, NY: Seven Stories Press.

Kivel, P. (2011). Fear and danger. In K. L. Koppelman (Ed.), *Perspectives on human difference: Selected readings on diversity in America* (1st ed., pp. 9-13). Boston, MA: Allyn & Bacon.

McIntosh, P. (1990). White privilege: Unpacking the invisible knapsack. Retrieved from http://www.case.edu/president/aaction/UnpackingTheKnapsack.pdf

Razack, S. (2006). *Looking White people in the eye: Gender, race and culture in courtrooms and classrooms.* Toronto, Ontario, Canada: University of Toronto Press.

Razack, S. (2008). *Casting out: The eviction of Muslims from western law and politics.* Toronto, Ontario, Canada: UTP.

Reilly, C. (2011). "To what extent am I part of the problem?" Strategizing identity politics while instructing a multicultural teacher education course. In C. Reilly, V. Russell, L. K. Chehayl, & M. McDermott (Eds.), *Surveying borders, boundaries, and contested spaces in curriculum and pedagogy* (pp. 123-139). Charlotte, NC: Information Age.

Romero, D. (2011). Crime. In K. L. Koppelman (Ed.), *Perspectives on human difference: Selected readings on diversity in America* (1st ed., pp. 176-178). Boston, MA: Allyn & Bacon.

Skiba, R. J., Michael, R. S., Nardo, A. C., & Peterson, R. L. (2002). The color of discipline: Sources of racial and gender disproportionality in school punishment. *The Urban Review, 34*(4), 317-342.

Smith, A. (2006). Heteropatriarchy and the three pillars of White supremacy: Rethinking women of color organizing. In INCITE! Women of Color Against Violence (Eds.), *Color of violence: The INCITE! Anthology* (pp. 66-73). Cambridge, MA: South End Press.

Smith, L.T. (1999). *Decolonizing methodologies: Research and Indigenous peoples.* New York, NY: Zed Books.

Spelman, E. V. (1988). *Inessential woman: Problems of exclusion in feminist thought.* Boston, MA: Beacon Press.

Srivastava, S. (2006). Tears, fears and careers: Anti-racism and emotion in social movement organizations. *The Canadian Journal of Sociology, 31*(1), 55-90.

Stoler, A. L. (1995). *Race and the education of desire: Foucault's history of sexuality and the colonial order of things.* Durham, NC: Duke University Press.

Tatum, B. D. (2011). The complexity of identity: "Who am I?" In K. L. Koppelman (Ed.), *Perspectives on human difference: Selected readings on diversity in America* (1st ed., pp. 31-35). Boston, MA: Allyn & Bacon

Van Dyke, A. (2002). Identity politics in NWSA: Memoirs of a lesbian caucus chair
["25 Years of NWSA: Vision Controversy, Transformation" issue]. *NWSA Journal*, *14*(1), 51-57.

Wuerth, S. (2011). Edwina left behind. In K. L. Koppelman (Ed.), *Perspectives on
human difference: Selected readings on diversity in America* (1st ed., pp. 36-38).
Boston, MA: Allyn & Bacon.

Zinn, H. (1980). *A people's history of the United States*. New York, NY: Harper and
Row.

CHAPTER 3

PERDIDA/LOST

Self-Reflections in Nepantla as Voice Emerges

Elva Reza-López
Boise State University

At the 2011 Curriculum and Pedagogy conference, we collectively brain-stormed the benefits of Patti Lather's (2007) concept of "getting lost." This brought to mind my own experiences and reflections in a space called Nepantla. A Nahuatl word meaning "in the middle or in-between" (Maffle, n.d.), a space that is destructive and creative, Nepantla surfaced during the Spanish post-Conquest in the late 1500s. It "characterized the religious beliefs and practices of ... Christianity and [the] Nahua religion as 'neither one nor the other'" (p. 2), providing resilience and time for the Nahuas to negotiate the tensions they were experiencing between their known world and the conquered world. Chicana activist, Gloria Anzaldúa (1987) writes, "you haven't got into the new identity yet and haven't left the old identity behind either—you are in a kind of transi-tion" (p. 237). Anzaldúa (2002) further defines Nepantla as:

> The place where different perspectives come into conflict and where you
> question the basic ideas, tenets, and identities inherited from your family,
> your education, and your different cultures. Nepantla is the zone between

changes where you struggle to find equilibrium between the outer expression of change and your inner relationship to it. (pp. 548-549)

For people of color, being in this liminal, transitional space can be chaotic, frustrating, and uncomfortable. Clashes with hegemony due to culture, language, socioeconomics status, sexual orientation and gender issues can provoke uncertainties of identity and belonging and contribute to a sense of being lost. Although it is a space of transformation, one seems lost in the process of how this transformation is evolving, as one is being "pulled between opposing realities": the power of White privilege and the oppression of the subaltern voice (Anzaldúa, 2002, p. 548).

"GETTING LOST" AND "NEPANTLA"

Patti Lather (2007) has flipped the understanding of the words "getting lost" to a more positive lens by positing an "inquiry process ethically grounded in *not* knowing" (Childers, 2008, p. 1). It validates research as a subject in process, in an unclaimed and "fertile ontological space" (Lather 2007, p. viii). This, from my perspective, parallels being in the space of Nepantla. Subjectivity is processing in an unclaimed and ontological space.

Lather's concept of "getting lost" positions critical scholars to confront and question their own (mis)understandings, (in)securities of what is occurring in their inquiry, and face the fact that they don't know. They are lost. Should the research process be trusted? Similarly, people of color in Nepantla are weaving, searching their own realities and identities in a space that is chaotic and so uncomfortable that one weaves in and out in order to survive, shifting between the before and after. Should Nepantla be trusted?

Both of these concepts, "getting lost" and "Nepantla," from my perspective, echo the reconceptualist method of *currere,* as both deal with the "self," the experiential, and the (auto) biographical (Pinar, 1975) in spaces that question the old and the new, the before and after from a present position. In Nepantla, however, tensions, complexities and misunderstandings that connect to the self and the experiential are at times counterhegemonic and difficult to address. As a result, there is a need to negotiate old and new knowledge to fuse or transform it in order for agency and voice to evolve from the oppressed and marginalized space (Freire, 2000). Thus, Nepantla is a space that can transform the *self,* but through a process that, as I discovered, encompasses reflection, resentment, and renewal; a parallel, I think, to the process of *currere*: regressive, progressive, analytical and synthetical (Pinar, 1975). I will elaborate this connection further in the next section as I relate my experiences of being lost in a nepantla space.

PERDIDA/LOST IN NEPANTLA: FINDING VOICE AND AGENCY

Reflecting in clashing worlds, I regress to my historical past to progress and define my present. My historical past is not pleasant. As an immigrant from Mexico, I have experienced counterhegemonic clashes and Nepantla. That is, I have felt lost, unsure of where I belonged (am I Mexicana or Americana or both?) and have searched for truths that connect to my realities. One example of these counterhegemonic clashes that I recall was my first days in an American school. My father had told me that I would be going to school to learn English. I was excited and looking forward to learning English. These first days at school were a Nepantla experience since I did not know the language and was totally lost in the classroom environment. However, another issue had me perplexed and I eventually asked my mother for an answer. "Why," I asked, "are *güeritos* going to school if they already know English?" My reality was that school was to learn English; if they already knew it, why attend?

My school experiences were painful and little connected to my home life. I struggled to fit between two worlds and two different lenses with different ideologies. At home I spoke the language that I was punished for speaking at school. At home I was told never to question the teacher, but at school I was scolded for not asking questions. At home I felt empowered, while at school I was oppressed. Now, as a professor of color, I am aware that my voice at times is not valued. My knowledge at times is questioned and doubted, until spoken by a White person. Then it becomes accepted. Anzaldúa (1987) recalls her experiences in doctoral classes at University of Texas in the 1970s: "In a lot of these classes I felt silenced, like I had no voice" (p. 230). This silence still continues in some of our institutions for many people of color. Thus, I resent an educational system that fails to value the voice of my ethnic group and their history. This clash has spiraled me into Nepantla where poetry writing has sanctioned voice and agency. The following poems evolved while being lost in Nepantla. This process has not been easy and continues to be filled with complexities, tensions and anxieties.

Voice and Agency Emerge in Poetry

I was tired of listening to White privilege telling me, "No, that's not the way it is done!" "No, that's not what the book stated!" These comments to me echoed the following: you are a Latina, what would you know? Oppression, felt as a second language learner.

There is much that people of color know, but it may not connect to mainstream *conocimientos* because it is the knowledge of the minority that mainstream curriculum continues to omit. The oppression mentioned earlier hurled me into Nepantla where agency and voice, among chaos, emerged. The result was the poem, "You're Latina, What do You Know?" that addresses my historical *conocimientos*.

You're Latina, What Do You Know?

I speak my mind with pride,
Teacher, teacher, I know the answer.
But a long cold stare shivers my spine as I hear a voice say,
You're Latina, what do you know?

Oh, I know, teacher, teacher. I know.

I know that once this southwest land was part of Mexico.
Santa Fe was its capital and the Camino Real its path to heartland.
I know, teacher, teacher, that the Gadsden Purchase changed its landscape,
One day Mexicana with pride, next day "Americana with shame."
No longer the land of Aztlan; no longer the land of native man.
Bought, Caramba No! Stolen, my native Mexican mother concurs,
A perspective 100 plus years has yet to change.

Oh, I know, teacher, teacher. I know.

I know that once Spanish was spoken with pride,
But, now spoken with shame for those who assimilate.
Subtracted from our education due to English Only,
But added for a few White elites, who now recognize
The need and power of speaking a second language in a global space.

Yes, teacher, I know that now my
Voice falls on deaf White ears,
When I speak with pride of my heritage.

Oh, I know, teacher, teacher, I know.

I know that now my voice falls on deaf White ears,
When I relate how best I learn,
Except of course when it is echoed by a White voice
Who now is the expert of how best to teach us Mexican kids.
Why should this be so, I ask?

It is hegemony, the status quo—the power at hand,
Or so I am told.

No more, ya basta, I shout!
The Latina voice MUST be heard!
But, how I'm asked?
You're just a Latina, what do you know?

Oh, I know teacher, teacher, I know.

I know about racism, marginalization and discrimination,
That robs my identity of what I wish to become,
But I also know about la familia, el hogar, and hermandad,
The network that supports my breath of everyday life,
I know about Nepantla, the space of possibilities dreams and hopes,
Nepantlando borderland realities of two worlds to behold.

I am Latina, teacher, teacher, I know, I know.

You are White….
What do you know about me!
Why don't you know about me?
I am Latina, teacher, teacher, I know, I know.

Processing concientization (Freire, 2000), problematizing and critically analyzing macrosociety, I discovered a world more complex and more inhumane. In Nepantla again, I reflected on issues of colonization and I found the courage to finally speak my mind! The poem, "Pido la Palabra" (*I ask for the word*), expresses my beliefs and hopes through a voice liberated after years of colonization and suppression, still seeking answers for unjust causes. I see this process as social activism, praxis in progress.

Pido la Palabra

Pido la palabra
To apologize no more about my history and my voice;
Pido la palabra…
For my agency to flow about my land with freedom instead of fear;
Pido la palabra…
To unleash my colonized mind and speak with pride that I too have value;
Pido la palabra…
So that I no longer will be silenced by racism, oppression and
    marginalization;
Pido la palabra…
To speak about the pain I still bear;
Pido la palabra…

To speak the language of my heritage;
Pido la palabra …
To define my identity as Chicana, Nueva Mestiza, Nepantlera;
Pido la palabra…
To no longer feel shame of my culture, my language, and my identity;
Pido la palabra …
Por la Raza Cosmica as it negotiates new pathways for a more humane
  world.
Pido la palabra…
To hope.

I know I hold half the Word,
Do you hold the half that connects?
Entonces …
Pide la palabra.

Most recently, I voice concerns about schooling and high-stakes testing. The latter, a dehumanizing (Freire, 2000) structure from my perspective that needs eradication. In, "Esperanza Hope," I question the humanity of our students, as they have become statistics, data and a money-making mechanism.

Esperanza Hope

I am Esperanza Hope,
A member of the human race
Who enjoys reading, writing
And sharing knowledge space.

I am Esperanza Hope,
A member of a global space,
Who smiles, laughs, cries and sings,
Emotions that display a humane face.

I am Esperanza Hope,
A proud member of the mestizo race,
Who prides herself in speaking two languages,
Bridging two cultures/fusing two worlds.

I am Esperanza Hope, I think?
Now seeking answers to this certainty
Due to those questioning my *color* identity,
And stating that I do not belong.

Am I Esperanza Hope?
Cheated by hegemony,
I am now a number, data, and a threat,
For those tracking my educational success.

No, no longer Esperanza Hope,
But a statistic, a money making machine,
For an education system that need the numbers
To boast about *their* success.

Do I dare be Esperanza ... Hope?

The three poems resonate with a renewal of the self at the microlevel, connecting the present via past and future: a parallel, from my perspective, to the synthetical stage of *currere* (Pinar, 1975). However, the self still doubts and seeks acceptance at the macrolevel.

CONCLUSION

Only by being in a space of tension and possibilities and "getting lost" was I able to allow my inner voice to surface. As pedagogues, I believe that we should weave together the tensions, complexities and possibilities encountered in schooling to create a more democratic, socially just curriculum for all. This means that the "colorless" classroom must become "colorful," as critical race theorists advocate (Delgado & Stefancic, 2001; Ladson-Billings, 2000). Being in Nepantla allowed me to see that oppression and suppression connects to color. Teachers must begin addressing issues of diversity by seeing color in their classrooms. They need to enter a Nepantla. When a teacher negates color, diversity is being negated. For students of different cultures, languages and socioeconomic class, schooling continues to be foreign. They continue to be silenced by a mainstream classroom that values middle class Eurocentric knowledge. Reconceptualizing curriculum to include the historical voice and agency of people of color needs to be addressed. Understanding the space of Nepantla as a *currere* for the underrepresented, segregated and discriminated groups may impact such an endeavor. But, one must also keep in mind that being in Nepantla is a spiral effect that continues to be impacted by the outer/inner clashes of macrosociety and, thus, is a never-ending cycle.

As I reflect on what I have just written, I find myself wondering and getting lost on another issue. Why are second language learners referred to as English language learners in the literature? Aren't we all English language learners?

REFERENCES

Anzaldúa, G. (1987). *Borderlands/La frontera: The new mestiza*. San Francisco, CA: Spinsters/Aunt Lute.

Anzaldúa, G. E. (2002). Now let us shift ... the path of conocimiento ... inner work, public acts. In G. Anzaldúa & A. Keating (Eds.), *This bridge we call home: Radical visions for transformation* (pp. 540-578). New York, NY: Routledge.

Childers, S. M. (2008). Methodology, praxis, and autoethnography: A review of *Getting Lost. Educational Researcher, 37*(5), 298-301.

Delgado, R., & Stefancic, J. (2001). *Critical race theory: An introduction.* New York, NY: New York University Press.

Freire, P. (2000). *Pedagogy of the oppressed.* New York, NY: Continuum.

Ladson-Billings, G. (2000). Racialized discourse and ethnic epistemologies. In N. K. Denzin & Y. S. Lincoln (Eds.), *The handbook of qualitative research* (2nd ed., pp. 257-278). Thousand Oaks, CA: SAGE.

Lather, P. (2007). *Getting lost: Feminist efforts toward a double(d) science.* Albany, NY: State University of New York Press.

Maffie, J. (n. d). The centrality of Nepantla in conquest-era Nahua philosophy. Retrieved from http://www.enkidumagazine.com/eventos/chimalpahin/art/0001_CH08.htm.

Pinar, W. F. (1975). The method of "currere." Retrieved from http://www.eric.ed.gov/ERICWebPortal/contentdelivery/servlet/ERICServlet?accno=ED104766

CHAPTER 4

GETTING LOST
IN LIFE/DEATH DISRUPTIONS

Reclaiming the Right of a Legal Space

Miryam Espinosa-Dulanto
Valdosta State University

This work recounts a life-story in which intersections of power and privilege are marked in every step. The U.S. Census Bureau (2010) reported that in the year 2009, *one* in *five* people were either a first or second generation U.S. resident—70 million people in all. Of those, about 12 million were unauthorized, undocumented immigrants (Hoefer, Rytina, & Baker, 2012). Maria's story clearly illustrates how legal immigration status not only defines social space and opportunities, but, more importantly, how it restricts basic human rights and creates an underclass, an unauthorized, undocumented population with no legal rights or legal protection. Within this population, gender occupies a central space as it is the reason for continuous abuse and discrimination—and in this story, death.

As a qualitative researcher, the choice of using poetic narrative allows me to trace the risky expeditions, literal and metaphorical, undertaken by Maria which bring to life a complicated cartography composed of the multiple death-defying journeys women—immigrant or not—take in their ordinary lives (Ellis, 2010). The poem that follows emerged out of a larger research project centered on the lives of immigrant women.

Excursions and Recursions Through Power, Privilege, and Praxis
pp. 35–45

Maria's story weaves the familiar and the extraordinary embodied in a woman's life. The story depicts the dreams, hopes, violence, and danger associated with the Mexican/U.S. border, which breathes and grows in the dreams of daughters, wives, sisters, mother, and lovers within both nations (Denzin, Lincoln, & Tuhiwai Smith, 2008). My hope when sharing this life story is for the reader to understand that self and other are intertwined and that it is not possible to know one without the other (Denzin & Girardina, 2010).

Getting Lost in Life/Death Disruptions: Maria—sin apellido

Maria was born crying
cries of fear, cold, and hunger
calmed by mother's warm tits
warmed by few found rags

Maria's childhood came with more
fear, cold, and hunger
Maria's life-long true companions
taught her tricks to get fed and clothed

Fear presented survival talents
cold demanded crawling into warm places
unbearable hunger coupled with begging

A child in a well-developed body
Maria became a woman before her time
raped by father, stepfather and other men
Maria learned more tricks to survive

Pushing a little cart with *mercaderia*
child Maria sold whatever she found
other times cleaned houses
learned what she didn't have
watched children older than herself
Maria took whatever job was offered
exchanging hard labor for
a few coins   a bite to eat   a warm corner for rest

Maria at nineteen
started walking *North*
odd jobs held her in-route
from Querétaro to San Miguel de Allende
a week became a month
she reached *Aguas Calientes*

While cruising Zacatecas
Maria's twenties and Juan arrived together
Queretano también

Juan and Maria shared *North* dreams
with 1800 more miles to go
al otro lado waiting for them
there it was—bold sunny California

Soon, there were others
Carlos and Camilo from Zacatecas
Lucila and Pedro from *la capital*
and Ernesto and Patricio from Yucatán
Maria was not alone anymore

Fear vanished as buddies protected her now
while waiting for a good time to cross
she found nicer clothes that showed off
the new tattoos - symbols of her newly attained family
that made other people afraid

One April night, dark as an empty hole
the group crossed *la línea*
that part wasn't as bad as stories Maria had heard
their *coyote* had water hidden in the desert
Juan brought tequila to keep them warm and alert
no one felt tired, no time was too long
tequila and darkness mixed well

Daylight found the group lost and drunk
near the Mission Valley Parkway
that was about 20 needed-to-be-walked desert miles
from the place where the Los Angeles family
(in *gringolandia* that is called "gang")
was to collect them

"You, hide here ... and you, better lay down ... now!
pinche cabrones ... never gonna learn ...
getting drunk while crossing ... are you fucking insane?"

Maria smiled at the *coyote*
of course she would lay down
no idea why the *coyote* was so upset
better find some shade ...
a *sueñito* would help

The day was all gone when the group woke-up
hungry and thirsty to no more water or food
to an angry *coyote* herding them
onto an invisible trail found on an imaginary map

Five, six, seven hours walking
pitch-black all around, reaching nowhere
made the group more tired, more thirsty, more hungry
less patient and even less compliant

Punches, kicks, whacks came down all over
then sighs, groans, *súplicas* … blood!
the *coyote* was begging Juan to stop
the *paliza* made him remember the path to HWY 5
also where he had hidden some water and food

In a peachy-grey almost-dawn light
the group reached the meeting point
a sharp curve took the road onto a small path
where a huge *troca* was parked
fulsome *bienvenidos* filled the quiet air
strangers' faces covered by tattoos—were the only thing Maria saw

Life in East *Los Angeles* was different
it was nothing like the movies Maria used to watch
no one spoke English
everyone had brown skin, dark hair, and black eyes
lived in big abandoned buildings
with worn-down furniture and no cathedral windows

Where are the *bolillos*? Maria kept asking herself

There were no bolillos at Cahuenga Boulevard
                    it was the *Salvatrucha*s' zone
don't want to get near the Maras, was the daily reminder
                    or the Camarillo Street full of *Norteños*
18th street was Maria's place to stay
                    and maybe Clanton at 14th was OK too

Maria learned where to stay safe
from other brown people like herself
but found no answer for where to find
the beautiful, tall, blonde people
she saw in the movies and used to called *bolillos*

Days passed by, weeks were leaving too
nothing to do but be ready for Juan's desires

he seemed to have good moments
yet spent long hours with the other men
and even more time with new younger girls

One night, Juan arrived brandishing a new "piece"
he bragged something about smashing a *chicken* and a *perro*
who had encroached on their street using their colors

Was he talking about animals?

Juan's clothes were ripped and stained
he was high with rough energy, loud with a horselaugh
waiving the gun as a valuable trophy
he caught Maria in a bear clasp

For the first time Maria was confused and afraid
couldn't understand what he said, his words made no sense
Maria was not at ease with his doings
he tore her blouse, leaving Maria's bosoms crudely exposed
to the "hommies" who were in the room

Firmly, Maria pushed Juan away
"*así no Juan, así no …*"
she begged, and pushed him harder—away from her
surprised by Maria's reaction, he tripped
an explosion of laughs and teasing noises
received him on his landing
Jose was now a running laugh for his *hommies*

Juan lost it   Maria paid for it

Badly wounded
Maria awoke in an emergency room
the YMCA midnight-cart driver found her, naked and bleeding
at the street corner where Juan tossed her
after he got tired of beating her

Maria's body needed to heal
one leg was broken in three parts
her face was swollen and engorged
her arms all bruised and scratched
her torso … ohhhh … Maria's torso
it felt horrible but looked worse
like Juan drew a *tic-tac-toe* game on it

Three days later, still weak
Maria was released from the hospital

an ambulance drove her to a women's shelter
a safe haven to recuperate away from the East L. A. *familia*
the building looked similar to the places she had stayed
but it was quiet and nobody wanted to get into her bed

Maria's body was healing, the bruises almost gone
her bones were getting healthier
dark purple scratches replaced the dreaded scars
the time to leave the shelter was near

Pointing at a map, one of the counselors told Maria,
"This is America, the United States is huge
we are here in California, in L.A.
but there are many other places to live"
—What is the farthest place from here?
"The East Coast," the lady responded
—Are there any jobs there? ¿*Hay trabajo allí?*
"I know someone in Georgia that may be able to help you"

Still on crutches, Maria was driven to the Greyhound station
the shelter's counselor gave her three $20 bills,
a ticket to Valdosta, GA, and a card with a name and a phone number
"She will help you," the lady whispered in Maria's ear
and, "be patient, it's a long ride, about three days
—tres días … ¿hay que caminar?
no walking—it's about 2500 miles."

The trip to Valdosta took longer than scheduled
Maria lost connections, transferred to wrong coaches
all that rollover on half day layovers
adding up miles and many hours to an already long trip
exhausted, but believing, she reached Southern Georgia
ready for the new challenges

Preparing soil to be sown
tomatoes, peppers, eggplants, peas, onions, carrots
planted under the steely Southern sun and intense humidity
weeding, picking, packing vegetables
produced the $ that leads to dreams

Time flew, it was Maria's twenty-third birthday
she baked herself a cake, called her mother in Querétaro
totaled-up her savings book, jotted notes and smiled
Maria had enough money for a used, single-wide trailer

The dreams were coming through
Working long days in the field was the first step

The carrot packing was later
Of course, that was also a step back
with that supervisor who wanted *foyarla*

Left the carrots for another packing factory
boxing tomatoes, peas, and green beans
the supervisors were bitchy Latinas
who liked long shifts and no answering back
but no sexual threats or exchanges
—and no stability either
no new crops   no more work
found another job

New birthday—Maria's 24th
she only remembered it the night before
alone at her trailer, yet she kept dreaming
Maria wanted to finish school, she had left it at 5th grade

English classes after work, opportunities would unlock
a factory job with controlled temperatures
Sunday to Friday—evening shifts
left Saturdays to attend Mr. Jimenez's Beauty School

Maria pushed forward towards her dreams
not easy, Maria was a haughty, eye-catching brown woman
was that a *maldición*? A curse?
at work, she could count on undesirable sexual advances
each time she asked for a raise, a shift, or more hours to work

She began learning English at work too
with Duane, a gorgeous *bolillo,* master welder at the factory
he tutored Maria during breaks then during lunch time too
Maria began to laugh, she opened her heart to this Duane
she told me, "It feels so good to be with him, I think I'm falling for Duane"

I watched them take care of each other
Duane bought the special chairs for Maria's beauty parlor
Maria cut Duane's hair and gave him a pedicure
they became inseparable, they looked happy

Reclaiming the Right of a Legal Space: Maria—Lobianco

To the courthouse entered Maria—no last name and Duane Lobianco
they exited as Mr. and Ms. Lobianco
she wrote a thousand times *Maria Lobianco Maria Lobianco*
Maria Lobianco Maria Lobianco Maria Lobianco Maria Lobianco
Maria Lobianco Maria Lobianco Maria Lobianco Maria Lobianco

it was her first legal name, Maria Lobianco

New plans, *nuevos* sueños
Duane's new job with a national welding company
took him welding all over the country
there were phone-calls and texting many times during the day
Maria stayed local, worked one shift,
earned her online elementary and middle school diplomas
Saturdays and Sundays, the house-parlor opened to clients
and, when there was time, painted memories

Duane found an immigration lawyer
"Work, pay taxes, get involved with your community, be good citizens"
to work for Maria's *papeles*, to resolve her immigration status
Maria and Duane worked as much as they could
saving money for Maria's papers
saving money for the life they were planning

Duane was back for the week
made a barbeque for Maria's friends
embracing and kissing they shared their news during lunch
"We are trying to get pregnant and... there is more,
Duane is looking for a job to stay in Valdosta"

The work routine continued for a couple months
only broken for preparations for the Art Show
Maria's effort to get involved, to use her legal name, to be identified
there Maria's paintings and my photography
were to be shown at a local art gallery, "Life through our eyes"

"Duane is back for good, he is making frames for the show"
                              Maria called to let me know
"Let's meet at the gallery, we need to decide on the show pieces."
but she never showed up,
nor responded to my phone calls...
my thought, Duane is back—they are probably making up

I was completely wrong

A phone call came late at night
It's Valdosta Police Department
          Ma'am, we want to ask if you know a female at ...
          —what? Maria?
          Is Maria the female on the poster for an art show?
          —WHAT ARE YOU SAYING?
          Can you describe Maria?
          —Maria, why Maria?

The tattoos will help us to identify …
—WHAT ARE YOU SAYING?
Madam, someone will be there pretty soon

Maria's dreams ended in an instant
a whack with a sharp object killed her instantly
her body found decomposed
identified by tattoos, as shown in the art show poster
especially a heart, with Maria & Duane's names

No documents meant no legal name
Maria held no legal space in the United States of America

It was not easy to identify her
on a pay-stub, Maria Cardenas
on a cashier check, Maria Rosales
on her tax-ID, Maria C. Rosales Lobianco
the marriage certificate, Maria Lobianco
none had Maria's finger prints
there were no identification records
no birth certificate, no social security
no naturalization procedures
Maria was the Latina Jean Doe
however, we all had shared and were part of her life

Maria's next of kin was the confessed killer
it was an accident, Duane Lobianco claimed
a premeditated attack, the Coroner reported

For whatever reason Maria is gone, forever
futile efforts for happiness led to a life cut short
with no relatives to claim the body
it would be sent to the pauper's unnamed grave
no documents meant no legal name
Maria's legal space in the United States of America is an unnamed grave.

As a nation, the United States is not a stranger to immigration; on the contrary, immigrants were the ones who built and worked to develop the country as we know it. However, the radical change in the national origin, race, and ethnicity of the current immigrants (Latin Americans versus Europeans), together with the federal government's incapability to regulate immigration at the Mexican border, has steered individual states into making decisions and passing harsh immigration-control laws.

In April 2010, the state of Arizona was the first to pass legislation regarding immigration—SB1070, "Support Our Law Enforcement and Safe Neighborhoods Act." Since then, five states have passed similar or more severe regulations (Utah, Indiana, South Carolina, Georgia, and Alabama) while 36 states have refused or rejected to advance similar bills (American Immigration Council, 2012). In May 2011, the state of Georgia advanced the HB 87—"Illegal Immigration Reform and Enforcement Act of 2011," a copycat of Arizona's SB1070 law. In the case of Georgia, almost 75% of the agricultural work is done by hired labor (Georgia Dept. of Agriculture, 2012). Usually the farmworker is also a migrant as s/he works as a full-time, temporary worker and moves all over the state and the country with the season's labor needs. Currently in Georgia, law enforcement officers have the authority to enforce federal immigration laws such as the verification of the immigration status of foreign nationals, leading to internment and deportation (Georgia General Assembly, 2012).

As a qualitative researcher and as an educator, I believe that giving a human face to the numeric data will help increase awareness about power and privilege. Furthermore, sharing this life can shed light on intersections of gender, ethnicity, socioeconomic and immigration status and give the reader the opportunity to understand that the self and the other are intertwined and that it is not possible to know one without the other.

REFERENCES

American Immigration Council. (2012, February). A Q&A guide to state immigration laws: What you need to know if your state is considering anti-immigrant legislation. Retrieved from http://immigrationpolicy.org/sites/default/files/docs/State_Guide_to_Immigration_Laws_Updated_021612.pdf

Denzin, N., & Girardina, M. (Eds.). (2010). *Qualitative inquiry and human rights.* Walnut Creek, CA: Left Coast Press.

Denzin, N., Lincoln, Y., & Tuhiwai Smith, L. (Eds.). (2008). *Handbook of critical and indigeneous methodologies.* Thousand Oaks, CA: SAGE.

Ellis, C. (2010). Telling moments in an autoethnographer's life. In N. Denzin & M. Girardina (Eds.), *Qualitative inquiry and human rights* (pp. 243-246). Walnut Creek, CA: Left Coast Press.

Georgia Department of Agriculture. (2012, January). Report on agriculture labor: As required by House Bill 87. Retrieved from http://agr.georgia.gov/AgLaborReport.pdf

Georgia General Assembly. (2012, March). HB 87 - Illegal Immigration reform and enforcement act of 2011. Retrieved from http://www1.legis.ga.gov/legis/2011_12/sum/hb87.htm

Hoefer, M., Rytina, N., & Baker, B. (2012, March). Estimates of the unauthorized immigrant population residing in the United States: January 2011. Retrieved from http://www.dhs.gov/xlibrary/assets/statistics/publications/ois_ill_pe_2011.pdf

U. S. Census Bureau. (2010). Current population survey: Annual social and economic supplement's foreign-born population. Retrieved from http://www.census.gov/apsd/techdoc/cps/cpsmar09.pdf

CHAPTER 5

BECOMING ELL TEACHERS

The Learning Trajectory of Two Preservice Teachers and Their Implications for Teacher Education Curriculum

Bridget A. Bunten
Washington College

INTRODUCTION

American public schools represent the cultural and linguistic diversification of the United States population. One of the challenges of this diversity is that the students speak more than 350 languages (García, Jensen, & Scribner, 2009; Goldenberg, 2008). Of the approximately 14 million language-minority students in public schools, 5 million of them are classified as English language learners (ELLs) (National Clearinghouse for English Language Acquisition, 2007a, 2007b). Teachers across the country are more and more likely to have students that need additional English language support in their classrooms than ever before.

The students that sit in our public school classrooms represent the astonishing increase in our nation's cultural and linguistic diversity. The PK-12 ELL population grew by 57% from the 1995-1996 school year to the 2005-2006 school year as compared to a 3.7% growth in the overall PK-12 population. During the 2005-2006 school year in particular, ELLs

Excursions and Recursions Through Power, Privilege, and Praxis
pp. 47–64

represented 10% of the total PK-12 enrollment (National Clearinghouse for English Language Acquisition, 2007a). In that same decade, the states that saw the highest percentage growth rates of ELLs in the nation were South Carolina (688%), Arkansas (361%), Indiana (350%), North Carolina (346%), and Tennessee (296%) (National Clearinghouse for English Language Acquisition, 2007b).

However, in spite of these growing numbers, there are only five states that have specific ELL coursework or certification requirements for all teachers. In seventeen states, the teacher certification standards for all teachers contain reference to the special needs of ELLs and another eight states refer to "language" as an example of diversity. There are 15 states that do not require all teachers to have expertise or training in working with ELLs (National Clearinghouse for English Language Acquisition, 2008). Both the student demographics and the limited state requirements for preservice teachers of ELLs clearly demonstrate that more attention needs to be placed on the successful preparation of teachers in order to provide them with the knowledge, skills, and dispositions required to meet the needs of our nation's children.

This research addresses key curricular issues in preparing preservice teachers to teach the growing ELL population in U.S. schools. Currently, an integral component of teacher education programs should focus on preservice teachers' development of skills, knowledge, and dispositions for teaching ELLs. Specifically, there is urgency for building "usable knowledge" among preservice teachers with regards to educating ELLs (Lindblom & Cohen, 1979; Snow, 2001). This urgency has become a key issue in U.S. teacher education programs.

The purpose of these two case studies is to explore the discourses that preservice teachers employ in order to describe their developing understanding of the teaching and learning of ELLs. Of particular interest are the moments in which they acknowledge a shift in their thinking from one discourse (that they held upon entering the course) to another version (that was impacted by course materials and experiences). Knowing how these two preservice teachers interacted with the topics, readings, and discussions of this particular course focused on teaching ELLs allows us, as teacher educators, to develop and enhance such courses, which are much needed in our teacher education programs countrywide. The two participants, chosen from a group of twenty, were selected because they represented a diversity of characteristics of the preservice teachers in the class: Michelle (a White female of European-American descent) was a senior seeking elementary education certification and Aidan (a White male of European-American descent) was a freshman seeking secondary education certification in mathematics. Their limited experiences with ELLs prior to the course were typical of most preservice teachers enrolled in the course. In the next section, I present a literature review in which issues surrounding ELL teacher education curriculum are considered and related to my research. In the following section, I provide the theoretical framework based on the work of Foucault (1978) and Bakhtin (1981) through which I examined the data. I then clarify my methods of data collection and analysis by describing the context within which the data emerged and the manner in which discourses were identified. The two participants' use of various discourses and their self-identified zones of contact are presented in the findings sections. Each participant self-identified three zones of contact that marked a shift in their thinking about ELLs throughout the course of the semester. Last, the implications section discusses three key implications of this research for teacher education curriculum: (1) It is crucial that more states integrate courses about teaching ELLs into their teacher education curriculum; (2) A key component of such a course is the inclusion of field experiences that allow preservice teachers to interact directly with ELLs, their families, and their teachers, as well as discuss and reflect upon these interactions; and (3) We, as teacher educators, need to consider going beyond the single semester experience of such a course because the development of the knowledge, skills and dispositions necessary to work with ELLs does not happen within the confines of a single semester.

LITERATURE REVIEW OF TEACHER EDUCATION AND ELLS

In response to these changing demographics and the struggles of schools and teachers to respond to them, researchers have sought out the voices of preservice teachers, current teachers, and teacher educators as a preliminary step to proposing a course of action. My review of the literature reveals five main areas that researchers address for working with preservice teachers in relation to ELL issues. The first area focuses on the necessity to consider and learn from the experiences and concerns of current ELL educators. Valuable insight can be gained from these educators as they share the challenges they faced, the solutions they devised, and the negotiations they made regarding ELLs, individual beliefs, school context and language policy. As a result, modifications in course offerings that reflect ELL teachers' experiences and concerns are a necessary and proactive stance on the part of teacher education programs (Batt, 2008; Isenbarger & Willis, 2006; Varghese & Stritikus, 2005).

The second area further supplements the first through the work of Costa, McPhail, Smith, and Brisk (2005) who argue that change in teacher education programs begins with the involvement of faculty. During a faculty institute on ELLs (held in Massachusetts), college and university faculty members identified the following aspects that preservice teachers need to develop in order to be effective teachers of ELLs: "(a) deeper respect for the culture of ELLs and their families, (b) the ability to question their own assumptions, and (c) the ability to discuss issues of identity, privilege, and ethnocentricity" (Costa et al., 2005, p. 109).

A third area in the literature addresses the importance of opportunities for preservice teachers to investigate their personal views and experiences with diversity by sharing their feelings about minorities, ELLs, and exposure to different races and cultures (Bunten, 2010; Lee & Dallman, 2008). The beliefs and practical knowledge of preservice teachers highlight the importance of teacher education programs to consider "various diversity issues from multiple perspectives ... constructing knowledge and practical teaching of diversity ... considering personal experience with diversity in teacher preparation ... [and having] field experiences with culturally diverse children" (Lee & Dallman, pp. 42-43). The above contributions demonstrate the necessity of including the ideas and perspectives of teachers, preservice teachers, and teacher educators while considering how to respond to the increasing diversity in the public schools.

The fourth area in the literature identifies the need for significant changes in teacher education programs due to an apparent mismatch between the cultural and linguistic background of the majority of teachers and their students. In the United States, the teaching force is relatively homogenous with a predominance of European-American teachers and preservice teachers (Commins & Miramontes, 2006; Costa et al., 2005; Giambo & Szecsi, 2005/06; Grant & Gillette, 2006; Zygmunt-Fillwalk & Clark, 2007) while the diversity of the student population is growing at an alarming rate. Commins and Miramontes (2006) assert that preservice teachers need to be prepared to work with students that traverse this wide range of cultural and linguistic diversity. In order to do so successfully, teacher education programs need to incorporate coursework and field experiences that integrate the application of knowledge and skills that are effective when working with ELLs (Commins & Miramontes, 2006; Giambo & Szecsi, 2005/06; Lucas, Villegas, & Freedson-Gonzalez, 2008; Varghese & Stritikus, 2005).

Finally, constant reflection and reexamination of one's own cultural beliefs and assumptions about people of different races, cultures, and languages is an integral part of the courses and field experiences that are being developed. For example, language shock classes (Washburn, 2008) and immersion experiences (Zygmunt-Fillwalk & Clark, 2007; Zygmunt-Fillwalk & Leitze, 2006) allow preservice teachers to develop empathy for ELLs, learn strategies for teaching ELLs, and construct a new reality for teaching in a multicultural, multilingual classroom. Within these contexts, the preservice teachers modify their educational philosophies in light of their new experiences, but this change does not occur neatly overnight or even in the confines of one semester (Bunten, 2010). Zygmunt-Fillwalk and Clark (2007) assert, "Becoming multicultural thus emerges as a recursive process rather than a destination. A cyclical process emerges as individuals encounter, reflect, deconstruct, and recreate worldviews. With novel experiences, individuals begin the process anew" (p. 292).

It is this fifth area of the literature that this chapter examines more deeply with a specific focus on the learning trajectories of two preservice teachers as they navigate their way through the curriculum of an undergraduate course about teaching ELLs. The discourses that preservice teachers use to describe the recursive, cyclical process of becoming (a teacher of ELLs) change and evolve over time. Within this evolution, the discourses can clash, altering themselves, each other, and the ways in which a preservice teacher articulates her/his developing knowledge and understanding. The identification of the theoretical moment or location of discourse conflict can be enlightening for both the individual subscribing to those discourses (the preservice teachers) and outside observers (professors, researchers, etc.). Poststructuralist theories presented by Foucault (1978) and literary theories presented by Bakhtin (1981) allow us the opportunity to examine these discourses, and where and how they may conflict, in order to better understand the potential ramifications for preservice teachers and the students they work with. By applying these theories to research focused on preservice teachers developing the knowledge, skills, and dispositions to thoughtfully work with ELLs, we will deepen our understanding of the inherently complicated and recursive nature of becoming a teacher who serves a rapidly expanding segment of the student population.

DISCOURSES WITHIN A "ZONE OF CONTACT"

The work of Foucault (1978) and Bakhtin (1981) provide a theoretical lens through which to view the discursive practices of preservice teachers as they engage with new ideas, pedagogies, and philosophies. Foucault asserts that, "there can exist different and even contradictory discourses within the same strategy" (1978, p. 102). Preservice teachers' use of varying discourses, both verbal and written, can be examined for possible contradictions and insights into their thinking and reflective practices. In this way, individuals can use discourses strategically and intentionally, and people can use multiple discourses to defend, support, and/or protect arguments or beliefs.

This existence of conflicting discourses allows us to examine the possible contradictions among preservice teachers' use of varying discourses within their own written work. In this sense, a discourse can be seen as "a hindrance, a stumbling block, a point of resistance and a starting point" (Foucault, 1978, p. 101) employed by a preservice teacher who is currently in between the multiple ways of being a college student, a future teacher, and a member of a particular family and community. Interwoven throughout their contributions are references to their own lives and experiences in school, which clearly play a large role in determining which discourses they engage in and how. It is partially through this lens that I will investigate the discourses that are evident in Michelle and Aidan's writing, and how they position themselves and others, define limits, and articulate possibilities.

According to Bakhtin (1981), the act of becoming (in this case becoming a teacher of ELLs) is a process of "assimilating the words of others" with our own and thus the discourses others use in an attempt to make sense of our own experiences (p. 341). Bakhtin's (1981) notion of *heteroglossia* contributes to our understanding of the occurrence of two or more conflicting voices (or discourses), and their assimilation, at any given time in an individual's particular context. Our world is inherently *heteroglossic* due to the often-conflicting coexistence of different discourses (Bakhtin, 1981). This *heteroglossic* process of meshing and partial reformation of others' discourses plays a significant role "in an individual's ideological becoming" (Bakhtin, 1981, p. 342). Therefore, we take up the discourses of others and use them as a basis for our own interactions with people and ideas in particular contexts, thus influencing our behaviors, actions, and words.

Within a heteroglossic world, Bakhtin (1981) discusses the antagonistic relationship that is evident between authoritative discourse and internally persuasive discourse, which exist simultaneously and impact one's ideological becoming. An authoritative discourse represents the "received and static knowledge" of others that functions as a particular way of thinking in a variety of social contexts and is often based on a line of thinking that comes from a theoretical deduction as opposed to actual experience (Britzman, 2003, p. 42). Therefore, an authoritative discourse could represent particular assumptions that one possesses about ELLs, their families, or English language acquisition prior to having direct contact with ELLs. In addition, the alternative discourses that I may present through class readings and discussions about ELLs can also be seen as authoritative discourses for the preservice teachers because they are the words, ideas, and beliefs of others, which they have not necessarily taken on as their own yet. Similar to Foucault's view of discourse as capable of arranging and mapping our words and behaviors, an authoritative discourse also creates "normative categories that organize and disorganize our perceptions," which can result in a competition between these normativities

(Britzman, 2003, p. 42). The extent to which an authoritati·
aids in determining our perceptions of the world is related
with which we examine these categories and refuse to view ⸏
playing the natural order or truth about something or someone.

In opposition to authoritative discourse is internally persuasive discourse, which acknowledges the existence of contradictory social practices that are often "in opposition to socially sanctioned views and normative meanings" (Britzman, 2003, p. 42). An internally persuasive discourse is an "everyday discourse" that reflects what one thinks and has the potential to change and evolve while interacting with others (Ball, 2006, pp. 66-67). One's own words, thoughts, ideas, and beliefs are present in an internally persuasive discourse and may not have its authority acknowledged by others. For Bakhtin (1981), an individual often experiences an inner struggle between the authoritative and internally persuasive discourses that takes place at a "zone of contact" where these discourses both partially belong to the individual while partially belonging to the other (p. 345). Therefore, the "internally persuasive discourse is a discourse of becoming" as we struggle to take what we already know and decide to expand it, abandon it, or maintain it (Britzman, 2003, p. 42). The zone of contact resembles Foucault's (1978) assertion that one individual can simultaneously be employing the strategic use of different and often contradictory discourses in a process of "trying things on" to see how they fit (or don't fit) with one's actions, behaviors, and beliefs.

In many ways, the internally persuasive discourses of the preservice teachers may mirror the authoritative discourses of the dominant culture that they brought with them to the university, which can be at odds with the academic and research discourses of ELLs that were presented in class. In the process of becoming a teacher, and in this case, a teacher who works with ELLs, both authoritative and internally persuasive discourses are evident and are often conflicting. The moment or space where divergent discourses collide is a *zone of contact*. The preservice teachers' choice of discourse within a zone of contact exhibits their sense of reflection and agency. Both Foucault (1978) and Bakhtin (1981) provide a framework within which to consider the point of conflict, or zone of contact, where the authoritative and internally persuasive discourses of preservice teachers collide, and are capable of providing insight into their experiences, pedagogies, beliefs, and intentions.

The self-identification of a contact zone and the discourses within that zone holds particular significance for preservice teachers. Tightly connected to the fifth area that I identified within the literature review, it is crucial for preservice teachers themselves to actively reflect on and reexamine their experiences with and beliefs about children. This process of reflection and reexamination is both recursive and cyclical, but even more so when it is stimulated by their own identification of how their authoritative and internally persuasive discourses have collided, aligned, and/or changed. If identification and acknowledgement of their discourses and contact zones came solely from me, as their professor, my thoughts and opinions could be considered another example of an authoritative discourse. Whereas discourses and zones of contact identified by the preservice teachers themselves have the power to be internally persuasive. This distinction is why the self-identified zones of contact presented in this research are so crucial; they increase the likelihood that the discourses used will develop into lasting, internally persuasive discourses for the preservice teachers that will (hopefully) positively influence their work with ELLs.

METHODS OF DATA COLLECTION AND ANALYSIS

The two preservice teachers, Michelle and Aidan (both pseudonyms), were enrolled in a course entitled "Teaching English to English Language Learners." This course is part of the teacher education curriculum at a large public university located in what is otherwise a rural area and was specifically developed to meet new mandates for teacher education programs in the state. Michelle, a junior in her early twenties, was studying to become an elementary school teacher. Aidan, a freshman in his late teens, was a mathematics major with the hope of becoming a high school math teacher. Throughout the semester, Michelle, Aidan, and their classmates engaged in various formal and informal writing assignments both in and out of the college classroom.

The course in which Michelle and Aidan were enrolled, EDUC 250 (pseudonym), was a brand new course that was required by the state for all education students in the early childhood, elementary, and secondary education programs. The professor who designed the course and I each taught a section of EDUC 250 during its first semester. Michelle and Aidan were enrolled in my section. Overall, EDUC 250 focused on the development of the foundational knowledge needed for preservice teachers to successfully assist ELLs in their future classrooms. The course was based on the principle that teachers play a crucial role in creating a positive classroom-learning environment, particularly for ELLs, which ultimately contributes to their academic and social success. The purpose of this course is for preservice teachers to develop essential dispositions, skills, and knowledge needed to fulfill their critical role of addressing the diverse needs of ELLs.

The major course topics included culture, language, learning contexts, and pedagogy. Culture focused on understanding the diversity of ELLs, their families, their communities, and their cultural values. Language focused on understanding the structure (i.e., morphemes, words, and syntax), functions, and variations of the English language, first and second language and literacy acquisition processes, and the connection between oral and written language in school contexts. Learning contexts focused on understanding the characteristics of school and classroom situations that support ELLs' successful learning. Pedagogy focused on understanding key principles of linguistically responsive teaching for ELLs. Students studied these four major course topics through course readings, class discussions, and cultural explorations of their own and others' cultures while engaging in individual, social, and experiential learning opportunities.

Three assessment measures were used to evaluate student understanding of the course content, and these measures included a research paper, a learning portfolio, and a curriculum-based test. Scores from these three assessment measures were aggregated to represent a final grade for the course for each student.

For the purpose of understanding Michelle and Aidan's individual learning trajectories, I examined the components of their learning portfolios, which included: a description of three cultural artifacts, their autobiography, eleven reading memos, ten quick writes, and their teaching statement. The cultural artifacts assignment was a brief description of three cultural artifacts that the students chose to represent themselves as a cultural being. They wrote a short autobiography that described their aspirations, identity, and personal experiences. The reading memos were one-page interpretations of specific readings that were turned in the day before we met to discuss those readings. The quick writes were written responses to prompts at the beginning or end of a class period that were intended to help students internalize class readings and discussions focusing on a specific course theme. Finally, the teaching statement assignment asked students to identify changes in their thinking throughout the semester, articulate their current pedagogy and philosophy regarding teaching ELLs, and describe specific curricular manifestations of these current beliefs within their future classrooms.

All of Michelle and Aidan's writing samples within their learning portfolios were scrutinized through content analysis to look for patterns and themes (Creswell, 2007). Particular attention was given to their development of knowledge, skills, and dispositions surrounding the teaching and learning of second language literacy skills to ELLs. This investigation provides insight into the development and reflective practices of two preservice teachers as they address issues of language acquisition, culture, and literacy instruction and assessment. Drawing from both Foucault (1978) and Bakhtin's (1981) notions of discourse and Bakhtin's notion of a "zone of contact," I present Michelle and Aidan's self-identified zones of contact. I identified potential zones of contact marked by the recognition of a change in thinking or introduction of new ideas. It is at these locations where their internally persuasive discourses were developing and either contradicted or aligned with previously held authoritative discourses. The implications for curricular decisions across and within teacher education programs will subsequently be discussed.

FINDINGS: SELF-IDENTIFIED ZONES OF CONTACT

Michelle

According to Michelle's autobiography, she originally wanted to be a nurse, but was struck by the intensity of the job after shadowing a neonatal intensive care unit nurse at a local hospital. While at the university, she started out pursuing courses focused on health care, but switched during her sophomore year to study elementary education. She admitted that her decision to switch was partially influenced by her mother who is a third grade teacher.

Michelle's cultural artifacts included a photograph of her and her two sisters, a pair of ski gloves, and the book she was currently reading, *Breaking Dawn* by Stephanie Meyer (2008). The photograph represents the strong bond she has with her sisters. The ski gloves stand for her enjoyment of skiing as a sport and a much needed stress reliever. Last, the book symbolizes her overall love of reading and desire to continue to read for pleasure as her academic responsibilities increase.

Throughout the rest of her learning portfolio, Michelle presented three significant self-identified zones of contact. Michelle's first self-identified zone of contact was where her own experiences and beliefs about culture were challenged by other discourses. In particular, Michelle refers to this realization in the first reading memo, which was a response to a chapter written by Geertz (1973). According to Michelle, "It is important to view and experience other cultures because it allows us to see into different ways of life. We have to accept others that believe in different things because we are all unique in our own ways" (9/2/09). Michelle returns to the same discourse at the end of the semester in her teaching statement by clearly defining this zone of contact, "My learning about different cultures and how important it is to be exposed to other cultures has definitely deepened this semester" (12/15/09).

Michelle identified her second zone of contact in two different quickwrites. This zone dealt with the language that ELLs should be immersed in and use while at school. Initially, Michelle advised that ELLs should predominantly be immersed in solely English: "ELLs learn best in schools when they are surrounded and immersed in the language that they are currently learning. Being around people who speak the language and interacting with them will help them pick up the language better and quicker" (8/25/09). Nearly two months later while Michelle was writing about effective classroom environments, she modified her original discourse to include the use of the students' native languages:

> An effective classroom environment for ESL students is a place where they are encouraged to talk and to participate. By having them talk, they gain practice in speaking in their second language. They should also be encouraged to use their first language. This will show them that their first language is a valuable resource they can use. (10/22/09)

Michelle's third self-identified zone of contact revolved around the pedagogical practice of establishing classroom communities. Michelle first mentioned this challenge in the fourth reading memo, which was the transcript of Gebber's (2007) award speech where the author talks about children being able to see "past the differences and focus on the friendships" (10/19/09). In her teaching statement, Michelle again employed a discourse that referenced the importance of a teacher of ELLs establishing a strong, trusting classroom community: "This is profound because this creates a caring community where kids are not worried about fitting in because they are different. It is so important to create a community within the classroom where students are encouraged to be themselves" (12/15/09).

In addition to the self-identification of the three aforementioned zones of contact, Michelle articulated in her teaching statement what these changes in her thinking would look like in her future classroom with ELLs. To begin, Michelle addressed her responsibility to her students:

> My philosophy is that all students can learn, but outside factors such as speaking a different language or having a disability can hider the speed and ability to learn ... we need to help these students succeed just as we would teach any other student. (12/15/09)

Michelle specifically referred to the fifth reading memo about Goldenberg's (1992) article on instructional conversations. In discussing the benefits of instructional conversations for the oral language and literacy development of ELLs, Michelle stated, "True education—real teaching—involved helping students think, reason, comprehend, and understand important ideas" (12/15/09). She continued by saying:

> We have to give a true education to all students including to ELLs so they can thrive as well. Every student has a right to real teaching and a real edu-

cation, and it is up to us, as teachers, to give this opportunity to them. (12/15/09)

In the excerpt above, Michelle is articulating her meaning of a "true education" for ELLs, which marks a shift from an authoritative to an internally persuasive discourse. Michelle concluded by reconnecting this responsibility to the establishment of a positive classroom community: "I want to establish a caring community between me and my students, as well as with the parents of my students" (12/15/09). Knowing more about other cultures, advocating for the use of ELLs' native languages, and creating an environment where all of her students can be open about themselves and their own beliefs were important to Michelle. In order to be successful as a teacher, Michelle acknowledged that her students needed to feel safe and view the classroom as a sanctuary. These three distinct self-identified zones of contact reveal how Michelle has appropriated the discourses of others (authoritative) and begun to make them her own (internally persuasive).

Aidan

In his autobiography, Aidan shared a great deal about his upbringing, which included his relationship with his two younger brothers, moving around a lot, his love of Power Rangers, and his parents' divorce. The divorce affected Aidan immensely in late elementary school and middle school as his household duties increased, his circle of friends decreased, and his weight began to climb. These pressures negatively affected Aidan's personal, social, and academic identities. During ninth grade, Aidan met a German exchange student who became a great friend and things started to improve for him personally and socially. Aidan lost weight, gained more confidence, did well in his classes, and overall, enjoyed his high school experience.

Aidan's cultural artifacts included his high school's "Terrible Towel," a tin box from Berlin, Germany, and a pom-pom from the university. The towel symbolized Aidan's love of sports, specifically football, and his strong connection to his high school. Aidan traveled to Berlin twice in high school, becoming good friends with the exchange student and his family. The tin represented his bond with another language and culture. The pom-pom stood for the new chapter in Aidan's life that recently began when he started at the university.

In his learning portfolio, Aidan presented three self-identified zones of contact. Aidan foregrounded the first zone of contact by admitting that he was initially hesitant to take EDUC 250 when his advisor suggested it.

Since the course was a new requirement, there wasn't much known about it, but Aidan stated that he wanted to take the risk and check it out. Aidan's first self-identified zone of contact revolved around a more thorough understanding of ELLs and how he, as a future high school math teacher, would be affected:

> The things I gained most from the class were the things my advisor did not mention to me. I gained a new perspective for the ELLs and for teaching them. Prior to this course, I had no idea what an ELL was (I had only heard of ESL) and I did not think this class was going to have much of an effect on me since my major is secondary education math. I was wrong. My thinking has completely shifted; I now grasp the importance of learning how to teach ELLs. (Teaching statement, 12/3/09)

In the excerpt above, Aidan clearly identified how the authoritative discourse he had ascribed to did not take ELLs into consideration. His experiences in EDUC 250 have resulted in a shift of his thinking to an internally persuasive discourse that includes his future professional goal of becoming a high school math teacher.

Aidan's second self-identified zone of contact was impacted by two "of the readings that morphed my thinking the most" (12/3/09). Aidan wrote about the Flynn (2004) article on curriculum-based readers theater and the reciprocal teaching (1989) excerpt in the sixth reading memo. He admitted to never having considered the use of these activities in a high school math class, but has now found great benefits in them for ELLs at all grade levels and in all subject areas (10/28/09). In his teaching statement, Aidan returned to these strategies and his intended use of them: "I feel that these two concepts will be very valuable to me as a future high school math teacher" (12/3/09). The resulting internally persuasive discourse is one that, for Aidan, is open to the possibility of using a variety of instructional strategies to meet the needs of his adolescent ELLs.

Aidan's third self-identified zone of contact was his newfound understanding and ability to articulate the knowledge, skills, and dispositions of teachers of ELLs. When discussing the increasing number of immigrants and languages spoken in the United States, Aidan asserted, "I believe that knowing how to teach ELLs is a necessity to all teachers" (Teaching statement, 12/3/09). Aidan continued by identifying qualities of an ELL teacher:

> A teacher with ELL students needs to be patient, nurturing and empathetic as well. A teacher needs to be able to adapt his/her teaching style to the ELLs and he/she needs to be able to connect with the ELLs in some way: emotionally, mentally, or culturally. (12/3/09)

The above excerpt displays Aidan's internally persuasive discourse that provided him with the ability to clearly articulate characteristics of effective ELL educators that he couldn't have identified as noticeably as before.

While reflecting on these self-identified zones of contact and their discourses in his teaching statement, Aidan articulated what the changes in his thinking would mean at a practical level: "I will do many group activities" (12/3/09). He explained that group work is also good math pedagogy and that he would be strategic about which groups he places the ELLs in. Additionally, Aidan intended to access his ELL students' prior knowledge and experiences with math: "I will ask the ELLs if there were any differences between the math they were taught in their home country ... even in math, cultures can do things very differently, and it can still be right" (12/3/09). By connecting with students in this way, Aidan believed that it would help him to "develop a better relationship with that student and increase his/her chances of success" (12/3/09). It is evident that through these internally persuasive discourses, Aidan is able to more effectively articulate many facets of both curriculum and pedagogy that will have positive outcomes for his ELLs.

IMPLICATIONS FOR TEACHER EDUCATION CURRICULUM

In making sense of Michelle and Aidan's learning trajectories through EDUC 250 and their self-identified zones of contact, it is crucial to reconsider the larger context within which this course took place. Their university is located within a state that is one of only five states across the country that requires ELL-specific coursework or certification requirements for all preservice teachers. Clearly, this course requirement and their experiences are the exception when compared to teacher education curriculum and preservice teachers, in general, in the other 45 states. The most prevalent and critical implication drawn from Michelle's and Aidan's experiences is that more states need to integrate courses about teaching ELLs into their teacher education curriculum. Such a course is of particular importance in the low-incidence states with the highest percentage growth rates of ELLs during the 2005-2006 school year: South Carolina, Arkansas, Indiana, North Carolina, and Tennessee (National Clearinghouse for English Language Acquisition, 2007b).

The second implication of this research focuses on the content of a course about teaching ELLs and how we go about helping preservice teachers develop the knowledge, skills, and dispositions necessary to address the diverse language and literacy needs of ELLs. Preservice teachers benefit greatly from field experiences in schools, classrooms, and community centers that allow them to have direct interactions with ELLs, their families, and their teachers. This component is something that EDUC 250 lacked. For the most part, my students only had limited contact with adult ELLs and indirect contact (through work samples) with elementary-aged ELLs.

Such field experiences would allow preservice teachers the opportunity to observe lessons, conduct interviews with teachers and students, and teach lessons of their own, among other activities. During these direct interactions, preservice teachers would have continued opportunities to engage with competing discourses about ELLs and teaching. This exposure would assist in the creation of meaningful zones of contact in which preservice teachers could self-identify the personal growth, evolution, and development of their being, thinking, and doing. Preservice teachers should then be encouraged to consider how they are taking up the discourses of others (authoritative) and meshing them with their own as they engage in the process of becoming a teacher of ELLs who can clearly articulate their own internally persuasive discourses.

In conjunction with these field experiences, the preservice teachers need ample opportunities to discuss and reflect upon their interactions with ELLs in academic and social settings. These debriefing sessions can happen in both oral and written form, individually and collaboratively throughout the course of the semester. Continuous reflection and reevaluation of self and others will greatly contribute to the preservice teachers' increased understanding of themselves as linguistic and cultural beings.

The third and final implication of this research highlights the need for us, as teacher educators, to go beyond the single semester experience. Change in educational philosophies and practices regarding ELLs does not happen overnight and is not a final destination, but should rather be viewed overtime as part of a larger developmental process (Bunten, 2010; Zygmunt-Fillwalk & Clark, 2007). Over the course of their teacher preparation experiences, preservice teachers engage in a constant negotiation of authoritative and internally persuasive discourses. EDUC 250 and the assignments examined in this research are only a few pieces of their infinite development as teachers. As a teacher educator, I should be thankful that this initial experience with ELL research and topics has sparked them to think about and respond to ELLs in a more comprehensive, thoughtful way.

In addition to the creation of more ELL-focused courses in teacher education curriculum, we must follow the preservice teachers after finishing the course. What happens during their student teaching experience? How do they interact with ELLs? What about their first year of teaching? Their first three years of teaching? How do they react when confronted with new authoritative discourses? Do new zones of contact emerge? If so, how and when? How does the teacher respond? What additional factors come into play as they consider the development of new internally persuasive discourses? These are only a few examples of questions that we, as teacher educators and researches, can ask as we continue to follow the learning trajectories of our preservice teachers.

Beyond the confines of our classrooms, preservice teachers interact with new and diverse schools, colleagues, student populations, families, communities, cultures, and languages on a daily basis. These interactions continuously shape the preservice teachers they are and the inservice teachers they will become by presenting myriad discourses to be accepted, challenged, refuted, and/or ignored. By accompanying our preservice teachers on their journey, we are afforded the opportunity to better understand their transformation and growth in order to improve our own teaching practice. If we, as an educational community, are to rise to the challenges posed by the increase in the linguistic and cultural diversity of our county and our student population, then it is imperative that we investigate our preservice teachers' experiences with ELLs more thoughtfully and over an extended period of time.

REFERENCES

Bakhtin, M. M. (1981). Discourse in the novel. In M. Holquist (Ed.), *The dialogic imagination* (pp. 259-422). Austin, TX: University of Texas Press.

Ball, A. F. (2006). *Multicultural strategies for education and social change: Carriers of the torch in the United States and South Africa*. New York, NY: Teachers College Press.

Batt, E. G. (2008). Teachers' perceptions of ELL education: Potential solutions to overcome the greatest challenges. *Multicultural Education, 15*, 39-43.

Britzman, D. (2003). *Practice makes practice: A critical study of learning to teach*. Albany, NY: State University of New York Press.

Bunten, B. A. (2010). Welcome to America, now speak English: Preservice teachers' discourses focus on native Russian-speaking students. *Multicultural Education, 17*(4), 2-9.

Commins, N. L., & Miramontes, O. B. (2006). Addressing linguistic diversity from the outset. *Journal of Teacher Education, 57*, 240-246.

Costa, J., McPhail, G., Smith, J. & Brisk, M. E. (2005). Faculty first: The challenge of infusing the teacher education curriculum with scholarship on English language learners. *Journal of Teacher Education, 56*, 104-118.

Creswell, J. W. (2007). *Qualitative inquiry and research design: Choosing among five approaches* (2nd ed.). Thousand Oaks, CA: Sage.

Flynn, R. M. (2004). Curriculum-based readers theater: Setting the stage for reading and retention. *The Reading Teacher, 58*(4), 360-365.

Foucault, M. (1978). *The history of sexuality: An introduction* (Vol 1.) New York, NY: Vintage Books.

García, E. E., Jensen, B. T., & Scribner, K. P. (2009). The demographic imperative. *Educational Leadership, 66*(7), 8-13.

Gebber, S. (2007). Acceptance remarks for the Spartan Village G.L.O.B.A.L. Education Award (East Lansing Education Foundation). East Lansing, MI.

Geertz, C. (1973). *The interpretation of cultures*. New York, NY: Basic Books.

Giambo, D., & Szecsi, T. (2005/06). Opening up to the issues: Preparing preservice teachers to work effectively with English language learners. *Childhood Education, 82,* 107-110.

Goldenberg, C. (1992). Instructional conversations: Promoting comprehension through discussion. *The Reading Teacher, 46*(4), 316-326.

Goldenberg, C. (2008). Teaching English to language learners: What the research does—and does not—say. *American Educator, 32*(1), 8-23 & 42-44.

Grant, C. A., & Gillette, M. (2006). A candid talk to teacher educators about effectively preparing teachers who can teach everyone's children. *Journal of Teacher Education, 57,* 292-299.

Isenbarger, L., & Willis, A. I. (2006). An intersection of theory and practice: Accepting the language a child brings into the classroom. *Language Arts, 84,* 125-135.

Lee, S., & Dallman, M. E. (2008). Engaging in a reflective examination about diversity: Interviews with three preservice teachers. *Multicultural Education, 15,* 36-44.

Lindblom, C. E., & Cohen, D. K. (1979). *Usable knowledge: Social science and social problem solving*. New Haven, CT: Yale University Press.

Lucas, T., Villegas, A. M., & Freedson-Gonzalez, M. (2008). Linguistically responsive teacher education: Preparing classroom teachers to teach English language learners. *Journal of Teacher Education, 59,* 361-373.

Meyer, S. (2008). *Breaking dawn*. New York, NY: Little, Brown and Company.

National Clearinghouse for English Language Acquisition & Language Instruction Educational Programs. (2007a). How many school-aged limited English proficient (LEP) students are there in the U.S.? Retrieved from http://www.ncela.gwu.edu/faqs

National Clearinghouse for English Language Acquisition. (2007b). *The growing number of limited English proficient students: 2005-2006 poster*. Retrieved from http://www.ncela.gwu.edu/stats/2_nation.htm

National Clearinghouse for English Language Acquisition. (2008). *Educating English language learners: Building teacher capacity*. Retrieved from http://www.ncela.gwu.edu/practice/mainstream_teachers.htm

Snow, C. E. (2001). Knowing what we know: Children, teachers, researchers. *Educational Researcher, 30*(7), 3-9.

Varghese, M. M. & Stritikus, T. (2005). "*Nadie me dijó* (Nobody told me)": Language policy negotiation and implications for teacher education. *Journal of Teacher Education, 56,* 73-87.

Washburn, G. N. (2008). Alone, confused, and frustrated: Developing empathy and strategies for working with English language learners. *The Clearing House, 81,* 247-250.

Zygmunt-Fillwalk, E., & Clark, P. (2007). Becoming multicultural: Raising awareness and supporting change in teacher education. *Childhood Education, 83,* 288-293.

Zygmunt-Fillwalk, E. M., & Leitze, A. (2006). Promising practices in preservice teacher preparation: The Ball State University urban semester. *Childhood Education, 82,* 283-288.

CHAPTER 6

RESTLESS AND LOST IN CURRICULUM AND PEDAGOGY

Excursions and Interventions

Jennifer L. Milam
University of Akron

Each of us has been a student.
     Many of us have been teachers.
          We are all curriculum workers.

And while the above is true, the messy, rewarding, chaotic, painful, deeply intellectual, spiritual, and yes, even physical work of curriculum has been largely ignored or exchanged for static notions of content and traditional, if not nearly always oppressive, ideas of what curriculum should be and who students, teachers and curriculum workers are (and, by default, who they are not). Nearly 35 years ago, Adrienne Rich and Andrea O'Reilly began the groundbreaking work of deconstructing the paternalistic and reductive ideals of motherhood to "release the creation and sustenance of life into the … realm of decision, struggle, surprise, imagination, and conscious intelligence" (O'Reilly, 2006, p. 11). In serendipitous synch with these works was/is the emergence of curriculum studies and curriculum

Excursions and Recursions Through Power, Privilege, and Praxis
pp. 65–71

theorizing in the reconceptualist movement that posits as unfinished and complicated the very nature of the lived, destabilized, and profoundly personal experiences of all of us. In this moment, the convergence of auto/biography, identities, subjectivities, reflexivities, praxis and discourse refuse the reductive and elude the definitive. As posited by Springgay and Freedman and their coauthors (2012), mothering is physically, emotionally, and intellectually, restless at its core—performative and demanding of reiteration. And, like curriculum and pedagogy, as an active practice it can become a "strategic site of political, economic, and cultural transformation" (p. 5).

Reconceptualized curriculum theorizing and pedagogy are living, breathing, birthing, and rearing texts and experiences that refuse previously articulated, overly simplistic, paternalistically exclusive, and impersonal narratives or stories about education. And while language on the following pages may appear linear and two-dimensional, as on the printed page it must be, curriculum theory, curriculum studies, and curriculum work, is a contested cultural space—unfree from cultural, political, historical, and hegemonic structures and categories that seek to discipline and contain curriculum and pedagogy. In each question we pose, every rally we attend, in the moments when we help our own children with their homework, when we prepare future teachers, or ponder a provocative theory, we can engage in acts of "deconstructing assumptions of a knowing subject, a known subject, and an unambiguous, complete knowledge outside of the unsaid and unsayable, the embedded fore-structures of understanding" (Lather, 2000, p. 104) to shine light on the un/conscious, multiple, and distinctly personal experiences of ourselves—and each other. The recognition of the un/knowable and in/comprehensible is to resist (re)presentation and finality—to push beyond what we think we know and what we believe to be possible.

RESTLESSNESS: A BEGINNING

On the one hand, we, human beings, are comforted by certainty, by predictability, by the ability to name and understand, with measurable and purportedly objective means, the world around us. On the other, we theorize experiences and challenge the very nature of our being in the world seemingly excited by the possibility of the unknown or unknowable. This contradiction, this restlessness, I contend is at the core of our wrestling, our contemplating, our searching for meaning—in nearly all aspects of our lives. This restlessness, exemplifies what Kinser (2008) described as the "ambiguity, tension, contradiction, and personal struggle in feminist mothering" (p. 11) but it's the same when "feminist mothering" is replaced with "curriculum" and the ambiguity, tensions, and contradictions therein. It is the endless search for a utopic space of existence and the realization that this space does not exist. For m/others, it is the realization that your idealized fantasies of what it means to be a parent, to unconditionally and mightily love (and receive the love of) child(ren), and to become every bit the parent you perhaps lacked, are impossible fantasies at best. At their worst, the fantasies are depressing delusions that inflict horrible pain and suffering on the psyche and physical body. For the curriculum worker, theorist, practitioner, it is coming to see the absolute absence of hope in spaces once viewed only as hopeful and optimistic, riddled with candy-coated phrases like "All children can learn" and "No child shall be left behind." Worse, it is realizing that our very position implicates us and holds us responsible for change.

Restless, we seek, we wonder, we imagine.
Lost, we mourn, we cry, we surrender.

The sense of loss—loss of control, loss of autonomy, loss of idealized notions of curriculum, loss of rationality—might reflect a mourning of the loss of a subject (of a self) "capable of fully conscious, fully rational action, a subject assumed in most liberal and emancipatory discourse" and s/he is replaced with a "provisional, contingent, strategic, constructed subject which, while not essentialized, *must* be engaged in processes of meaning-making given the bombardment of conflicting messages" about what it means to teach, to learn, to work, to think, to theorize, and be responsible for the education of other human beings (Lather, 2000, p. 120, emphasis in original). And perhaps, it is in the moment of meeting a child, our child(ren)—our own and those in schools—that we see a reflection of the unknowable, fragmented, and irrational self we had previously left unattended. Lather (2007) suggests, as echoed by Springgay and Freedman (2012) with regard to mothering, that a double(d) reading of curriculum "intervenes in what it critiques by not only overturning the classical opposition but by a general displacement of the system" (p. 6). It does not insist on a new (re)presentation but rather to challenge the possibility of (re)presentation at all.

RESTLESSNESS: EXCURSIONS AND INTERVENTIONS

While on first read, one might recognize this space as theoretically and intellectually productive (I certainly do), even pregnant with pedagogical possibilities for growth and learning (Maudlin, 2012), it is also a space that for those who have never previously encountered it, or for those who have been enmeshed in it for some time, an exhausting place where foundational knowledges, taken-for-granted ways of being in the world, are swept away like the sands on a beach with each breaking wave. It is an encounter with a self that "is constituted and reconstituted relationally, its boundaries repeatedly remapped and renegotiated" (Scott, 1987, p. 17). We question things once assumed as truth and posit new truths in relation to and with our world, our theories, and our experiences. In essence, we are engaged in a postmodern (Grossberg, 1987), "post-post-structuralist" project (Johnson, 1986, p. 69) rejecting a tendency to reify any singular, even fractured, self (or notion of curriculum) while constantly, *restlessly*, engaging in discursive self and social (re)production in an attempt to illuminate some coherence and continuity in our world—if even for a moment in time, a particular event, or interaction.

In the midst of radical contingencies and indeterminancies, we must dis/locate our selves—be lost, seeking, still always feeling just out of arms reach of some sense of stability, of knowing. In the harshest and most compassionate way, we must confront what many already know—to work in curriculum, in classrooms, is to live in the presence and power of the real, and to live a restless life is inescapably fraught with discomfort and alienation. And while these are experienced alongside moments of great joy and immeasurable exhilaration, to feel them, to recognize and name them, is difficult because it requires an acknowledgement that the grandiose notions of curriculum or theoretical idealism present in our culture, memory, and social consciousness are falsities built on grand narratives that neglect the contradictions and complexities of living—and more often than not, privilege some while marginalizing many. It is worth acknowledging that troubling, resisting, and theorizing in/with/through discomfort and alienation is insufficient—an oft deployed critique of many critical perspectives including critical theory, postmodernism, and other post discourses—and can render conversations (and action) about curriculum, identities, and positions paralyzed. Where does one go if all knowledge is tentative? If all positions are contested? Is wandering through restlessness enough? Perhaps not, but what I am suggesting here is what Foucault (1989/1996) proposed when he put forth a different ethical position for transformative intellectuals:

> The role of the intellectual is not to tell others what they must do.... The work of an intellectual is not to mold the political will of others; it is ... to reexamine evidence and assumptions, to shake up habitual ways of working and thinking, to dissipate conventional familiarities, to reevaluate rules and institutions. (p. 462)

While there is no singular model or (re)presentation for how restlessness might be employed, called upon, or used as a tactical and contemplative

approach to curriculum and being in the world, we migh
cault's "shaking-up" to include Malewski's (2009) curriculu
cultural work, advocacy, critical study, and intervention—acti
by theory, cultural work informed by curriculum studies, advo
the "tyranny of the normative" (p. 16). Interventions that incl
study of language, structures, and knowledge, and interventions in curriculum that allow for "opportunities to think teaching and learning
through a growing number of perspectives" (p. 23). What I am suggesting
here, as an extension of restlessness, are interventions that allow for a
(re)framing of disciplinarity beyond similarity and consensus and move
toward praxis and a purposeful (un)bounding of the field based on difference, divergence, and (dis)location. More, interventions are moments of
thoughtful integration of curriculum studies in unexpected places (e.g.,
traditional teacher education programs or the high school curriculum),
advocacy work on political committees and community organizations
(e.g., opt out movements), and activism with and among groups working
toward equity, democracy, and social transformation (e.g., occupy movement, teach-ins, community organizing). In these moments of intervention and proliferations, restlessness is reflected in commitments to
dissensus and divergent (re)presentation of our "human inventiveness ...
that necessarily brings together seemingly incompatible ideas without col-
lapsing them into each other" (Malewski, 2009, pp. 23-24).

Beyond interventions, one might also consider excursions of/into/with
restlessness—ventures into (un)known territories, of un(der)studied histories, and with (un)common knowledges. "Curriculum theorizing in
postreconceptual times then is caught up at the crossroads of a certain
undecidability as to what to do so as to engage in political mediation and
remain flexible enough to accommodate nuance and ambivalence"
(Malewski, 2009, p. 537). While we are necessarily constrained by material
and symbolic forces in neoliberalism, when we (re)focus our thoughts, our
actions, our language toward a "mutual, dialogic production of a multi-
voice, multicentered discourse" (Lather, 1991, p. 112) we can ponder,
posit proliferations of theory and practice, in a world where not all people
are the same, and we are not all oppressed (and oppressing others) by and
with the social scripts and objectifications that envelope us now and have
for the entirety of our past. The goal is not arrival at some ideal utopia or
aimless idle awaiting revolution, but rather a dynamic, engaged discourse
and dialogue that recognizes the possibilities and potential in its entire
people and that renders "suspect bounded theories of teaching and learning and highlights the political and gendered dimensions of canoniza-
tion" (Malewski, 2012, p. 356) and paternalistic, hegemonic, and
reductive curricula.

Restless.

Unable to stay still or quiet.

Ceaselessly active or moving.

Worried. Anxious. Uneasy.

Not restful.

Without repose.

Restless and Lost.

Lost and Restless.

In the twilight, the moments between darkness and daylight, restlessness resides. In the spaces between static notions of curriculum and pedagogy, restlessness is found. It can be debilitating in its omniscience or liberating in its refusal to relinquish simple answers to our deepest, most pressing questions. Curriculum work, like mothering, is restless. It is the constant searching for explanation, articulation, and illumination, for one's self and others. It is the courageous, radical and rebellious understanding that nothing is ever finished and nothing should ever be. For the joy, the power, the excitement and the promise lies in the unknowing, the restless searching through unfamiliar terrains and journeys through a "reflexive cycle in which thought bends back upon itself and thus recovers its volition" (Pinar & Grumet, 1976, pp. 130-131). As Springgay and Freedman (2012) posit, a "double(d) movement" that urges us through tensions and structures and toward fertile ground for new practices allows us to embrace restlessness and the dis/comforting "struggles for self-representation and self-determination" (Visweswaran, 1994, p. 32; as cited in Pillow, 2003, p. 93). For the restless, it is comforting and reassuring to know that others share the journey—will you?

REFERENCES

Foucault, M. (1996). Concern for truth. In S. Lotringer (Ed.) & L. Hochroth & J. Johnston (Trans.), *Foucault live: Collected interviews, 1961-1984* (pp. 455-464). New York, NY: Semiotext(e). (Original work published 1989)

Grossberg, L. (1987). The in-difference of television or, mapping TV's popular economy. *Screen, 28*(2), 28-47.

Johnson, R. (1986-1987). What is cultural studies anyway? *Social Text, 16*, 38-80.

Kinser, A. E. (Ed.). (2008). *Mothering in the third wave.* Toronto, Ontario, Canada: Demeter Press.

Lather, P. (1991). *Getting smart: Feminist research and pedagogy with/in the postmodern.* New York, NY: Routledge.

Maudlin, J. G. (2012). Pregnant pedagogy. In S. Springgay & D. Freedman (Eds.), *Mothering a bodied curriculum: Emplacement, desire, affect* (pp. 34-50). Toronto, Ontario, Canada: University of Toronto Press.

Malewski, E. (Ed.) (2009). *Curriculum studies handbook: The next moment.* New York, NY: Routledge.

Malewski, E. (2012). M/othering as un(der)studied in curriculum studies: An epilogue. In S. Springgay & D. Freedman (Eds.), *Mothering a bodied curriculum: Emplacement, desire, affect* (pp. 341-360). Toronto, Ontario, Canada: University of Toronto Press.

O'Reilly, A. (2006). *Rocking the cradle: Thoughts on feminism, motherhood and the possibility of empowered mothering.* Toronto, Ontario, Canada: Demeter Press.

Pillow, W. (1994). Confession, catharsis, or cure? Rethinking the uses of reflexivity as methodological power in qualitative research. *Qualitative Studies in Education, 16*(2), 175-196.

Pinar, W., & Grumet, M. (1976). *Toward a poor curriculum.* Dubuque, IA: Kendall Hunt.

Scott, J. (1987). Critical tensions (Review of Teresa de Lauretis, *Feminst studies/critical studies*). *Women's Review of Books, 5*(1), 17-18.

Springgay, S., & Freedman, D. (Eds.). (2012). *Mothering a bodied curriculum: Emplacement, desire, affect.* Toronto, Ontario, Canada: University of Toronto Press.

Visweswaran, K. (1994). *Fictions of feminist ethnography.* Minneapolis, MN: University of Minnesota Press.

RECURSIONS

Introduction

James C. Jupp
Georgia Southern University

INTRODUCTORY NOTES AND COMMENTS

As a curriculum worker who is interested in intellectual history and who spent 18 years teaching in Title I schools, it is with great pleasure that I write the introductory notes and comments to this section titled "Recursions"—which we have divided into two parts, "Re/Turning to History" and "Re/Turning to Praxis." The present field, as I witness it in curriculum studies conferences and in the American Educational Research Association's (AERA) Division B sessions each year, appears increasingly ahistorical and troublingly divorced from authentic dialogue with teachers, educators, and policymakers.[1] The authors in this section, *against the grain* of the present field, engage and rework historical concepts and representations along with historical notions of curriculum praxis currently diminished in the field. The first group of essays, organized under the notion of *re/turning to history,* engage and rework concepts and representations in ways that articulate historical sensibilities for the field. The second group of essays, organized under the notion of *re/turning to praxis,* approach the arduous task of articulating curriculum theory that could reanimate and reengage teachers' understandings of their practice. Both groups of essays take important steps toward re/turning to history and re/turning to praxis and begin to articulate what an historicized and practical field might look like as graduate students and younger scholars take center stage in the years that come.

Excursions and Recursions Through Power, Privilege, and Praxis
pp. 73–78

RE/TURNING TO HISTORY

Regarding an ahistorical curriculum studies, I see—with a few exceptions such as the work of Petra Munro Hendry, Anne G. Winfield, Bernadette M. Baker, and myself—very little historical sensibility in curriculum studies as a field. Rather than historical sensibilities, the field engages cultural studies content and continually asks *What's new in cultural studies? Who will bring it to curriculum studies?* Seemingly mimicking the ahistorical capitalistic cultural production of guidebooks and "how-to" management guides in educational leadership that persistently and ahistorically ask and answer the question *what works? ... what works? ... what works?*, curriculum studies scholars persistently and ahistorically ask and answer the question *what's new? ... what's new? ... what's new?* without developing the historical sensibilities that might condition historicized work with cultural studies literatures and produce work that might engage a broader community of educators.

Since the reconceptualization of AERA's Division B Curriculum and Objectives as Curriculum Studies in 1982 (documented in Jackson, 1992; Pinar, Reynolds, Slattery, & Taubman, 1995; Schubert, 2008), one of the vulgar aspects of curriculum studies scholarship emphasizes the continual introduction of cultural studies concerns into curriculum studies. William Schubert (2008), in briefly outlining the development of curriculum studies since its reconceptualization, characterizes the trajectory of curriculum studies over the last 40 years:

> For more than 30 years, curriculum studies have offered alternative concep-
> tions of curriculum that focus on lived texts (currere) through perspectives
> of history, politics, race, gender, phenomenology, poststructuralism (decon-
> struction and postmodernism), autobiography or biography, aesthetics or
> the arts, theology or religion, institutions, international perspectives, and
> more. (p. 391)

Inherent in Schubert's (2008) characterization and important to the argument that I am making is that curriculum studies has continually imported (almost mimicked) cultural studies' epistemological concerns and associated "intellectual politics." Recently, João Paraskeva (2012) has observed that this parade of cultural studies epistemological concerns (one after another) competing for space in curriculum studies preclude a more thoughtful and progressive engagement in alternative politics, knowledges, worldviews, *and their praxis for educational reconstruction.* Presenting a similar critique, William Pinar (2007) has called for a return to intellectual history outside and inside curriculum studies in articulating what he termed "verticality" (p. xiv) as a correction to the ahistorical curriculum studies field that has developed during the reconceptualization.

Problematic in a field predominated by the ahistorical importation of cultural studies concerns is that curriculum studies loses not only previous scholars' conceptual content and trajectory, but—perhaps more damagingly—new scholars felicitously assume old questions with long intellectual trajectories outside and inside curriculum studies ahistorically as "originators" instead of scholars working thoughtfully in conceptually rich traditions of curriculum inquiry. What the first group of essays have in common, as they are organized under the notion of re/turning to history, is that they engage historical concepts or representations outside and inside curriculum studies.

First in this group, Raygine DiAquoi's "'Hopefully They Will See You in a Different Light': A Critical Race Analysis of Double Consciousness" reengages W.E.B. Du Bois' notion of double consciousness as it relates to her mother's counsel and story convincingly indicting the postracial order. Second, Boni Wozolek's "The Nested Nature of M/Othering: Complicating Curriculum Conversations" provides an historicized understanding of feminist relationality through contemporary and historical discussions of m/othering conceptualized, particularly, through Nel Noddings, Madeleine Grumet, Janet Miller, and Stephanie Springgay and Debra Freedman's work focusing, in particular, on a notion of knowing self, society, and others as textually kneaded, interpenetrated, and embodied. Third, Monique Cherry-McDaniel's "(Re)Righting the Script: Speaking Back to Public Curriculum to Secure a More Humanizing Citizenship for African American Women and Girls" creates an historical and contemporary montage of what the author calls "racist regimes of representation" in arguing for a countercurriculum through which African American women and girls can achieve humanizing citizenships and identities. Fourth, and rounding out re/turning this history, Elinor A. Scheirer's "Vision, Practice, Reflection: The Influence of Four Women on Progressive Education" provides biographical sketches and pedagogical stories of four women progressive educators—Marietta Pierce-Johnson, Laura Zirbes, Sybill Marshall, and Margaret Willis—in exercising an important memory of the protofeminist intelligence in progressive education as these exceedingly independent and determined women taught children, raised families, developed curriculum, administrated schools, and, most importantly for Scheirer, engaged in open-ended experimentation that Schwab later termed practical inquiry. Though only one of these studies is formal "history," all together they re/turn to history through engaging historicized concepts and representations traditional to the field of curriculum studies, and by doing so, they provide historical sensibilities or verticality (Pinar, 2007) to the field.

RE/TURNING TO PRAXIS

As I have argued (Jupp, 2007a, 2007b) along with others (Grumet, 2010; Helfenbein, 2011; Huddleston, Job, Powell, & Vaughan, 2011; Job & Huddleston, 2011; Job, Sams, Appelbaum, Sloan, McDermott, 2011; Price, Helfenbein, & Job, 2012; Sams & Job, 2011), curriculum studies scholars should return to praxis in K-16 curriculum, teacher education programs, and practical policy discussions. Re/turning to praxis for curriculum studies scholars, transcending the bifurcated field that split traditionalists from reconceptualists in the 1970s (documented in Jackson, 1992; Pinar et al., 1995; Schubert, 2008), appears a productive move in reclaiming the historical roots of curriculum's progressive-critical praxis orientation (e.g., Counts, 1932; Dewey, 1902; Kilpatrick, 1918; Rugg & Schumaker, 1928; Tyler, 1949). Nonetheless, re/turning to praxis, again *against the grain* of the present field, requires a change in how curriculum studies scholars speak, what scholars value, and what the field produces as research. The stakes of this re/turning to praxis seem increasingly high as I am reminded of Curriculum and Pedagogy's tenth annual meeting in 2009. During the business meeting of the 2009 conference, a teacher from Atlanta berated the conference's cliquish feel and insider lingo, and, much to my dismay at the time, several of curriculum and pedagogy's predominant scholars walked out during this teacher's comments—very much confirming her complaints. The Curriculum and Pedagogy Group, despite its espoused efforts, still has a long way to go before it productively realizes its ideals of influencing K-16 curriculum, teacher education programs, and practical policy concerns. Nonetheless, what the second group of essays have in common is that they evince a re/turn to praxis so important in curriculum and pedagogy's mission statement.

First in this group, Chris Loeffer's "Purple Crayons, Wild Things, and Dots: Getting Lost in Children's Literature and Curriculum," extending a direction developed by Peter Appelbaum's (2008) *Children's Books for Grown-Up Teachers*, provides a philosophical reading of children's literature that both deepens teaching and learning of those books and develops teachers' understandings of curriculum as a result. Second, Susan L. M. Bartow's "Troubling Teaching: Learning From Social Media," making school strange through historic representations of public schooling's ever-present Industrial Era arrangements alongside contemporary representations of fluid and interactive digital media, urges public school teachers to see and take advantage of digital democracy in developing a Deweyan democratic vision of teaching and learning in classrooms. Third, Laura Rychly's "Receptive Praxis," engaging poststructuralist discourses in critiquing static identities in culturally responsive pedagogy, returns to curriculum studies traditions of teacher pedagogy in suggesting a praxis of *being with, dwelling with,* and *living with* students' in inter- and copenetrating ways. Fourth and rounding out this group, Katrina F. Cook's "Agency and Choice in Two Second-Grade Classrooms," presenting teachers' understandings of agency as they are reflected in classroom practices and projected on students' agency, makes a strong case for developing preservice and professional teachers' agency as possibility for extending agency in classrooms and to students.

The essays in this section, grouped under subsections *Re/Turning to History* and *Re/Turning to Praxis,* do just that. Collectively pushing *against the grain* of the current field, they articulate new directions that re/turn to old ones, and by doing so, provide key trajectories for the field's advancement. In contemplating new scholars' research in this section—as I read and reread the papers, I became convinced that what is required in the present historical moment is *re/turning to praxis* and that the language we need to return to praxis will require *re/turning to history.*

NOTE

1. At AERA 2012 in Vancouver, Division B was physically marginalized from other divisions by use of conference space leaving Division B sessions almost a mile from the Vancouver Convention Center. This use of conference space that physically marginalizes Division B members and sessions from other AERA members and sessions manifests AERA's appraisal of Division B members and sessions and simultaneously reifies an insular Division B community and releases other AERA Divisions from the critical content of Division B's sessions.

REFERENCES

Appelbaum, P. (2008). *Children's books for grown-up teachers.* New York, NY: Routledge.

Counts, G. S. (1932). Dare progressive education be progressive? *Progressive Education, 4*(9), 257-263.

Dewey, J. (1902). *The child and the curriculum.* Chicago, IL: University of Chicago.

Grumet, M. (2010, October). *Looking for proposal in curriculum theory.* Keynote speech presented at the annual meeting of the *Journal of Curriculum Theorizing* conference, Dayton, Ohio.

Helfenbein, R. (2011, October). *They jacked the message: Strategies and tactics in the war on public education.* Paper presentation at the annual meeting the Curriculum and Pedagogy Group, Akron, Ohio.

Huddleston, G., Job, J., Powell, J., & Vaughan, K. (2011, April). *Discussing the committee for curriculum theory in policy.* Panel given at the American Education Research Association conference, New Orleans, Louisiana.

Jackson, P. W. (1992). Conceptions of curriculum and curriculum specialists. In P. W. Jackson (Ed.), *Handbook of research on curriculum* (pp. 3-40). New York, NY: MacMillan.

Job, J., & Huddleston, G. (2011, October). *Defining a call for curriculum theorists.* Presentation given at the annual meeting of the *Journal of Curriculum Theorizing* conference, Dayton, Ohio.

Job, J., Sams, B., Appelbaum, P., Sloan, K., McDermott, M. (2011, October). *Creating a position statement for the Committee for Curriculum Theory in Policy.* Working group at the Curriculum and Pedagogy Conference, Akron, Ohio.

Kilpatrick, W. H. (1918). The project method. *Teachers College Record, 19*(4), 319-335.

Jupp, J. (2007a). Gramsci, critical pragmatism, and praxis experiments. *Journal of Curriculum and Pedagogy, 4*(1), 65-71.

Jupp, J. (2007b). Toward reconceptualist work in K-12. *Journal of the American Association for the Advancement of Curriculum Studies, 3*(1), 57-75.

Paraskeva, J. (2012, April). *Theories after theory: Toward an itinerant curriculum theory.* Presentation given at the annual meeting of the American Association for the Advancement of Curriculum Studies, Vancouver, British Columbia.

Pinar, W. F. (2007). *Intellectual advancement through disciplinarity: Verticality and horizontality in curriculum studies.* Rotterdam, The Netherlands: Sense.

Pinar, W. F., Reynolds, W., Slattery, P., & Taubman, P. (1995). *Understanding curriculum.* New York, NY: Peter Lang.

Price, T., Helfenbein, R., & Job, J. (2012, April). *Critical conversations around the Common Core State Standards.* Panel given at the annual meeting of the American Association for the Advancement of Curriculum Studies, Vancouver, British Columbia, Canada.

Rugg, H., & Schumaker, A. (1928). *The child-centered school: An appraisal of the new education.* New York, NY: World Books.

Sams, B., & Job, J. (2011, June). *Discussing the committee for curriculum theory in policy.* Panel given at the Curriculum Studies Summer Collaborative, Savannah, Georgia.

Schubert. W. (2008). Curriculum in theory introductory essay. In F. M. Connelly, M. F. He, & J. Phillion (Eds.), *The Sage handbook of curriculum and instruction* (pp. 391-398). London: SAGE.

Tyler, R. (1949). *Basic principles of curriculum and instruction.* Chicago, IL: University of Chicago Press.

PART I

RE/TURNING TO HISTORY

"HOPEFULLY THEY WILL SEE YOU IN A DIFFERENT LIGHT"

A Critical Race Analysis of Double Consciousness

Raygine DiAquoi
Harvard University

It was not just revolutionary; the concept of the divided self was profoundly mystical, for Du Bois invested this double consciousness with a capacity to see incomparably further and deeper. The African American … possessed the gift of second sight in this American world, "an intuitive faculty (prelogical, in a sense) enabling him/her to see and say things about American society that possessed a heightened moral validity. Because he dwelt equally in the mind and heart of his oppressor as in his own beset psyche, the African American embraced a vision of the commonweal at its best. (Lewis, 2009, as cited in Ladson-Billings & Tate, 2006)

My mother is cleaning her bedroom while the cordless phone rests precariously in the space between her left shoulder and her ear. From the mischief in her eyes, I can tell that she is on the phone with her best friend. Even though I set a specific time for this interview I know that she will not rush her conversation. As I sit on top of her large bed, I am reminded of many of the conversations that my mother had with me here,

Excursions and Recursions Through Power, Privilege, and Praxis
pp. 81–95

quiet lessons about my racialized body and the way that all of my actions would be perceived. Along with telling me that I could do anything, she explained that there was a lot that I could not do because of the scrutiny that my brown skin would attract. This was my education. Looking back, I realized that my mother employed a very specific curriculum. She often recalls those times fondly since I am out of the house now; she believes that her efforts were necessary to my success. The assignment that I am working on at the time of this interview is focused on understanding the motivation behind those early lessons. Several minutes into the interview, she begins to share the thoughts that informed her parenting style and philosophy:

> I said you know for one thing if my children were going to be born here ... I don't want the world to look at them as Black Americans and think of them in that way. I wanted them to be different. I wanted them to be decent human beings who contribute to society. I wanted them to be well-behaved children so they could be well-behaved adults. I didn't want them to become delinquents, thieves, drug dealers, disrespectful people, killers, assassins you know ... annoying neighbors, people who want to fight, people who look for war all the time. I didn't want them to be that way so therefore I went on a mission.

My mother's narrative, though shocking despite its familiarity, reflects what Lewis (2009, as cited in Ladson-Billings & Tate, 2006) describes when he explains Dubois' concept of the African American's ability to see herself and the world through both her own eyes and the eyes of dominant society.

Born in Haiti, my mother realized that her children, who would be born in the United States, would be seen as Black Americans and were therefore entitled to a bitter inheritance of low expectations and contempt. She explains that she was focused on and occupied with ensuring that we would somehow be noticeably different by equipping us to disprove the expectations that others were sure to have of us because of the color of our skin. Her explanation of how and what she wanted us to be is indicative of her awareness and internalization of the dominant gaze. Possibilities for our future selves are refracted through and against the very same set of lenses from which she hopes to hide us.

Though she never overtly connects the negative attributes at the end of her comment with the term African American, I know that when she says that she didn't want the world to think of her children "in that way" she is thinking about what Toni Morrison (1992) calls "American Africanism" or "the denotative and connotative Blackness that African peoples have come to signify, as well as the entire range of views, assumptions, readings, and misreadings that accompany Eurocentric learning about these people" (pp. 6-7). At the end of her comment, she explains that she "went on a mission." When I ask her to explain, she shares:

> I kept telling you … you're a beautiful girl, you got nice hair, you got nice skin, oh you look like a little princess. You know a little dark princess. That's what you are and you're gonna be very smart … a dark girl that is very smart and you know you gonna be smarter than anybody in your class … anybody who sees you … you gonna be so smart, you gonna be very smart in whatever you do.

Though aware of the way that she and her children would be perceived by wider society, my mother's description of her "mission" reveals the way that she sees or would prefer to see herself and have her daughters see themselves. The repetition of certain words is indicative of the mantra-like phrases that she showered upon us. Here, my mother focuses on our beauty. However, even in praising our features, it is still apparent that her knowledge of dominant society's conceptions inform her own. She must tell us that we have nice hair and skin because she is aware that we will hear otherwise, that we will be seen differently, that we may come to believe otherwise. Her mention of "anybody who sees you" evokes the Duboisian "sense of always looking at oneself through the eyes of others" (1903, p. 3). Through her words, my mother tries to explain the narratives that she shared with us, narratives to nourish and embolden us, stories about ourselves that would help us to fashion positive Black identities.

When taken as a whole, the pieces of her narrative suggest that she vacillated between feeling pride in her identity and feeling shame, if not anger. Even in crafting a narrative for us it is clear that she continued to define and indeed measure herself by "the tape of a world that looks on in amused contempt and pity" (Dubois, 1903, p. 3). As a Black person she embodies Dubois' "two souls, two thoughts, two unreconciled strivings; two warring ideals in one dark body" and highlights the continued impact of racism on the lived experiences and education of African Americans (p. 3). Though I am analyzing the persistent duality inherent in an African American identity, it is important to note that the concept of double consciousness is applicable to "all people who are constructed outside of the dominant paradigm" (Ladson-Billings & Donner, 2005, p. 282). In a period that has been prematurely labeled "postracial" and is "characterized by slipperiness, apparent nonracialism and ambivalence" it is important to continue to foreground the educational experiences of individuals who are continually swept to the margins (Bonilla-Silva, 2002, p. 41). The counterstory presented here reveals my mother's experience with racism, and her efforts to counter its effects in the lives of her children. It is my hope that by sharing this narrative, I can complicate conversations that insist that race and racism bear little consequence on the lives of African Americans, and encourage educators to think about the limitation of embracing a colorblind stance among populations that are imbued, from an early age, with a heightened sense of the importance of race.

TODAY'S RACISM

The late Manning Marable (1992, as cited in Solorozano & Yosso, 2002) explains that racism is "a system of ignorance, exploitation, and power used to oppress African Americans, Latinos, Asians, Pacific Americans, American Indians and other people on the basis of ethnicity, culture, mannerisms and color" (p. 24). In the United States this system is mapped onto the American subconscious through race-making policies and institutions, effectively placing whole communities outside of humanity (Wacquant, 2001, p. 98). Today "institutionalized racial inequalities created by the long era of slavery followed by Jim Crow racism are now properly accepted and condoned under a modern free market or laissez faire racist ideology" (Bobo, Kluegel, & Smith, 1997, p. 16), which locates racial inequality within minority communities and allows for the denial of the existence of racial phenomena and discrimination while simultaneously reflecting "the ways in which race and racism continue to be deeply embedded within the framework of American society" (Omi &Winant, as cited in Parker & Lynn, 2002). Bobo's description of laissez faire racism coincides with the subtle and disarming colorblind racism that Bonilla-Silva (2002) describes as "the dominant racial ideology of the post-civil rights era" (p. 42).

Colorblind racism is an ideology fitting of a social, political and cultural context that is invested in the mythologies of meritocracy and individualism and increasingly presented as an ideal. Under colorblind racism, racial inequality is normalized through the rhetoric of liberalism, and situated within the cultural deficiencies of communities of color further reifying White privilege and invalidating the experiences of people of color (Bonilla-Silva, 2002). The nationally constructed rhetoric of colorblind racism obscures the "hidden transcript" of the lives of communities of color and strategies used by these communities in their responses to racism (Scott, 1990, as cited in Dawson, 2006, p. 242).

Delgado and Stefanic (2001) explain "that members of this country's dominant racial group cannot easily grasp what it is like to be non-White. Few have what W.E.B. Dubois described as "double consciousness" (p. 39). This ability to see "further and deeper" is a result of living under racism and oppression. It allows the oppressed the gift of a kind of dual vision; she is able to see the world through the perspective of the dominant class while simultaneously seeing the world through her subordinate status. Her "doubleness" is her strength and her gift to a society that is not ready for this kind of contribution (Margulies, 1997, as cited in Dixson, 2006, p. 219). It is what allows her to "see the limitations, flaws, weaknesses and contradictions of spaces and structures that appear transparent and accessible, but are not" (Dixson & Rousseau, 2006, p. 19). However, it is also her weakness. Appearing whole, she is divided within, fighting and resisting herself and the oppressor, living and reviling herself within the same breath. The consequence of prevailing discourses like colorblindness is that we, as a society, fail to see the "intimate terrorism," or the ongoing battle between the oppressed and resistant self, occurring in those possessing a double consciousness (Anzaldua, 1987, p. 42).

CRITICAL RACE THEORY: COUNTERING DOMINANT DISCOURSE

Critical race theory (CRT) emerged in the 1970s as lawyers and legal scholars realized that the "heady advances of the civil rights era of the 1960s had stalled and in many respects, were being rolled back" (Delgado & Stefanic, 2001, p. 4). They recognized the inability of Critical Legal Studies to accurately understand and respond to the impact of race and racism in the United States and developed CRT to challenge dominant legal claims of racial neutrality and objectivity, which have been bolstered by discourses of meritocracy and liberalism (Decuir & Dixon, 2004). The main tenets of CRT are that racism is ordinary and permanent (Delgado & Stefanic, 2001, p 7.), basic civil rights are afforded to communities of color "in as much as they converged with the self-interests of Whites" (Decuir & Dixon, 2004, p. 28), Whiteness functions as property (Decuir & Dixson, 2004, p. 28; Ladson-Billings & Tate, 2006), liberalism as it is manifested in "the notion of colorblindness, the neutrality of the law, and incremental change" must be critiqued and challenged (Decuir & Dixson, 2004, p. 29), and counterstories, or narratives documenting experiences from the margins are an important tool for disrupting dominant discourses. The experiences of people of color are too often marginalized by "majoritarian stories about merit, causation, blame, responsibility and social justice" which we have come to internalize as truth (Delgado, 1993, p. 666). CRT recognizes prevailing discourses about race and racism as the descendants of a "host of stories, narratives, conventions, and understandings that today, through repetition, seem natural and true" (p. 666). As such, CRT is calling for new stories rooted in the "experiential knowledge of people of color" (Matsuda, Lawrence, Delgado, & Crenshaw, 1993, p. 6). These narratives can be used as pedagogical tools in teaching about racial oppression and the strength required of those who resist it (Solorzano & Yosso, 2002).

METHODOLOGY

I use counterstory to explore and analyze my mother's stories about experience with and responses to racism in the choices that she made about how to raise her daughters. In CRT, the counterstory, or "the method of telling the stories of those people whose experiences are not often told, " is used to counter the stories that are often told about people of color in the social sciences (Solorzano & Yosso, 2002, p. 32). These counterstories, which become the data, are important because of their power to present a different way of knowing and naming racism (Fernandez, 2002). As Fernandez (2002) explains, storytelling "allows the participant to reflect on his or her lived experience ... allows the marginalized participant to speak or make public his or her story ... subverts the dominant story or the reality that is socially constructed by Whites" (p. 49). The counterstory recenters race and racism and open up spaces for the discussion of racism as a pillar of oppression, and the way in which people continue to resist racism. In the field of education, counterstories are increasingly used by scholars to better understand the experiences of students of color and challenge "claims of neutrality, objectivity, colorblindness and meritocracy" (Ladson-Billings & Tate, 2006, p. 20; see also Decuir-Guinby, 2007; Parker & Lynn, 2002). In this chapter, the method of counterstory is used to illuminate one parent's attempts to mitigate the effects of racism on her children through specific strategies, which demonstrate the significance of the CRT notion of Whiteness as property to her own life. By exploring this parent's narrative we gain valuable insight into one parent's attempts at racial socialization. This counterstory adds to the literature on the socialization practices of parents of students of color (Brown, Bruce, Lesane-Brown, Chase, & Tanner-Smith, 2010; Cross & Fhagen Smith, 2001; Hughes, Witherspoon, Rivas-Drake, & West-Bey, 2009; Ward, 2000).

DATA COLLECTION AND ANALYSIS

The narrative explored in this paper draws upon data gathered as part of an earlier project on racial socialization and academic success. I triangulated various sources of data, including interview transcripts, photo albums, yearbook pictures, letters, and drawings that my mother had collected throughout the years. Using the three-interview series method

(Seidman, 2006), I conducted three, in-depth, semistructured interviews with my mother, and explored themes that my mother brought up during the course of the interviews. All interviews were conducted at my mother's home, audiotaped, and transcribed. I asked my mother to describe those of her efforts that she thought contributed to our success. I also asked my mother to provide a rationale for her efforts and provide concrete examples of the way that she constructed a specific identity for us. Her answers formed the basis for the counterstory presented, corroborated my recollection of my experiences growing up, and revealed the great extent to which race and racism had informed the way that she carried herself and the way that she instructed her children to conduct themselves.

I used a grounded theory approach to understand my mother's beliefs about education, race and racism (Strauss & Corbin, 1998). This approach enabled me to develop an analytic framework that came out of the data (Maxwell, 1996). While I used concepts from the literature on racial self-concept, academic achievement, and racial socialization in my initial analysis, open and focused coding allowed for themes to emerge from the data regarding double consciousness and the importance of racial identity.

FINDINGS

My mother's story reflects both her acceptance of majoritarian stories about African Americans and her resistance to these stories. At times, her double consciousness is a crippling liability, and she is able to only see herself through the gaze of others. At other times, it functions like Margulies' (1997, as cited in Dixson, 2006, p. 219) "doubleness," a talent allowing my mother the ability to truly see the world as it is and thus critique it in ways that could not occur if not for her double consciousness. Indeed, it is through her own struggle with her double consciousness that we are able to see the ways in which the CRT notion of Whiteness as property dominate her reality. We are also able to observe the ways that she speaks back to and lives in spite of this othering discourse. Ultimately, her story is also a critique of the normalized liberal discourse of colorblindness, a testimony to the continuing significance of race.

THROUGH THEIR EYES

Arriving in the United States from Haiti, my mother quickly inferred the meaning attached to her race and the scrutiny that would always follow her and her children:

> People observe you, neighbors coworkers … as little as you were in school I remember people telling me, "wow your children … they are very exceptional. Were they born here?" I said why? Why are you asking me were they born here? "Well they are very smart, their behavior, they're very calm, they are well behaved." So obviously they expect Black children to be disruptive … they expect Black children to be difficult, to be troublemakers at all times which is not true. All children are children. So therefore I had to tell my children be the best that you can be so people could … so you could earn respect from others.

Apparent in her words is the struggle to make her self believe that all children are given equal treatment despite simultaneously holding knowledge of the fact that "obviously they expect Black children to be disruptive … to be difficult, to be trouble makers at all times." Later she says, "you don't have to do anything to show the world or to prove yourself but be the best that you can be … so you could earn respect from others". Again, her words betray her inner gaze, her own self-perceptions, and an outer gaze, the perception of others.

The way that others see her, as object, ultimately affects the way that she sees herself and her children; the two gazes become intertwined and she is able to express the sentiments behind both within the same breath (Fanon, 1967). Ultimately this outer gaze is what informs the kinds of behaviors that she encourages in her daughters. She teaches her daughters ways to carry themselves that will ensure that they are not inappropriately judged or labeled. She instills dispositions that are definitely rewarded in school. Recalling a teacher's comments about her exceptional children, it is clear that she can only hear the subtle and slippery insult of a microaggression (Solorzano, Ceja, & Yosso, 2000). The way in which "proper" behavior is subtly constructed as being outside of the purview of Black children demonstrates how Whiteness and the cultural practices which have come to define Whiteness have been constructed as "the ultimate property" (Ladson-Billings & Tate, 2006, p. 58). Implicit in the compliments that my mother received is what Ladson-Billings and Tate (2006) refers to as the right of disposition, a concept integral to the construction of Whiteness as a form of property. We were being rewarded for demonstrating dispositions that had been labeled White property: being well-behaved and seeming intelligent. In suggesting that we could not possibly be born here because of our seemingly White dispositions, we are set apart from other African Americans, who are subtly othered. The seemingly benign praise stings and reminds her of how she is really seen.

Education, though not necessarily an equalizer, emerges throughout my mother's narrative as a tool that *might* enable her daughters to have some respite, however brief, from constantly looking at themselves through the eyes of others:

In this world ... you are already ... Black ... they have certain preconceptions ... so therefore they put you somewhere, they don't even give you a chance to prove yourself as to who you are so therefore you have to make sure you are educated, you have to make sure that you know how to express yourself. You don't have to prove yourself to anyone because you know who you are but you having this ... you have the skills and the profession ... that could represent you ... I think that in itself would give you respect of others ... and um hopefully they will see you in a different light.

Consistent with earlier parts of her narrative, my mother speaks from both sides of her halved self. She seems to resign herself to the fact that many people hold preconceived notions about Black people and their capabilities. These notions, though limited, have the power to limit as she explains that "they put you somewhere." Whereas everyone else is given a chance to prove themselves through various pathways, my mother's words indicate that education is perhaps the only manner through which African Americans can be respected. In her last sentence she reveals that having the right skills may garner respect. However, this respect is not guaranteed. She could not guarantee that her children would be respected. She could only hope that they would be seen differently; she hoped we would be seen as she saw us.

THROUGH HER EYES

A picture of my sister, mother, and me at church, neatly coiffed, reminds me of early weekday mornings, before the lights came on, when I stood timidly at my mother's door, waiting for her to brush my hair before I left for school. She always marveled at how I had inherited my father's thick hair, expressing playful envy for the mane that framed my face, turning me around so I could marvel at the bun that formed a crown on my head. Every act involving ourselves went this way, with her making sure to praise us and remind us that we were not what others projected:

I always tell you ... that you girls, you all are beautiful, you have beautiful hair, beautiful brown skin and besides there is something even more beautiful that you all possess, it's your brain. You all are very smart.

Between her legs, getting our hair combed, or in department stores trying on new clothes or buying toys, my mother frequently reminded us of what she saw when she looked at us. In addition to letting us know that we were beautiful, she also made sure to always refer to our intelligence. She laughs when she remembers how, at a very young age, I had started internalizing and repeating what she had been telling me. When asked my age

I would share my age and add that I was very smart. Again, my mother's practice occurs against the backdrop of the notion of Whiteness of property. She is aware that our particular intelligence would never be recognized, because it has been constructed as an inalienable right of those in possession of Whiteness (Decuir & Dixon, 2004; Ladson-Billings & Tate, 2006). She bolstered her words with training in dispositions that had been constructed as White. She recalls, "I tell you all when you are little ... I expected you to know how you all should behave when you go to school ... I showed you all how to present yourself." In school, she expected us to demonstrate our mastery of "unauthorized conceptions of knowledge" (Ladson-Billings & Tate, 2006, p. 59). She knew that there would be rewards for possessing these behaviors. She is both conscious of the way that her identity is constructed by others and the way we will be constructed as Other. She shares, "society sometimes in this country doesn't give certain children a chance ... before they see the child they just label them." I realize that even when she is looking at us through her eyes she is seeing her self reflected back at her through the prevailing opinions of others. Her words are the product of her duality, bearing the stamp of the internal and external battle that define her reality. I recognize now that these words were targeted attempts to counteract the effects of living in a racist society. Preparing us for experiences of discrimination, through training in dispositions constructed as White, was one of the many strategies that my mother used to equip us to manage racism (Cross & Fhagen-Smith, 2001; Harris-Britt, Valrie, Kurtz-Costes, & Rowley, 2007; Neblett, Philip, Cogburn, & Sellers, 2006). Her strategies ensure that we can survive and succeed "in a world which yields *him* [the African American] no true self-consciousness" (Dubois, 1903, p. 10).

FOR OUR EYES

A picture of my 3-year-old self reading a book causes both of us to smile. She recalls the praise she received from others for our love of reading. I remember that we read certain kinds of books; I was exposed to and only had access to books that covered subjects relating to people who looked like me. My mother often brought picture books and workbooks about Africa and Haiti.

During one interview, I produce a red, green, and black children's book, from my bag, which causes her smile to widen. She cannot believe that I still have this book and so many of the others that she brought home for me. When I ask her to explain her rationale for buying books that only featured African and African American history, she explains:

> Yes I buy books. I buy a lot of books because I wanted you to become famil-
> iar with your own self, because I've heard other children … they see them-
> selves through what the world is showing. They see a White doll and they
> say "oh this is me" and I didn't want you to go that route. I didn't want you
> to feel that way. I wanted you to know exactly who you are.

Recognizing her own experience as one with double vision, my mother
wants us to learn about our racial and ethnic identity, culture and heritage
from an African centered perspective, a worldview with the reality and
experience of the African in America at its center (Asante, 1988; Pollard &
Ajirotutu, 2000).

This type of subtle racial socialization practice, worked in tandem with
my mother's very explicit discussions about race and racial discrimination
to convey a message of racial pride while also preparing us to counter the
bias and discrimination that we were sure to encounter (Neblett, Smalls,
Ford, Nkuyen, & Sellers, 2009). However, it was not only what we read
that provided a strong counternarrative to the misinformation that we
received in school; it was that we read:

> I always explained to my children when you go somewhere whether in
> school whether a church at the doctor's office, in the subway, you sit quietly,
> sit properly, you know observe your surroundings be vigilant be quick to lis-
> ten slow to talk. You know … and um always carry a book with you when you
> are in public where there is going to be a lot of people you carry books with
> you, you keep yourself busy you don't mind other people business you know,
> be quiet.

My mother often lectured us on the stereotypes that existed about African
Americans. At a very young age she told us that people thought that we
were stupid, lazy and generally inferior and that as a result we had to
make sure that we always challenged these stereotypes. As she talks, I
remember always carrying a bag with me that was filled with the latest
book that I was reading or story that I was writing. Knowing that our
Black bodies were constantly being surveilled she tells us to bring a book
with us "where there is going to be a lot of people." Though I genuinely
enjoyed reading, I remember feeling that there was a performative aspect
to our behavior.

My mother reveled in the way that our behaviors and the way that we
comported ourselves disrupted widely held assumptions about Black children. We were not simply reading to educate ourselves. She wanted us to
enact postures of intelligence so that others could see us differently. We were
always educating others. Additionally, she was teaching us to challenge the
way that Whiteness, and the rights attributed to Whiteness, function as
property (Decuir & Dixon, 2004; Harris, 1995; Ladson-Billings & Tate,

2006). She wanted us to internalize the idea that our identities were congruous with dispositions that had been subsumed under a conception of Whiteness that excluded everyone who was not White. While she wanted us to only see ourselves through our own eyes, many of her plans were formulated with the gaze of White society in mind. Many of her rules for our behavior are a direct response to negative messages about Black people. However, I would not characterize them as reactive. On the contrary, I think that she was proactive in preparing us for bias and discrimination. She wanted to imbue us with an awareness of racial inequalities and provide us with an arsenal of tools that would enable us to face any situation. The most important tool in our kit was our sense of self. My mother explains:

> I always tell you you gotta be smart. You gotta look at people in their eyes when you talking to them and I tell you don't be afraid of nobody. Not in the sense that you gonna fight them but don't let people intimidate ... make you feel that you less because of your *skin color.*

These words highlight my mother's awareness of bias and illustrate what Neblett et al. (2009) calls "racial barrier messages." She instructs us on how to interact with the world because she knows that it will try to convince us that our skin color entitles us to inferior treatment and services. Not only does she want us to be aware of inequality, she wants us to confront it.

CONCLUSION

It is very easy for many to assume that racism no longer impacts the lives of people of color. Colorblind racist discourse allows society to deny that "racism is a permanent component of American life," that it dominates all domains of interaction (Bell, 1992, p. 13). It is difficult for those who are not in the margins to understand how racism seeps into the most intimate details of the lives of those excluded from the center, othering them even when they are seemingly free from the gaze of dominant society. My mother's counterstory centers the discussion of racism demonstrating its impact on her life and the strategies she employs to counter its ability to affect her children. Through CRTs notion of Whiteness as property, we gain insight into the manner in which my mother navigates the duality that defines her, a duality that she ends up passing on to her children.

I now understand and am advantaged by my unique perspective. At times, I wonder what it would be like not to have this constant awareness of racism, to be able switch it off, but I know that it is my birthright as an African American. Anzaldua explains that "those who are pushed out of the tribe for being different are likely to become more sensitized (when not being brutalized in insensitivity)" (p. 60). My mother succeeded in heightening this "acute awareness" in me and I now know that I am "excruciatingly alive to the world," imbued with the "capacity to see in the surface phenomena the meaning of deeper realities, to see the deep structure below the surface" (Anzaldua, 1987, p. 60). Unfortunately, many never learn the power of their "doubleness." The "doubleness" that children and families of marginalized populations carry with them remains underutilized in our discussions about the way that race and racism operate in American society.

With this narrative, I hope to put forth an alternative way of knowing and being in the world, a uniquely African American perspective that is born out of a very intimate and intergenerational familiarity with a racism. I hope that it will serve as a bridge between communities, a starting point for challenging the dominant discourses that prevent us from acknowledging and dismantling the oppressive realities that live in communities of color, realities created when dominant society embraces fantasies like colorblindness.

DEDICATION

I dedicate this chapter to the family of Trayvon Martin and to the day when Trayvon Martins are seen in a different light.

REFERENCES

Anzaldua, G. (1987). *Borderlands/la frontera: The new mestiza*. San Francisco, CA: Aunt Lute Books.

Asante, M. K. (1988). *Afrocentricity*. Trenton, NJ: Africa World Press.

Bell, D. A. (1992). *Faces at the bottom of the well: The permanence of racism*. New York, NY: Basic Books.

Bobo, L., Kluegel, J. R., & Smith, R. A. (1997). Laissez-faire racism: The crystallization of a kindler, gentler, antiblack ideology. In S. Tuch & J. K. Martin (Eds.), *Racial attitudes in the 1990s: Continuity and change* (pp. 15-41). Westport, CT: Greenwood.

Bonilla-Silva, E. (2002). The linguistics of color blind racism: How to talk nasty about Blacks without sounding "racist." *Critical Sociology, 28*(1-2), 41-64.

Brown, T., Bruce, M., Lesane-Brown, Chase L., & Tanner-Smith, E. (2010). Negotiating boundaries and bonds: Frequency of young children's socialization to their ethnic/racial heritage. *Journal of Cross-Cultural Psychology, 41*, 457-464.

Cross, W. E., & Fhagen-Smith, P. (2001). Patterns of African American identity development: A life-span perspective. In C.L. Wijeyesinghe & B. W. Jackson

III (Eds.), *New perspectives on racial identity development: A theoretical and practical anthology* (pp. 243-268). New York, NY: New York University Press.

Dawson, M. C. (2006). After the deluge: Publics and publicity in Katrina's wake. *Du Bois Review, 3*(1), 239-249.

Decuir, J. T., & Dixson, A. D. (2004). "So when it comes out, they aren't that surprised that it is there": Using critical race theory as a tool of analysis of race and racism in education. *Educational Researcher, 33*(5), 26-31.

DeCuir-Gunby, J. T. (2007). Negotiating identity in a bubble: The experiences of African American high school students at Wells Academy. *Equity & Excellence in Education, 40*(1), 26-35.

Delgado, R. D. (1993). On telling stories in school: A reply to Farber and Sherry. *Vanderbilt Law Review*, 46V and L. Rev. 665.

Delgado, R. D., & Stefanic, J. (2001). *Critical race theory: An introduction.* New York: New York University Press.

Dixson, A. D. (2006). The fire this time: Jazz, research and critical race theory. In A. D. Dixson & C. K. Rousseau (Eds.), *Critical race theory in education: All God's children got a song* (pp. 213-232). New York, NY: Routledge.

Dixson, A. D., & Rousseau, C. K. (Ed.). (2006). And we are still not saved: Critical race theory ten years later. In A. D. Dixson & C. K. Rousseau, *Critical race theory in education: All God's children got a song* (pp. 31-56). New York, NY: Routledge.

Dubois, W. B. (1903). *The souls of Black folk.* New York, NY: The New American Library.

Fanon, F. (1952). *Black skin, White masks.* New York, NY: Grove Press.

Fernandez, L. (2002). Telling stories about school: Using critical race and Latino critical theory to document Latina/Latino education and resistance. *Qualitative Inquiry, 8*, 44-63.

Harris, C. I. (1995). Whiteness as property. In K. Crenshaw, N. Gotanda, G. Peller, & K. Thomas (Eds.), *Critical race theory: The key writings that formed the movement* (pp. 357-383). New York, NY: The New Press.

Harris-Britt, A., Valrie, C., Kurtz-Costes, B., & Rowley, S. (2007). Perceived racial discrimination and self-esteem in African American youth: Racial socialization as a protective factor. *Journal of Research on Adolescence, 17*, 669-682.

Hughes, D., Witherspoon, D., Rivas-Drake, D., & West-Bey, N. (2009). Received ethnic/racial socialization messages and youths' academic and behavioral outcomes: Examining the mediating role of ethnic identity and self-esteem. *Cultural Diversity and Ethnic Minority Psychology, 15*(2), 112–125.

Ladson-Billings, G., & Donner, J. (2005). The moral activist role of critical race theory scholarship. In N. K. Denzin & Y. S. Lincoln (Eds.), *The SAGE handbook of qualitative research* (3rd ed., pp. 279-302). Thousand Oaks, CA: SAGE.

Ladson-Billings, G., & Tate, W., IV. (2006). Toward a critical race theory of education. In A. D. Dixson & C. K Rousseau (Eds.), *Critical race theory in education: All God's children got a song* (pp. 11-30). New York, NY: Routledge.

Matsuda, M. J., & Lawrence, C. R., III, Delgado, R., & Crenshaw, W. K. (1993). *Words that wound: Critical race theory, assaultive speech, and the first amendment.* Boulder, CO: Westview Press.

Maxwell, J. A. (1996). *Qualitative research design: An interactive approach.* Thousand Oaks, CA: SAGE.

Morrison, T. (1992). *Playing in the dark: Whiteness and the literary imagination.* Cambridge, MA: Harvard University Press.

Neblett, E. W., Smalls, C. P., Ford, R. K., Nkuyen, X. H., & Sellers, M. R. (2009). Racial socialization and race identity: African American parent's messages about race as precursors to identity. *Journal of Youth and Adolescence, 38,* 189-203.

Neblett, E. W., Jr., Philip, C. L., Cogburn, C. D., & Sellers, R. M. (2006). African American adolescents' discrimination experiences and academic achievement: Racial socialization as a culture compensatory and protective factor. *The Journal of Black Psychology, 32*(2), 199-218.

Parker, L., & Lynn, M. (2002). What's race got to do with it? Critical race theory's conflicts with and connections to qualitative research methodology and epistemology. *Qualitative Inquiry, 8*(1), 7-22.

Pollard, D., & Ajirotutu, C. S. (Eds.). (2000). *African-centered schooling in theory and practice.* Westport, CT: Bergin and Garvey.

Seidman, I. (2006). *Interviewing as qualitative research: A guide for researchers in education and the social sciences.* New York, NY: Teachers' College Press.

Solorzano, D., Ceja, M., & Yosso, T. (2000). Critical race theory, racial microaggressions and campus racial climate: The experiences of African American college students. *Journal of Negro Education, 69,* 60-73.

Solorzano, D. G., & Yosso, T. J. (2002). Critical race methodology: Counter-storytelling as an analytical framework for educational research. *Qualitative Inquiry, 8*(1), 23-44.

Strauss, A., & Corbin, J. (1998). *Basics of qualitative research: Techniques and procedures for developing theory* (2nd ed.). Thousand Oaks, CA: SAGE.

Wacquant, L. (2001). Deadly symbiosis: When ghetto and prison meet and mesh. *Punishment and Society, 3*(1), 95-133.

Ward, J. V. (2000). *The skin we're in: Teaching our children to be emotionally strong socially smart, spiritually connected.* New York, NY: Free Press.

CHAPTER 8

THE NESTED NATURE OF M/OTHERING

Complicating Curriculum Conversations

Boni Wozolek
Kent State University

VIGNETTE: BE/COMING TO MOTHERHOOD

A few weeks after my daughter was born I had a family friend come to visit. She asked me, "So … has becoming a mother changed your life?" For a moment I looked at her through eyes weary from having a colicky baby. In that moment I had a surreal daydream where I took off my shirt, pointed to my linea negra, the black line from pregnancy that runs from my ribcage to just above my pubic bone and said, "This is my linea negra. As a woman of color it shows a part of me that some White women will never experience. Like my ethnicity, it's the first thing I bet people would see if they were to look at my stomach now. Like my ethnicity, at first I was slightly embarrassed by it, by being different, but now I take pride in that difference." Then I would point to the stretch marks at my side and say, "These are my stretch marks. They will, for the rest of my life, serve as a visual reminder of what my body went through for this pregnancy. A reminder of one of the first sacrifices a mother makes for her child. All of

Excursions and Recursions Through Power, Privilege, and Praxis
pp. 97–113
Copyright © 2012 by Information Age Publishing
All rights of reproduction in any form reserved.

these things are suddenly all at once together within and on me. That's how motherhood has changed my life."

Perhaps then I would go on to explain that the dark circles under my eyes were not just from being woken up every 45 minutes in the night, but were from sleep-deprived thoughts of my studies and my baby that crept into my taxed mind. Instead I kept covered, not revealing any of my thoughts. Not because I felt more comfortable that way. Up until the moment my doorbell rang I had honestly not been wearing a shirt. Not because I was following the etiquette taught to me by grandmother who felt it was important to be not only dressed but dressed in a conservative elegance for company. I could not count the number of times that rule had been broken as I negotiated breastfeeding and motherhood in general. I kept covered because at the end of the day, that is what many m/others[1] (Springgay & Freedman, 2009) do. Often in these first few months I felt compelled to cover the physical and emotional changes that motherhood has brought into my life. The push to lose the weight gained during pregnancy in order to fit the mainstream American image of an attractive young woman, or the effort to socially downplay the complex life of being a working mother are two examples of how I've covered these changed parts of myself in order to put on a mask that feels comfortable in public. As mothers we are expected to prattle over our new bundle of joy and shamefully hide the reality of recovery. Instead, to answer my friend's original query about how my life has changed, I simply smiled and said, "In more ways than I could possibly express."

INTRODUCTION: LOST IN THE POSTPARTUM HAZE

While it is said that it takes time for things to change, I disagree. It takes time for *some* things to change. Other things, in my recent experience, can change in a matter of twelve minutes of learning how to push a watermelon out of a straw. I was told that having a baby would crystallize my priorities in life. I disagree. Having a baby has complicated my priorities in wonderful, although sometimes painful, ways. The vignette above only serves as a physical reminder of how becoming a m/other has changed me. Having to step down from positions on committees and giving up the almost obsessive-compulsive nature to which I approached my studies are professional and personal reminders of this process. As the postpartum dust settles, I find that the complications of motherhood—the binaries created in the friction of my mother and other roles, a (re)conception of self through these roles and my recent experiences, and a complication of personal ideas and ideals—pull me into exceptionally visceral experiences that live with/out my once tidy personal, professional and scholarly lives.

The purpose of this paper is twofold: to talk about the embodied experiences I have had since becoming a m/other (Springgay & Freedman, 2009) and to draw the parallels that these experiences have had on my view of education. While I have always identified myself as a female, my recent experience as a mother has presented me with a set of gendered roles that are vastly more concrete than my previous premother experiences. For example, before motherhood I could participate in my studies without much judgment as my husband helped with the housework that was neglected as I spent time writing and studying.

As I have pushed on with my studies, the general reaction has been surprise when people learn that I have not decided to stop or postpone my work. This is in part because some are surprised I find the energy to continue while others are shocked that I would charge my husband with the role of sole caregiver several nights a week. While I respond to these reactions to my decisions, I cannot help but wonder if the reaction would run parallel if I was a father. As I seek to honor the tensions that exist between the superficial formalities in academia and the messiness behind the public façade which is my personal reality, I attempt to add to the conversation of reconceptualizing curriculum from the perspective of m/othering and problematize the disembodied space that has allowed me to live comfortably in a binary infested lifestyle; a lifestyle that preserved my professionalism but displaced the aesthetic artistry of my lived experience from the classroom (Dewey, 1934; Eisner, 2002). In other words, as I had previously conceptualized myself as a wife, daughter, teacher and student, I had been able to keep these pieces of myself separate. Becoming a mother helped me to openly examine how those lines could be blurred and in turn complicate my epistemological beliefs in ways that have brought a sense of the artistic and the sensual to my conception of the curriculum.

As one means of explicitly drawing the reader's attention to such complications, I have elected to frequently disrupt the text throughout this chapter with quotes that have informed my thinking for at least the following three reasons. First, these interruptions represent the disruption that life often brings to itself, obscuring our original path with other ideas, making us reconsider our original intentions. Much in the way that my child's cry interrupts my sleep, these quotes both support and complicate my narrative and add to the parallels I am drawing to the curriculum. Second, it is in my reading that I find myself and in myself that I identify with my reading and scholarship. By this I mean that these spaces allow me to identify with a type of inquiry in which I have always engaged but have seldom connected with my work as a public school teacher or my recent focus on teething and poopy diapers. In this cyclical process, I find that each part of myself is separate and yet together, connected as I once was and yet always will be with my child. My intention is to both complicate and clarify my experiences through these texts as they ground my experiences in the theoretical which in turn serves to ground my practice.

Finally, the use of these quotes is to situate my work within an intertextual framework (Gershon, Lather, & Smithies, 2009; Lather & Smithies, 1997) which has the following purposes. First, it is to call to attention the juxtaposition of my narrative and scholarship that run parallel and yet are still disruptive to each other. Second, it is to add a sense of the nuanced nature of motherhood that is reflected in various ways, from lived experience to the text. A final point is to offer transparency in my reflexivity as I explore the intersections of these parts of myself and this journey as it relates to the curriculum. One of these intersections is within Pinar's (2007) notion of verticality and horizontality which aims to align one's scholarship with the vertical, the historical topography of a discipline, and the horizontal, the analysis of current internal intellectual trends as well as external political and social milieus (Ng-A-Fook, 2011). From this perspective, these quotes serve as a respectful reminder of how past literature influences my current epistemological view of the curriculum and my studies as I begin to move past simply *knowing* to a state *being* (Pinar, 2007).

The use of a personal narrative in my writing works to serve at least the three following purposes. First, it is a personal reflection, which serves to reconcile my ontological and paradigmatic shift from preparenthood to motherhood. Second, by being transparent with my experiences, this account is an iteration of what Ellsworth and Milner (1996) refer to as situated responsiveness, an understanding that the story itself is situated within the context of the complexities of lived experience. Through this construct and its attention to complexity, the narrative inherently serves to work against certain social structures which may otherwise dismiss women's multiple positions in the world that "compel us to speak from between the boundaries of certain positions" (Bloom, 1996, p. 195). Finally, the narrative adds to a history of female voices that, as Hendry (2011) asserts, have worked tirelessly to be heard against a social system that has normalized women's current societal role by downplaying her historical significance.

The general exclusion of women's voices in the curriculum, policy, and histories are more than a mere oversight (Grumet, 1988). Rather, this exclusion is a part of a hidden curriculum and agenda in education that has been hidden not only from students and colleagues but also from the women who have been intimately affected by this silence (Grumet, 1988; Miller, 2005). As Grumet (1988) notes, there is a vital dialectic between the "domestic experience of nurturing and the public project of educating the next generation" (p. 5). Here Grumet is describing a tension between *domestic* and *public* projects and lives that is found at the intersection of mothering at schooling.

This tension between domesticity and a public presence manifests itself in several ways throughout my narrative. To that point, this piece balances between the parallels I draw between my experiences and the implications I feel those experiences have for the curriculum. If the counternarrative of women is integral to correcting a historical exclusion and there is a tension between the lived and public experience of mothers, then I feel that a transparent disclosure of personal experience in relation to rather than in opposition of public work functions as an active resistance to social structures which bind mothers to tension and silence.

Working from a perspective that histories give our current epistemological state a secure foundation on which to stand (Pinar, 2004, 2007), it is important to note the undertones that support the conversation of m/othering. While the open dialectic of m/othering is fairly recent (see Connelly & Ghodsee, 2011; Katz, 2009; McDermott, 2011; Pillow, 2004; Springgay & Freedman, 2007, 2009), the overall conversation is nuanced by the senses, aesthetics in education, and the ethics of othering; interrelated themes that serve as an integral part of feminist literature (Dewey, 1934; Eisner, 2002; Gershon, 2011a; hooks, 1994; Jipson, Hendry, Victor, Froude-Jones, & Freed-Rowland, 1995; Lather, 1991; McDermott, 2011; Miller, 2005; Quinn, 2011; Springgay & Freedman, 2007, 2009). While the primary focus of m/othering in relation to reconceptualizing curriculum work comes from the academy, I wish to provide a voice as both a graduate student and a public school teacher because the practice of parenthood simultaneously affects my scholarly and professional journeys.

COMPLICATING THE INTERSECTIONS OF SELF

I used to believe that I lived with/in certain intersections of my being. I was a teacher and a scholar. A wife and a daughter. An American with Goan and Norwegian roots. Becoming a mother has challenged these well-structured binaries and I find that more often than not they tend to clash in exquisite and complicated ways. These clashes have given rise to questions not only about myself but also about my conception of myself as an educator and the content I learn as a doctoral student. What is more important, education or schooling? What kind of education do I find valuable? How will I facilitate my daughter unpacking particular ways of knowing? How will my actions affect the kind of citizen she will become? How will culture play into our lives? As I sit rocking her at hours of the night that I forgot existed after my undergraduate program, a jumbled mess of everything from postmodern literature to poopy diapers creeps into my mind. Suddenly these parts of my being are not disconnected but rather my new experiences give me the privilege of embodying once separate parts of myself in the same moment.

Before I was graced with the complexities of motherhood, I had begun my graduate studies in curriculum and instruction. It is a degree that I feel is both practical and theoretical. As I progressed through the first year of my program, I struggled with the space that I saw between theory and practice and worked to reconcile applying my studies for the benefit of my students. I had wanted my students to explore the curriculum, to come to speak the language I was teaching in palpable ways rather than through individually packaged lessons. I wanted to bridge my teaching with the artistry with which I approached my studies. When I became a mother, my urge to build these connections only intensified as I began to realize that my daughter would eventually experience what I often view as a static, rigid conception of education that often presents singular packaged pieces of a broader curriculum.

> *"I am here because I am a woman of the border: Between places, between identities, between languages, between cultures, between longings and illusions, one foot in the academy and the other out" (Behar, 1996, p.162).*

Suddenly the neatly drawn structures through which the formal curriculum is most often approached seems to be a very unnatural process. In this space, science rarely interrelates with English, health functions separate from math and lived experience yields quietly and obediently to the text. Like an ethnographer who has just experienced a rich point (Agar, 1996), I stand in partial disbelief and ponder the strange normalcy as my students mechanically move from one subject to another, forgetting one lesson to begin the next. Much like my experience prior to becoming a mother, my students have compartmentalized their academic lives through a binaried curriculum. By this I mean that subjects are viewed in opposing terms, like math verses English. The opposition of these subjects binds disciplines into independent structures that are reified by policy such as the need to cover material for testing. These boundaries tend to silence voices and perspectives that are not required for standardized testing while trumping students' basic interpretive inquiry (Panayotidis, 2011).

Panayotidis (2011) discusses the deconstruction of this binaried system as learning to speak in multiple tongues. She states that if a discipline is a way of "languaging the world then ... perhaps in taking up our work in/ through a multi/interdisciplinary perspective we will learn to think and teach in multiple tongues" (p. 54). As a world language educator, I can identify with the disorientation that occurs as my students negotiate the art of language learning. As my students weave their tongue in ways that have been introduced to them since birth with the trill of a new perspective, they often discover a space of both confidence and confusion. Rose (2009) reminds us that education should help us "make sense of the world and find our way in it" (p. 31). Scholars have long argued for a fluid, multiple tongued conception of education to aide in this journey (Bakhtin, 1981; Grumet, 1988) but education remains steeped in a system of compartmentalizing schools that pushes students to first catalogue their subjects then separate their academic, social and familial lives. I often ask myself, does this disjointed nature of schooling reflect our students' as they exist outside of the bubble of schools? Will it take until they have a pivotal moment, like bringing a life into this world, to realize that life is not always "either/or" but more frequently "both/and" or even "neither/nor"? It is living in the curriculum of opposites that students come to see themselves in the same light—school/home, us/them, body/mind.

I lament over the inevitable binaried lifestyle to which my daughter will be indoctrinated through schooling. In particular, I have a growing concern for the Cartesian split and the hierarchy of the senses through which she may view herself and her world (Gershon, 2011a). Being the product of

> "To unravel the snarl of questions that surround my practice, to examine the interconnection between the roles I inhabit as a teacher, researcher, artist, mother, mentor, and to negotiate a path of meaningful inquiry that shifts both inward and outward is no simple task" (Lymburner, 2004, pp. 75-76).

a dominant educational paradigm, I cannot say that my epistemological view has been much different. It was not until recently that I have (re)considered the power of the senses and the paradigm through which I was indoctrinated. When my daughter was born, I took a walk shortly after the delivery. When I returned to the recently sterilized room, there was an unmistakable scent that sat heavily in the air. I asked if anyone else could smell it, they just shook their heads. I inhaled again and without thinking walked to my daughter. I pulled her close to me and smelled her. This scent, which was more overpowering than anything else I think I've ever experienced, was her. I can only describe it as strangely familiar, as if I had known it my whole life and yet it was entirely new. When they brought her back to me from the nursery, I would smell her every time. It was, through this form of comfort and silent communication, that I would initially come to know my daughter. For the first time in my life, I came to know something through a sense other than sight or hearing. As she grows, I've come to rely on touch to comfort her and taste to double check every bottle before giving it to her. Through these experiences I have awakened senses which may not be highly valued in Western settings, such as a feeling of intuition that my daughter needs me before she cries, which have become important as I negotiate the tension between fulfilling the needs of my child with my previous ways of knowing.

Yet these are not the senses that I was taught to value in school. The underpinnings of the ethnocentric, Western model of education tends to lean first toward sight (Gershon, 2011b; McDermott, 2011), which has been anthropologically linked with intellectual activity, while taste, touch, and smell show a predilection for the "primitive" senses (Howes, 2003). Within the traditional schooling structure I find that the prepackaged curriculum is inextricably linked to dominant Western senses through text and lecture (Gershon, 2011b). As McDermott (2011) explores, mothering can push us toward a curriculum of the senses, one which honors the "noise" of life (Gershon, 2011b) and seeks wisdom through the practice of being oriented to others through a bodied curriculum (Springgay & Freedman, 2007). A curriculum of the senses imbues the once bodiless landscape of knowing with a kind of wisdom (Gershon, 2011b; Hendry, 2011) that permeates the soul. Unfortunately, the same sociocultural norm that considers teaching as women's work because it is "natural" for them (Apple, 1985, 1986; Hendry, 2011; Park, 1996), limits sensual ways of knowing in the classroom.

> "I will try to make a plausible case for the beginnings of a distinctive moral approach arising from maternal instinct. Capacities such as the ability to 'read' the infant and its needs develop ... but how might a moral subject or agent emerge from these instinctive beginnings?" (Noddings, 2007, p. 6).

McDermott (2011) states that the richness of those "experiences have been left behind ... leaving us with [an] abstract, sterilized reinterpretation of sensory experiences" (p. 133). To this point, Grumet (1988) argues that part of the tension, the bitter milk, of education is the ways in which certain experiences and ways of knowing which are often particular to women yield to male dominated discourse and practice. The limitation of these sensual ways of knowing therefore speaks strongly to the ways in which girls' constructions of knowledge is often othered, pushing women to forget that "knowledge from and about the body is also knowledge about the world" (Grumet, 1988, p. 3).

I have found that similar sociocultural norms in the Midwest make the most natural parts of mothering difficult as well. For example, a few weeks after my daughter was born I had taken her to the mall to run a quick errand. While I was out she became hungry and started to cry. Fearing a public reaction to breastfeeding, a concern that this example will document as generally not unfounded, I ducked into a fairly empty clothing store and asked to use a fitting room to feed my child. As I could see, the fitting rooms were empty with the exception of one occupied room. The saleswoman looked at the empty hallway and explained that she did not have room for me to use, that there was a bathroom in the mall designed for nursing mothers. I cried that day as I nursed my newborn child in a dirty wooden chair located in a small, damp, single-stall bathroom without ventilation as my feet stuck to the urine stained floor. While I could have stopped and protested the treatment I had received, the pull of my child's cry made the very fiber of my being ache in a way that drove me to quickly nourish my child. On the other hand, another part of me was surprised that this treatment had come from another woman who, for all I knew, could be a mother herself. Was she acting on store policy? Was she embarrassed by the thought of me feeding my child, even though it would be behind closed doors? While I decided not to make her uncomfortable in her decision to deny my request, questions about policy, power and sociocultural values still play in my mind as I reflect on that moment.

This account is not atypical for the context in which I live. Since I have decided to breast feed I have been criticized numerous times for not using formula; I have been told that I am being "barbaric"; I have been given countless dirty looks by both women and men; and I have had children's eyes shielded from me despite the fact that I have always used a cloth of some kind to cover my breast and child's head in order

> "Suhaila tasted the air, too, and through tasting, she knew more than she had known before" (Soetoro-Ng, 2011).

to remain modest. At our daycare we are required to mark our bottles with a bright red label since they are filled with a bodily fluid and the workers are required to give the bottle using a glove to avoid contact with the contents of the bottle. As I drop my daughter off each morning, I am reminded that in this specific context, we are the only family using breast milk as I line up our bright red bottle with the other white-labeled bottles in the refrigerator. To be clear, I acknowledge that my experiences are highly contextualized and that in other spaces breastfeeding is the norm, as is the case abroad with my family members in Goa as well as in the United States where my cousin in San Francisco has relayed a very different narrative. However, this speaks to the point that this choice has to be carefully considered based on the context rather than the comfort of the mother. As I continue to make decisions that I feel benefit my daughter, such as not allowing her to watch any television, I find that while looking past sociocultural norms may be difficult, it is often the best for her and for our family.

The same can be said of education. While the curriculum is often used as a static space that is reached through prepackaged texts and tests in order to present particular kinds of information to children, I propose a more fluid conception of schooling that takes time and deliberation to satisfy (Dewey, 1934; Eisner, 2002). Here the concept of *currere* (Pinar, 1975) offers the ideal of an active journey rather than a static set of instructions (Slattery, 1995). This fluid space presents a "perpetual struggle" as practitioners and scholars reconcile the fact that the path is "never a finished product that can be finally mastered and passed along to an awaiting new generation" (Kincheloe, 1998, p. 130). If the curriculum is viewed as a fluid being rather than a static structure then there is a kernel of importance in running this course in the way called for through the *currere* (Pinar & Grumet, 1976). If practitioners are complicit in these norms then a historical call for the deconstruction of othering (Hendry, 2011; hooks, 1994; Kozol, 2005) and the attention to deliberation and artistry (Dewey, 1934; Eisner, 2002; Greene, 1988) in public education which tends to be reified through these norms will be left unanswered.

In more ways than one, mothering is a form of *currere*. It is certainly an active process, a path that is never quite finished (Pinar, 1998). Undoubtedly it is a challenge that meets with the resistance of life on a daily basis. On this path I find that I am frequently bombarded with loving suggestions from friends and, especially, family. Some are helpful, like being reminded that even babies have bad days. Some are absurd and cheekily ribald, like being told to eat a lot of ice cream to "grease the chute" to help induce labor. And some, while well intended, are useless, like being told that "this too shall pass." At the end of the day I am reminded that these suggestions are also interpretations of a situation. Despite my inherent exhaustion, these interpretations must be considered carefully, analyzed and, if warranted, acted upon.

> "Bitter milk, fluid of contradictions: love and rejection, sustenance and abstinence, nurturance and denial" (Grumet, 1988, p. xi).

This is also often the case with the texts through which students are provided in contemporary American education. Unfortunately, these texts often present interpretations as Truth, leaving little room for critique through the prepackaged curriculum. Written through a White-male perspective (Brunner & Peyton-Caire, 2000), texts frequently engage in a one-sided cultural analysis. Ignoring the fact that cultural analysis is intrinsically incomplete (Geertz, 1973; Ortner, 2006), these texts tend to map out a bodiless landscape of knowledge for students to bank rather than critique. As Morris (2011) argues, even the photographs designed to give context within a text are inherently wrought with the interpretation of the artist and must therefore be examined critically. In other words, one can never be sure what images escaped the frame or what voices were not written into the text. What pedagogical views are being filtered through these words and images? When left unexamined by teachers and students, constructions of both "others" and ourselves can be conceptualized as big "T," universal, Truth instead of the interpretations they are. It is, as Grumet (1988) states, a curriculum that is the presence of an absence. The main implication for teachers here is that a monovocal text that only offers a single point of view remains flat, lifeless, and shorn of dialogue (Fettes, 2011) and opportunities for student inquiry. In the same way that a monotongued disciplinary approach silences voices and opportunities for students, the one-sided nature of texts also has the power to silence and marginalize those who do not fit a unitary perspective.

As is the case with many individuals who are the product of public education or even the general construction of knowledge, I had always taken the interpretations of others and constructed my world view on their understanding of particular spaces, places and people. Admittedly, I saw text as Truth and felt that knowledge was best gained through a "proper" education. After all, I have spent several years and more money than I care to discuss on a "proper" education. I have gone from sitting in straight rows to memorizing facts to sitting in groups while I unpack ideas with a community of students. Certainly it has been a worthwhile journey but it has been my recent experience that has helped me come to understand the difference between education and schooling.

> "As if an instant, I learn what I know" (Hildegard of Bingen, quoted in Newman, 1987, p. 7).

For the first two months after my daughter's birth, my aunts from India came to live with my husband and me. For them, this is not culturally unusual. For the individualistic American in me, this initially brought about great anxiety. Nevertheless, we welcomed the additional help. Prior to her birth I had taken every prenatal course imaginable—breastfeeding, Lamaze, infant care—and I had read volumes of books on what to expect during the first year. After all that preparation I was ready to have a baby. However, I quickly realized that I was completely unprepared for a newborn. Luckily my aunts, along with my parents and in-laws, were there. In the months following her birth I learned through observation, stories and gentle lessons that proved to be more concrete and valuable than the courses I had taken during my pregnancy. For example, it is one thing to watch a video of a woman breastfeeding or even hold a doll in a cross-cradle position but it is entirely another to have several women give personal accounts of successful feeding positions or have an experienced woman explain how the latch is not conducive for the comfort of mother or child. I believe this is why despite offering courses, many hospitals offer lactation consultants and why midwifes are popular among breastfeeding mothers.

There is a notable history of the struggle between schooling and education (Au & Jordan, 1981; Levinson & Holland, 1996; Rival, 2000; Skinner & Holland, 2009). The Western tradition of schooling has often rendered the opinion that the best learning takes place within the classroom (Sommer & Becker, 1974). Realistically it is difficult, if not impossible, to define "good" education. Who is it "good" for? Who has the privilege of deciding what is "good"? What makes a "well-rounded" education? What facts are worth knowing (Spencer, 1859)? Macdonald (1974) suggests a "centering" of education that calls for the "completion of a person" (as cited in Marshall, Sears, Allen, Roberts, & Schubert, 2007, p. 122). If one seeks the completion of a person, surely she must look past basic facts and figures that pervade modern education. Who decides what completes a person? If life is a *currere*, are we ever "complete"? Certainly I felt less complete without the knowledge so patiently given to me by my family regarding the rearing of my newborn. In this sense, our system is inherently incomplete as it currently stands. There is knowledge that a student simply cannot gain through schooling. As I have explored, there is wisdom to be found in culture and past generations that can be brought into schools and used to help "center" our students (Au & Jordan, 1981; Lather, 2009; Rival, 2000).

> *"Wisdom was understood as a process (through intuition, divination, ritual, myths, art, and dance) that sought connection, not separation, from the universe" (Hendry, 2011, p. 35).*

CONCLUSION: (RE)CONSIDERING THE BODY OF CURRICULUM

What has been rearticulated throughout this chapter is a (re)consideration of our system of schooling as it relates to the wisdom found at the intersection of the personal and public narrative of women and mothers. Springgay (2008) regards this type of curriculum as *bodied,* meaning that attention is given to the "exploration of the production of subjectivities not premised on self/other dichotomies" (p. 31). If I move away from the prescriptive, the binaried, and toward the everyday, the bodied, then I find space that is alive and nutritive for myself and my students. It is a space that is called for by Addams, Flagg Young, Grumet, Greene, Lather, Miller, Springgay, Hendry, Noddings, and other scholars who found discomfort in the disconnected nature of schooling. Just as I have gone through a process of (re)imagining the purpose of my body, the interconnected roles to which I tend and my previous ways of knowing and interacting with my world, I also must attend to the often overlooked possibilities that exist within our system of schooling and to the complications that this system presents. For example, in a place where the curriculum is monolingual for the sake of efficiency (Labaree, 1997), which voices, senses and perspectives are lost in that mother tongue? There is a kernel of importance in the idea of complicating the normal and making it strange, in moving past what has already been done (Bourdieu 1993; Spinder & Spindler, 1982; Winfield, 2011) and toward a system of the messy, sensual every day. For me, the old was made new by the experience of becoming a mother. It is an experience which has simultaneously disrupted and centered my life. Just as a balance can be met through my most intimate experiences and public missions, I would suggest that schooling may find strength in unclear spaces (Lather, 2007).

Wright (2011) points out that the world is dirty but, as Behar (1996) notes, one must not be afraid to get down into the mud, to come into contact with the messiness of lived experience. From the physical to intellectual changes, nothing in my life has brought me closer to the mud than becoming a mother. Through text, independent interpretation and a binaried experience, schools have effectively sterilized a space that should be just as overtly messy and complicated as the world that it affects. The experience of these tensions in this space allows the reconsideration of what is normal and how it came to be normalized.

Too often practitioners are distracted by extraneous things in schools like test scores and implementing the newest policy. As an educator, I am driven by a more instinctive need to nourish my students with something more substantial than the foremilk of the prescribed cur-

> "We may take epistemological paths to reach this place, but where we arrive is a living breathing place of being" (Pinar, 2006, p.xii).

riculum. While it would be easy to be seduced by something so sweet and easily attainable, I realize the need to stay latched until I can find the hind milk that will nourish myself and my students. In light of my experiences I find myself working to nourish my students as a mentor, to guide but not control, to offer support and care that facilitates, not forces, growth. In this moment of teaching as an art of mentorship, I find that my students are hungry for a type of education that deeply connects them with their world in the intimate, palpable way that my daughter and I connect as I feed her. It is my hope that my experiences help me to be fully present in a space where I am not one but all parts of myself. A space where I feel engorged with the nested possibilities of mothering and education.

My narrative is nested within my physical, emotional and intellectual selves. In similar ways, I have argued for a curriculum that is nested within its sensual, experiential and braided forms. This nested and layered understanding of curriculum is similarly evident in the intertextual framework of this chapter, a juxtaposition of my narrative and scholarship. These polyglot ways of knowing are indicative of such multiple constructions of presence, the multiple ways of embodying and knowing mothering.

NOTE

1. This construction of "m/other" is selected from Stephanie Springgay and Deb Freedman's work and implies exactly what it suggests, that as mothers women are often othered in ways that are unique to their societal role as not only a woman but as caregivers. While I discuss the difficult process of becoming and living in the margins created by m/othering, I do not wish to overlook the important role of fathers and guardians in general. However, despite being a woman of color I have seldom felt so "othered" in my life. It is from this extremely personal journey that I wish to speak and complicate curriculum conversations.

REFERENCES

Agar, M. H. (1996). *The professional stranger: An informal introduction to ethnography* (2nd ed.). San Diego, CA: Academic Press.

Apple, M. W. (1985). Teaching and "women's work": A comparative historical and ideological analysis. *Teachers College Record, 86*(3), 455-473.

Apple, M. W. (1986). *Texts & teachers: A political economy of class & gender relations in education.* New York, NY: Routledge.

Au, K. H., & Jordan, C. (1981). Teaching reading to Hawaiian children: Finding a culturally appropriate solution. In H. Trueba, G. Guthrie, & K. Au (Eds.), *Culture and the bilingual classroom: Studies in classroom ethnography* (pp. 139-152). Rowley, MA: Newbury House.

Bakhtin, M. M. (1981). *The dialogic imagination: Four essays* (C. Emerson & M. Holquist, Trans). Austin, TX: University of Texas Press.

Behar, R. (1996). *The vulnerable observer: Anthropology that breaks your heart.* Boston, MA: Beacon Press.

Bloom, L. R. (1996). Stories of one's own: Nonunitary subjectivity in narrative representation. *Qualitative Inquiry, 2*(2), 176-197.

Bourdieu, P. (1993). *The field of cultural production.* New York, NY: Columbia University Press.

Brunner, C. C., & Peyton-Caire, L. (2000). Seeking representation: Supporting black female graduate students who aspire to superintendency. *Urban Education, 35*(5), 532-548.

Connelly, R., & Ghodsee, K. (2011). *Professor mommy: Finding world-family balance in academia.* Lanham, MD: Rowman & Littlefield.

Dewey, J. (1934). *Art as experience.* Rahway, NJ: The Barnes Foundation Press.

Eisner, E. (2002). From episteme to phronesis to artistry in the study and improvement of teaching. In E. Eisner (Ed.) *Reimagining schools: The selected works of Elliot W. Eisner* (pp. 193-204). New York, NY: Routledge.

Ellsworth, E., & Milner, J. L. (1996). Working difference in education. *Curriculum Inquiry, 26*(3), 245-263.

Fettes, M. (2011). Senses and sensibilities: Educating the somatic imagination. *Journal of Curriculum Theorizing, 27*(2), 114-129.

Geertz, C. (1973). *The interpretation of cultures*. New York, NY: Basic Books.

Gershon, W. S. (2011a). Introduction: Toward a sensual curriculum. *Journal of Curriculum Theorizing, 27*(2), 1-16.

Gershon, W. S. (2011b). Embodied knowledge: Sounds as educational systems. *Journal of Curriculum Theorizing, 27*(2), 66-81.

Gershon, W. S., Lather, P., & Smithies, C. (2009). Troubling the angles redux: Tales of collaboration towards a polyphonic text. In W. S. Gershon (Ed.), *The collaborative turn: Working together in qualitative research* (pp. 3-34). Rotterdam, The Netherlands: Sense.

Greene, M. (1988). *The dialectic of freedom*. New York, NY: Teachers' College Press.

Grumet, M. (1988). *Bitter milk: Women and teaching*. Amherst, MA: University of Massachusetts Press.

Hendry, P. M. (2011). *Engendering curriculum history*. New York, NY: Routledge.

hooks, b. (1994). *Teaching to transgress: Education as the practice of freedom*. New York, NY: Routledge.

Howes, D. (2003). *Sensual relations: Engaging the senses in culture and social theory*. Ann Arbor, MI: The University of Michigan Press.

Jipson, J., Hendry, P. M., Victor, S. Froude-Jones, K., & Freed-Rowland, G. (1995). *Repositioning feminism and education: Perspectives on educating for social change*. Westport, CT: Bergin and Garvey.

Katz, L. G., & Katz, S. J. (2009). *Intellectual emergencies: Some reflections on mothering and teaching—And a family*. Lewisville, NC: KPress.

Kincheloe, J. L. (1998). Grounding the post-formal notion of intrapersonal intelligence. In W. F. Pinar (Ed.), *Curriculum: Toward new identities* (pp. 129-142). New York, NY: Routledge

Kozol, J. (2005). *The shame of the nation: The restoration of apartheid schooling in America*. New York, NY: Crown Books.

Labaree, D. F. (1997). Public goods, private goods: The American struggle of educational goals. *American Educational Research Journal, 34*(1), 39-81.

Lather, P. (1991). *Getting smart: Feminist research and pedagogy with/in the postmodern*. New York, NY: Routledge.

Lather, P. (2007). *Getting lost: Feminist efforts toward a double(d) science*. Albany, NY: SUNY Press.

Lather, P. (2009). Response to Jennifer Gilbert: The double trouble of passing on curriculum studies. In E. Malewski (Ed.), *Curriculum studies handbook: The next moment* (pp. 73-77). New York, NY: Routledge.

Lather, P., & Smithies, C. (1997). *Troubling the angels: Women living with HIV/AIDS*. Boulder, CO: Westview.

Levinson, B. A., & Holland, D. (1996) *The cultural production of the educated person*. Albany, NY: State University of New York Press.

Lymburner, J. (2004). Interwoven threads: Theory, practice, and research coming together. In R. L. Irwin & A. de Cosson (Eds.), *A/R/Tography: Rendering self through arts-based living inquiry* (pp. 75-88). Vancouver, British Columbia, Canada: Pacific Educational Press.

Marshall, J. D., Sears, J. T., Allen, L. A., Roberts, P. A., & Schubert, W. H. (2007). *Turning points in curriculum: A contemporary American memoir* (2nd ed.). Upper Saddle River, NJ: Merrill/Prentice Hall.

McDermott, M. (2011). Curriculum of the eye/I. *Journal of Curriculum Theorizing, 27*(2), 130-144.

Miller, J. (2005). *Sounds of silence breaking: Women, autobiography, curriculum.* New York, NY: Peter Lang.

Morris, E. (2011). *Believing is seeing: Observations on the mysteries of photography.* New York, NY: The Penguin Press.

Newman, B. (1987). *Sister of wisdom: St. Hildegard's theology of the feminine.* Berkley, CA: University of California Press

Ng-A-Fook, N. (2011). Provoking curriculum theorizing: A question of/for currere, Denkbild and aesthetics. *Media: Culture: Pedagogy, 15*(2). Retrieved from http://mcp.educ.ubc.ca/v15n02DigitalGeneration_Article09_Ng-A-Fook

Noddings, N. (2007). *Philosophy of education* (2nd ed.). Boulder, CO: Westview Press.

Ortner, S. B. (2006). *Anthropology and social theory: Culture, power and the acting subject.* Durham, NC: Duke University Press.

Panayotidis, E. L. (2011). Thinking/teaching in multiple tongues: The interdisciplinary imagination. *Journal of Curriculum Theorizing, 27*(1), 48-63.

Park, S. M. (1996). Research, teaching, and service: Why shouldn't women's work count? *Journal of Higher Education, 67*(1), 46-84.

Pillow, W. S. (2004). *Unfit subjects: Education policy and the teen mother.* New York, NY: Routledge Falmer.

Pinar, W. F. (1975). *The method of currere.* Lecture presented at American Educational Research Association, Washington, DC.

Pinar, W. F. (2004). *What is curriculum theory?* Mahwah, NJ: Erlbaum.

Pinar, W. F. (2006). The lure that pulls flowerheads to face the sun. In D.W. Jardine, S. Friesen, & P. Clifford (Eds.), *Curriculum in abundance* (pp. ix-xxii). Mahwah, NJ: Erlbaum.

Pinar, W. F. (2007). *Intellectual advancement through disciplinarity: Verticality and horizontality in curriculum studies.* Rotterdam, The Netherlands: Sense.

Pinar, W. F., & Grumet, M. (1976). *Toward a poor curriculum.* Dubuque, IA: Kendall/Hunt.

Quinn, M. (2011). "No room in the inn?" The question of hospitality in the post (partum)-labors of curriculum studies. In E. Malewski (Ed.), *Curriculum studies handbook: The next movement* (pp. 101-117). New York, NY: Routledge.

Rival, L. (2000). Formal schooling and the production of modern citizens in the Ecuadorian Amazon. In B. Levinson (Ed.), *Schooling the symbolic animal: Social and cultural dimensions of education* (pp. 108-122). Oxford, England: Rowman & Littlefield.

Rose, M. (2009). *Why school? Reclaiming education for all of us.* New York, NY: The New Press.

Skinner, D., & Holland, D. (2009). Schools and the cultural production of the educated person in a Nepalese hill community. In P. Bhatta (Ed.), *Education in Nepal: Problems, reforms and social change* (pp. 295-332.). Kathmandu, India: Martin Chautari.

Slattery, P. (1995). *Curriculum development in the postmodern era.* New York, NY: Garland.

Soetoro-Ng, M. (2011). *Ladder to the moon.* Somerville, MA: Candlewick Press.

Sommer, R., & Becker, F. (1974). Learning outside the classroom. *The School Review, 82*(4), 601-607.

Spencer, H. (1859). *Education: Intellectual, moral and physical.* New York, NY: J.B. Alden

Spindler, G., & Spindler, L. (1982). Roger Harker and Schonhausen: From the familiar to the strange and back again. In G. Spindler (Ed.), *Doing the ethnography of schooling* (pp. 20-46). New York, NY: Holt, Rinehart and Winston.

Springgay, S. (2008). *Body knowledge and curriculum: Pedagogies of touch in youth and visual culture.* New York, NY: Peter Lang.

Springgay, S., & Freedman, D. (2007). *Curriculum and the cultural body.* New York, NY: Peter Lang.

Springgay, S., & Freedman, D. (2009). M/othering a bodied curriculum: Sleeping with cake and other touchable encounters. *Journal of Curriculum Theorizing, 25*(2), 25-37

Winfield, A. (2011, October 14). *Bringing history back: Curriculum theory's lost Memory.* Panel discussion presented at Bergamo, Dayton, OH.

Wright, H. (2011, October 14). *Keynote 1.* Keynote address presented at Bergamo, Dayton, OH.

CHAPTER 9

(RE)RIGHTING THE SCRIPT

Speaking Back to Public Curriculum to Secure a More Humanizing Citizenship for African American Women and Girls

Monique Cherry-McDaniel
Miami University

I recently read a novel by Dolen Perkins-Valdez, entitled *Wench: A Novel* (2010). It is a historical fiction about four Black women who are taken as concubines by their slave masters during the mid-19th century. Each of the women struggle with being forced into sexual relationships with their masters and having to live their lives ostracized from both the White and Black communities as a result of their unwanted positions. They also struggle with the reality that their own needs, dreams, and aspirations were second to the desires of their masters, who claim to love them. One of the main characters, Lizzie, who is "more humanely" forced into being a concubine by her master, Drayle, has a difficult time making sense of her ambiguous relationship. Lizzie believes that she and Drayle have a genuinely loving relationship but her position is always very uncertain. Drayle does not hesitate to beat Lizzie when she does something he dislikes; he does not hesitate to chain her up when he fears her escaping; and he does not hesitate to rape her when his desires get the best of his

Excursions and Recursions Through Power, Privilege, and Praxis
pp. 115–129
Copyright © 2012 by Information Age Publishing
All rights of reproduction in any form reserved.

otherwise genteel nature. Lizzie lives her life precariously perched on a line between human and animal, as people, including her beloved Drayle, define her very worth in terms of body parts.

I was saddened as I read the novel and meditated on what it must have been like to have no voice and a fragmented sense of self. I also found myself angered at the thought that today, over 100 years later, African American women and girls are still understood as a collection of body parts, our humanity and worth as people questioned and problematized through politics and public policy (Ibura Salaam, 2002; Sharpley-Whiting, 2007; Shende, 1997), and our identities spelled out for us through popular media and public ideology (Carroll, 1997; Hill Collins, 2004; Morgan, 2000). The legacy of American chattel slavery is not simply a piece of our history to be taken up in works of fiction, but instead, still haunts African American women and girls as we struggle to help the world see us outside of the roles related to work, sex, and motherhood. In this piece, I explore the power of the public curriculum in the creation and maintenance of damaging ideologies, discourses, and practices as it relates to the intersections of race and gender, and I encourage scholars and cultural workers to take seriously our need to "get lost" in the critical examinations of the histories and interests that have necessitated such ideologies, discourses, and practices.

In our quest to define ourselves, our greatest enemy is a public curriculum that is called upon each time a person or a system interacts with or acts upon us. Public curriculum is defined by Cortes (1983) as "that massive, ongoing, informal curriculum, of family, peer groups, neighborhood, organizations, occupations, religious institutions, and other socializing forces" (p. 25). While those in the educational field are familiar with curriculum, and often conceptualize it as deliberately constructed material for the purpose of teaching skills, dispositions, and concepts, very few concern themselves with the pervasiveness of the public curriculum and its contributions to how citizens are made and socialized into society. Public curriculum is arguably more powerful that any other curriculum in preparing people to take up citizenships, because it is present in all institutions in the civil society and is often made up of an endless supply of images and narratives that are rarely attached to the histories which produced them. These images and narratives create the frameworks people use to construct their identities, which are, at all times, in relation to the identities they construct for others. These identities are then used in order to define the levels of citizenship that are afforded to different people. They determine the amount of power and influence certain groups of people have over the scope, depth and evolution of their identities, as well as the ways that their interests and histories are adopted or rejected as the interests and histories of the greater society. For African American women and girls, the public curriculum has deemed us slaves in relationship to masters, whores in relationship to ladies, objects in relationship to subjects, and, in order to maintain these binaries, the images and narratives of old are recycled in present day cultural mediums.

In today's society, the public curriculum is made even more powerful through the pervasiveness of the media. Movies, music, television, news outlets, billboards, magazines, social media sites, Youtube, and blogs all serve to reinforce and re-present the images and narratives about African American women as the loud, coarse, uneducated, anomalies of American genteel womanhood. If you read a newspaper article, turn on the nightly news, suffer through a 30-minute sitcom, or allow yourself to be entertained/indoctrinated by a television crime drama, African American women will be portrayed as the sole reason for the so-called demise of the Black family, the main culprit of exorbitant governmental spending, and the most egregious offenders of American cultural norms. The media spells out who we are, and to be anything else would make our very existence rebellious. To use a concept from Judith Butler (1990), we are unintelligible outside of the tropes of Black womanhood that have been created for us. In fact, many of the efforts African American women and girls engage in to change the public curriculum of African American womanhood or girlhood, such as the Black Girls Rock Campaign, are understood as anomalies, and not given substantial media coverage.

Some scholars have written about the use and misuse of cultural images and representations, and, while their work has been taken up differently, the way they understand the nature of their work is very similar. For instance, Stuart Hall (1997) discusses racist regimes of representation and how they work to create knowledge about people of color. He argues that images and objects "can function as signifiers in the production of meaning" as long as familiar context, rules and codes are there to frame them (p. 37). Hall defines representation as the production of meaning through language and symbols, and uses this statement to define what he calls systems of representation.

> A system by which all sorts of objects, people, and events are correlated with a set of concepts or mental representations which we carry around in our heads. Without them we could not interpret the world meaningful [sic] at all. Meaning depends on the system of concepts and images formed in our thoughts which can stand for or "represent" the world, enabling us to refer to things both inside and outside our heads. (p. 17)

Hall also wrote that people have the capability to make meaning of very obscure and abstract ideas because people have ways of "organizing, clustering, arranging, and classifying concepts and of establishing complex relations between them" (p. 17).

Most important, Hall asserts that people who share the same culture(s) have the same concept maps, the same code by which to read and interpret language and signs. This certainly alludes to public curriculum, as one's experiences as a cultural being determine the concept maps and codes with which to read and interpret language and signs.

Similarly, Patricia Hill Collins (2000) discusses controlling images. She argues that stereotypes can function to hide or normalize oppression, or coerce people into behaving in particular ways by creating the points of reference people use to define normalcy. Controlling images are used currently to justify the oppression of African American women and serve as warnings and examples to other minority groups. These images are not only powerful in themselves; they gain greater influence and traction as they are employed within a sociopolitical context. For instance, she talks about the controlling image of the *mammy*. Slave masters and cultural authorities portrayed the mammy as an asexual, docile, accommodating, and often unattractive slave woman who cared for the slave master and his family. The roots of the controlling image of the mammy can be traced as far back as the early 1600s before the end of indentured servitude.

> English accounts of women of West Africa as heavily burdened drudges —a staple of most English colonial literature by the second quarter of the 17th century—may have influenced the predominantly cosmopolitan owners of African labor to set their female slaves to work in the fields. (K. Brown, 1996, p. 115)

This lack of consideration for the femininity of African women led to the complete "subordination of African women to the needs of English labor" (p. 116). Not only did slave owners and cultural authorities use the mammy image to justify the exploitation of African women's labor, but they also used it to hide the fact that the women who worked closely with the slave master and his family were often sexually abused and made to be silent about such abuses (Jordan-Zachery, 2009).

Today this same image is appropriated to justify much of the same treatment of African American women or women of African descent (Omolade, 1994). The mammy image has been preserved and rearticulated in the current American public curriculum. As a result, the thought that African American women should work like slaves persists. Additionally, the normalcy of African American women working in hazardous and vulnerable service positions also persists. Because African American women and other women of color are more likely be ill-educated, undereducated or in some way more vulnerable to labor exploitation, it seems "normal" and "commonsense" that we work in low-paying and dangerous jobs.

When African American women remain in a perpetual state of poverty, based on income or relationship status, which are the two main reasons women apply for welfare benefits, there is a clamor to remedy the "problem" of poverty, but not the circumstances that support poverty, hence welfare-to-work programs. These programs stand on the shoulders of another controlling image within the public curriculum, the *welfare queen*. Over the course of the last half century, the creation and use of the welfare queen has justified punitive welfare reform which helped to continue to blame African American women for never having had access to adequate education, employment, housing and healthcare, even though programs to provide services were available. Ronald Reagan created and heavily exploited the image of the welfare queen, whom he described as a woman who fraudulently collected hundreds of thousands of untaxed dollars in welfare benefits. She was an ill-educated African American mother who used her fertility to collect more benefits with the births of countless illegitimate children. She was intent on working the system instead of seeking gainful employment (Hancock, 2004; Neubeck & Cazanave, 2001; Roberts, 1995; Smith, 1987).

The combination of the mammy and welfare queen as controlling images inspired welfare reform programs, such as the Personal Responsibility Act and the Work Opportunities Reconciliation Act, which mandated a 2-year cap on benefits, required recipients to perform 40 hours of work or community service per week, and required job training (Clawson & Trice, 2000). These policies and others like them have denied women the benefits they needed to care for themselves and their children and essentially amounted to state mandated child neglect and abuse. Moreover, these policies have turned the bodies of poor women and children into state property mandating that they give up their rights to choice and privacy in exchange for food, shelter and medical care. These women are further humiliated and marginalized by a public curriculum that has depicted them as failures who are morally bankrupt, lazy, selfish, and often sexually irresponsible. Public curriculum has opened them up to additional victimization from the state and other entities that see these women as a subhuman and expendable population. As an example, service and care occupations were aggressively pushed in the job training programs, and service and care positions were made readily available to satisfy the work mandate of welfare to work programs. The mammy and welfare queen controlling images produced a public curriculum of African American women needing to be cured of their laziness and returned to the hard-working caricatures of who they were in early American history (Campbell Adair & Dahlberg, 2003; Hancock, 2004; Roberts, 1996). Essentially, the problem of poverty was solved by creating a plan to "fix" the impoverished. However, the sad result was that it did not protect

African American women from labor exploitation or from work hazards; it just normalized it as an unfortunate consequence of poor women having not made better life choices and continued the practice of forcing African American women to work, against our own mental, physical, psychological and emotional health, to care for society in underpaid and generally exploited service positions.

Another example is the recent case of Nafissatou Diallo, the hotel maid who accused Dominique Strauss Kahn of sexual assault. She was overworked, underpaid, and very vulnerable to sexual assault, but the likelihood of her being vindicated rather than punished for speaking out about the life she lead, as a result of what is expected of her as a woman of color, was slim. Although the prevailing public opinion is that Diallo lied about her attack, others argue that the lies she did tell, such as claiming a fictitious child on her taxes or underreporting her income to qualify for subsidized housing, were used against her and should not have played a major role in determining the veracity of her case, especially given the fact that Strauss-Kahn was known to be sexually violent with other women (Davidson, 2011; Dickey & Solomon, 2011; Katersky, 2011; Melnick, 2011).

Other controlling images, such as the *Jezebel* (the sexually wanton slave girl that justified the sexual abuse and institutionalized rape of African American women well into the 21st century), *Sapphire* (the angry, dubious slave woman that justified the violent silencing of African American women well into the 21st century), *Matriarch*, *Bad Black Mother* (the emasculating heads of household that justified the blaming and shaming of African American women for the state of their families and communities), and the *Lady* (the polite and accommodating antithesis of sapphire that nonetheless justified the silencing of African American women) work the same way (Hill Collins, 2000). They provide a framework for how to read the African American female body as a text embodying everything that is or could be wrong with the moral fabric of American society. We are made public enemy number one, our bodies lusted after and loathed simultaneously, as we are seen as not quite woman, not quite American, and not quite anything deemed normal and worthy of respect and protection.

Siapera (2010) discusses this phenomenon in her work, and, in a move to extend Hall's racist regimes of representation, she has created additional ways to see the representations of minorities, particularly women of color. She situates her work by calling on Foucault's term "regimes of truth," which denotes the idea that images and representations are part of larger networks of power which virtually turn those images and representations into true depictions of who or what they represent. She, like Hall, argues that there are always multiple regimes of representation at work simultaneously, and no regime of representation is equal in power, thereby making the argument that certain regimes of representation win over others in naming and defining institutions and groups of people.

In terms of how regimes of representation are used to construct racialized and gendered individuals in the United States and abroad, Siapera argues that there are different types of regimes of representation that forward different facets of the agenda to withhold full citizenship to certain groups of people, African American women and girls included. There is the (1) racialized regime of representation and the (2) domesticated regime of representation which are the precursors to the more violent and overt (3) racist regime of representation. There is also the (iv) regime of commodification (Siapera, 2010).

The racialized and domesticated regimes of representations are those regimes of representation that rely on age-old stereotypes of people of color. The stereotypes do not seem violent or particularly egregious, but they nonetheless lay the groundwork for ideologies, discourse and practices that are materially detrimental to people of color. Consider the previously mentioned Black lady controlling image. This image is of a genteel, polite, mild-mannered, and accommodating African American woman. It was birthed out of the politics of respectability. The stereotype is not negative at face value, but it serves to force African American women into a binary of behavior. When African American women walk into a hostile situation, in which anger is a legitimate and fitting response, the controlling image of Sapphire arrives before us in the minds of those who share in the problem. African American women immediately have a choice: do we "conform" and "confirm" the Sapphire image, or do we opt for the Black lady image. The Black lady will respond in a "less aggressive" manner, often denying or disregarding the seriousness of the offenses committed against her, for the sake of maintaining a more palatable image of African American womanhood. In this situation, which Hill-Collins recently wrote about in her newest book, *Another Kind of Public Education* (2010), African American women can "choose" to be "Blackened" by assuming the controlling image of the Sapphire, or we can choose not to be "Blackened" and assume the controlling image of the Black Lady. In either case, we have to silently endure having our voices and our responses predetermined for us, our identity crafted for us, as we negotiate our citizenship with individuals and institutions.

The racist regime of representation is much more apparent and is mobilized to justify the creation and maintenance of strict laws, policies, and institutions. This regime

constructs alterity [otherness] primarily as irrational, or not rational enough, and therefore brutal, violent and sexualized; it is further constructed as generally unable to speak, while, when it does speak, it is seen as demanding but not deserving because of its irrationality, hence, it must be treated primarily through power. (Hill Collins, 2010, p. 133)

The second characteristic of the racist regime of representation is that it generally removes agency and autonomy from gendered and racialized subjects which "works to justify the political, social, and cultural exclusion of ethno-culturally different women" and renders us "unable to represent [ourselves] autonomously and participate in political processes as equal citizens" (p. 137). Within a racist regime of representation, African American women are essentialized as part of a culture that has been negatively racialized as lazy, backward, stupid, incompetent, sexually irresponsible and dirty. We are also gendered in a way that further solidifies our position as a group needing to be civilized, spoken for, and ruled over.

A racist regime of representation becomes particularly problematic for African American women and girls because of its function as a double-edged sword. We are silenced because we lack the agency to speak for ourselves in public, but, if we do find a way to voice our concerns and our interests, our voices are deemed irrational and not worthy to be acknowledged (Siapera, 2010). Therefore, many of our attempts to resist other equally detrimental regimes of representation are thwarted, due to our seemingly absent voice(s).

This is particularly damning as it pertains to what Siapera calls the regime of commodification. This regime seems to welcome and accept difference—only in as much as that difference can be pimped for a profit. In this regime, difference is accepted but is reduced to identities which are then "made into things exchanged, bought and sold, thereby losing their complexity and humanity" (Siapera, 2010, p. 143). The market is placed above social justice, and for the sake of making or saving a dollar, the societal inequities that accompany difference is erased as identities are judged equally for their profitability. The signs and symbols that are linked to certain identities are amplified while the material circumstances of those identities are ignored. It is perfectly normal in this instance to exploit hypersexualized images of African American womanhood for the sake of selling anything, from music to apparel, like Beyonce's latest album or a House of Dereon shoulder bag. It is equally as normal to sell ideas and politics in the same way as material goods, such as the Life Always campaign, which used an image of an African American girl, barely out of pampers herself, to create billboards naming African American women as the number one threat to unborn African American children.

The billboards were sponsored by various religious organizations in the cities that they appeared in. The billboard was most controversial in New York's SoHo community, where Reverend Michael Faulkner, an African

American pastor who sponsored the billboard, argued that it was not meant to encourage hate against African American women, but to bring attention to abortion as genocide in the African American community. However, the billboards were impossible to read absent of a historical narrative of African American women being interpreted as sexually insatiable and irresponsible. It cannot be glossed over, either, that the billboards were released amid talks about defunding Planned Parenthood and the passing of the Protect Life Act. It should also not be ignored that the little girl was used, in the tradition of the regime of commodification, as a symbol for the "growing" problem of African American womanhood. In fact, the pastor who sponsored the billboard, Mr. Michael Faulkner, used market language to justify his decision, claiming that he legitimately *purchased* the picture, to be used as a *prop*.

There are countless other examples of the ways in which images and stereotypes of African American women are used to define our citizenships, and there are many examples of African American women creating counternarratives to speak back to the dehumanizing public curriculum. Among them was Audre Lorde, who understood the need for women of color to self-define. She says in her book, *Sister Outsider* (1984) that "it is axiomatic that if we do not define ourselves for ourselves, we will be defined by others—for their use and to our detriment" (p. 45). At this point, however, I think that it is necessary to detail a plan by which this work can be done in lasting and transformative ways, which begins with making sure that African American women are able to understand, articulate and strategize against the ways that these controlling images are currently being used in order to influence the citizenship(s) that we experience.

Burrell (2010) argues that, "even today, we have woefully inadequate countermeasures, no permanent cultural mechanisms to undo what a 400-year marketing campaign has achieved [against the reputation of African Americans]" (p. xiii). However, I would argue, the problem is not that there isn't a counternarrative available, but that it is largely consistent of the voices of African American women and girls who have been systematically excluded from the places and spaces that knowledge is created, refereed, legitimated and consumed by the larger public.

African American women have infiltrated literature, music, art, and other disciplines, and have maintained a quiet yet tenacious hold on folk knowledge in order to influence the ways that other African American women and girls see themselves. They have left a blueprint, so to speak, for future generations of African American women and girls to mount a defense against the onslaught against our character and humanity, but it is largely a defense. This defense is kept strong in the relationships that African American women have with each other. It is a defense that is made stronger around kitchen tables, in church pews, in beauty shops, and in other sacred spaces where violent understandings of Black womanhood cannot infiltrate unchallenged. While I do believe that a defense against such violence is necessary, particularly for African American girls who find themselves in the position to negotiate their citizenships in ways that their ancestors could not, I believe that it is just as necessary to actively and more publicly mount a public offense.

This offense must include public declarations of the ways in which the controlling images of Black womanhood influence the material lives that African American women and other women of color lead. This offense must be created from an understanding that "though the hypersexual images of Black ... women were created centuries ago ... once images are established, they change very slowly if at all. They become part of our collective culture, the DNA of even viler images" (Burrell, 2010, p. 52). Therefore a countercurriculum must explicitly and publicly historicize these controlling images and draw connections between the jezebel image and its influence on the institutionalized racism, classism, and sexism in the justice system and in health care. It must explicitly and publicly draw connections between the mammy image and its influence on the raced, gendered, and classed exploitation in the economy and work force. It must explicitly and publicly draw connections between the bad Black mother and the matriarch image and how these images have justified the unfair persecution of Black mothers, and the neglect and hypocrisy we show to Black children in the welfare system, education system, and the justice system.

In order to create such an offense, there needs to be an intentional and aggressive effort to create spaces and opportunities for African American women and girls, and their allies, to study the work and lives of African American women. The first step in this endeavor would be to create a curriculum for African American women and girls, replete with past and present representations of controlling images, which are historicized, and contextualized in ways that reveal the themes, and underlying purposes of such images in maintaining hegemony. Such a curriculum would do what Gramsci suggested in his work, of creating class consciousness, a historic bloc, and, finally, a war of position, whereby the hegemonic narrative of Black womanhood can be replaced with more positive and complete narratives. Moreover, a calculated and replicable plan for challenging and changing hegemonic narratives about gender, class, and race would be available to many groups of people who must negotiate negatively gendered, classed, or raced identities and citizenships. This work is very difficult, and includes a multifaceted, multilayered approach.

Some of the work has already started. African American women are providing spaces for African American girls and the larger public to explore the ways that White supremacy and patriarchy come together to make their lives difficult. Women like Glenn Paul (2003), Sharpley-Whiting (2007), and Morgan (2000) are writing in accessible ways about how media-influenced cultural phenomena are complicating the ways that African American women and girls negotiate citizenship in both public and publicly private spheres. Glenn Paul, in her book *Talkin' Back*, speaks specifically to the role the community plays in making sure that African American girls are taught to be financially independent, that they are supported in healthy ways through adolescence, and that they receive guidance on how to value themselves appropriately despite the disparaging image(s) the rest of the world has of them. Morgan goes even further, in her book *When Chickenheads Come Home to Roost*, when she speaks very clearly about the agency that African American women and girls have within the cultures that prove to be simultaneously empowering and dehumanizing. Other African American women are providing spaces for African American girls to create counternarratives of controlling images, and speak to their experiences with being Black, young and female in a western context. Carroll, in her work, *Sugar in the Raw* (1997), carved out a substantial space where African American girls, and girls from within the African Diaspora, speak candidly and critically about how they understand themselves in relationship to the American public curriculum. The girls who gave interviews recounted stories about being excluded, being perceived as dangerous, as ugly, and as passive, and the coping mechanisms they have formed in order to survive and thrive with dignity. Even more African American women are making the celebration of Black girlhood an important emancipatory project. A specific example is Ruth Nicole Brown's work with SOLHOT (Saving Our Lives Hear Our Truths), a space specifically dedicated to celebrating the lives of African American women and girls with the use of a hip-hop feminist paradigm of continued empowerment (R. N. Brown, 2008).

Much of these efforts are happening outside of the scope of public curriculum, in that these projects are not widely known and are not affecting the way the larger public understands African American womanhood or girlhood. This is not problematic in itself, but it does raise questions for those of us who believe that public curriculum plays a major role in the ways that all of America's citizens take up identity and citizenship for themselves and in relationship to others.

It is important that while African American women and girls are struggling to redefine and rearticulate ourselves, the rest of society is preparing to embrace new narratives of who African American women are, and to confront the histories and narratives that have heretofore made it difficult for African American women and girls to define ourselves as human and worthy of our nation's fullest extension of citizenship and respect.

However, we must understand that to accept new and more complete identities of African American women and girls would require us to challenge the identities of others. This is work that African American women and girls cannot do alone.

Therefore, we must work to infuse the public curriculum with more complete histories of race and gender relations and explore critically the interests that have dictated those relations. Educational leaders and other cultural workers must use any platforms available to us to ask the questions and search the public curriculum for the fissures in history that have created the material and symbolic circumstances that African American women and girls struggle against. One specific step that should be taken is working with intentionality and purpose to include the voices and wisdoms of African American women in larger academic and societal conversations. This does not mean that we read bell hooks only when we are talking about alternative versions of feminism. This means that when we are having conversations about discourses of beauty and womanhood, Gwendolyn Brooks' *Maud Martha* and Angela Davis' *Women, Race and Class* are central to the conversation. This means that when we are talking about women and labor exploitation, Ann Petry's *The Street* is central to the conversation. This means that when we are talking about violence in society, West's *Wounds of the Spirit* and Ntozake Shange's *Sassafrass, Cypress and Indigo* are central to the conversation. We cannot expect the voices, scholarship and activism of African American women to be taken seriously when the spaces that claim to be progressive and antioppressive are still relegating African American women's knowledge and wisdom to the catchy conference sessions located in the smallest venues at a conference.

We must also hold ourselves accountable for examining the research we do with or on behalf of African American women and girls, and acknowledge the uniquely raced and gendered bodies that African American women and girls live in. We must also task ourselves with creating knowledge for the express purpose of improving the lives of those we research, and be bold enough to stretch ourselves far beyond academia to do so.

This means that we must search our own subjectivities and our own motives in engaging an already exploited community, and avoid the pitfall of trying to fit African American women into the research we do on White women or on African Americans. Our research must start with the understanding that African American women have, since the beginning of this country, been positioned at the epicenter of debates on what "normal" gender, race, and sexuality is, and the work to mend that mangled foundation takes dedication, commitment, and real belief that the liberation of raced and gendered beings within our public curriculum is intricately tied to the liberation of African American women.

We must involve ourselves intricately in the apparatus of the public curriculum, and work to challenge and change the knowledge called upon in the process of identity creation and citizenship formation. We must make it difficult and uncomfortable for society to continue understanding African American womanhood as the antithesis of American normalcy. Most importantly, we must be prepared to support people who will inevitably question who they are as a result of how they now see others. The work is difficult but necessary, and of utmost importance because it requires that we leave the "comforts of academia" for the "real world." We must change our language to be more accessible; we must go into or create spaces where communities feel safe; we must engage and "empower" communities to interrogate their identities and their interests, and to, at times, work toward goals that are not immediately attached to their interests but towards social justice. We must be public intellectuals.

African American women and girls have lived with diminished citizenships for too long, and we deserve to know the same thing that Lizzie realized at the end of Perkins-Valdez's novel, which was that "she was more than eyes, ears, lips and thighs. She was heart. She was mind" (Perkins-Valdez, 2010, p. 290). African American women and girls have the right to know that we are powerful enough to define ourselves as whole subjects and not fragmented objects, and we have the right to experience the fullest citizenship possible. However, educational leaders, cultural workers, and allies, have to be brave, strategic, and diligent enough to help in bringing this project to fruition.

Who Look At Me

Black skinned female, 145 pounds,
supple, with womanish wisdom, ready
for work or sex, and sees more than just
my body?
Truth is, I am all nose and eye lashes,
and sun-kissed skin. I am also heart and soul.
I am spirit and will and wisdom and truths
too many to count.
See me! Seek to know *with* me and *from* me.
But ... please, please, please, stop trying to just know me.

REFERENCES

Brown, K. (1996). *Good wives, nasty wenches, anxious patriarchs.* Chapel Hill, NC: University of North Carolina Press.

Brown, R. N. (2008). *Black girlhood celebration: Toward a hip-hop feminist pedagogy.* New York, NY: Peter Lang.

Burrell, T. (2010). *Brainwashed: Challenging the myth of black inferiority.* New York, NY: Smiley Books.

Butler, J. (1990) *Gender trouble: Feminism and the subversion of identity.* New York, NY: Routledge.

Campbell Adair, V. & Dahlberg, S. (2003). *Reclaiming class: Women, poverty, and the promise of higher education in America.* Philadelphia, PA: Temple University Press.

Carroll, R. (1997). *Sugar in the raw: Voices of young black girls in America.* New York, NY: Crown.

Clawson, C. J., & Trice, R. (2000). Poverty as we know it: Media portrayals of the poor. *The Public Opinion Quarterly, 64*(1), 53-64.

Cortes, C. (1983). The mass media: Civic education's public curriculum. *Journal of Teacher Education, 34*(6), 25-29.

Davidson, A. (2011, July 25). Nafissatou Diallo's face. Retrieved from http://www.newyrker.com/online/blogs/closeread/2011/07/nafissatou-diallo.htm

Dickey, C., & Solomon, J. (2011, May 14). The maid's tale. Retrieved from http://www.thedailybeast.com/newsweek/2011.07/24/dsk-maid-tell-of-heralleged-rape-by-strauss-kahn-exculsive.html

Glenn Paul, D. (2003). *Talkin' back: Raising and educating resilient Black girls.* Westport, CT: Praeger.

Hall, S. (1997). *Representation: Cultural representations and signifying practices.* London, England: SAGE.

Hancock, A. M. (2004). *The politics of disgust: The public identity of the welfare queen.* New York, NY: New York University Press.

Hill Collins, P. (2000). *Black feminist thought: Knowledge, consciousness, and the politics of empowerment.* New York, NY: Routledge.

Hill Collins, P. (2004). *Black sexual politics: African Americans, gender and the new racism.* New York, NY: Routledge.

Hill Collins, P. (2010). *Another kind of public education: Race, schools, the media, and democratic possibilities.* Boston, MA: Beacon Press.

Ibura Salaam, K. (2002). How sexual harassment slaughtered, then saved me. In D. Hernandez & B. Rehman (Eds.), *Colonize this!: Young women of color on today's feminism* (pp. 326-342). New York, NY: Seal Press.

Jordan-Zachery, J. (2009). *Black women, cultural images, and social policy.* New York, NY: Routledge.

Katersky, A. (2011, July 24). Dominique Strauss Kahn accuser tells her story in exclusive ABC news interview. Retrieved from http://www.abcnews.go.com/Politics/Dominique-strauss-kahn-accuser-tells-story-exclusive-abc/story?id=1414829#Tv0irjDbd2B

Lorde, A. (1984). *Sister outsider.* Berkeley, CA: Crossing Press.

Melnick, M. (2011, July 26). No longer the perfect victim? Nafissatou Diallo defends herself. Retrieved from http://healthland.time.com/2011/07/26/no-longer-the-Perfect-victim-nafissatou-diallo-defends-herself/

Morgan, J. (2000). *When chickenheads come home to roost. My life as a hip-hop feminist* New York, NY: Simon and Schuster.

Neubeck, K., & Cazenave, N. (2001). *Welfare racism: Playing the race card against America's poor.* New York, NY: Routledge.

Omolade, B. (1994). *The rising song of African American women.* New York, NY: Routledge.

Perkins-Valdez, D. (2010). *Wench: A novel.* New York, NY: Harper Collins.

Roberts, D. (1996). Welfare and the problem of Black citizenship. *The Yale Law Journal, 105*(6), 1563-1602.

Sharpley-Whiting, T. D. (2007). *Pimps up, ho's down: Hip hop's hold on young Black women.* New York, NY: New York University Press

Shende, S. (1997). Fighting the violence against our sisters: Prosecution of pregnant women and the coercive use of norplant. In C. Cohen, K. Jones, & J. Tronto (Eds.), *Women transforming politics: An alternative reader* (pp. 123-135). New York, NY: New York University Press.

Siapera, E. (2010). *Cultural diversity and global media: The mediation of difference.* West Sussex, United Kingdom: John Wiley & Sons.

Smith, T. (1987). That which we call welfare by any other name would smell sweeter: An analysis of the impact of question wording on response patterns. *The Public Opinion Quarterly, 51*(1), 75-83.

CHAPTER 10

VISION, PRACTICE, REFLECTION

The Influence of Four Women
on Progressive Education

Elinor A. Scheirer
The University of North Florida

The history of progressive curriculum and pedagogy within public schooling offers educators opportunities to consider the role of teachers, especially women teachers, in shaping both theory and practice. The work of
four women, spread over many decades, exemplifies how commitments to
philosophical beliefs about the nature of schooling in a democracy are
honed through innovative and thoughtful practice that, in turn, leads to
reflective analyses to share with others. These progressive women educators exemplify different types of contributions to the development of progressivism in schooling.

Marietta Pierce Johnson established the Organic School in Fairhope,
Alabama, that became known worldwide. Laura Zirbes, as a teacher and
then teacher educator, developed, described, and nurtured progressive
pedagogy. Sybil Marshall experimented with and reflected on her teaching practice in public-school settings. And Margaret Willis supported the
development of progressive practice, not only through her teaching but
also through her efforts in supporting deliberation among colleagues
regarding schoolwide curriculum development. These activities are the

Excursions and Recursions Through Power, Privilege, and Praxis
pp. 131–142

challenges faced by practitioners in their efforts to develop progressive education as a viable and rigorous curricular approach.

The careers of three of the women selected for discussion in this chapter—Marietta Pierce Johnson, Laura Zirbes, and Margaret Willis—represent the period during which progressive school practices developed in the United States to a point when the approach gained recognition as a particular form of curricular experiences, flowered, and then waned under post-World War II critique and later Sputnik fears (Cremin, 1961; Kliebard, 1987). Their practice as a group spanned many decades, from the early 1900s through the mid-1960s, during which the development and acceptance of progressive curricular and pedagogical practices varied greatly across the United States in both form and substance. Against this historical backdrop, the work of these women was rooted in philosophical beliefs associated with progressivism. Even though one must acknowledge that the concept of progressive schooling is itself abstract and many versions of progressive school reforms existed during this long period of time, the progressivism they practiced emphasized child development, individual differences in growth, emergent concepts regarding human learning, the importance of children's experiences and interests in the process of learning, and goals for schooling in a democracy (Zilversmit, 1993). The careers of these women took different turns, but all of them began with classroom teaching, where they quietly experimented with pedagogy designed to reach children's interests and achievement levels regardless of their social and economic backgrounds. Likewise, Sybil Marshall's career in England represented a commitment to children's development, their interests, and their membership within a larger community outside the school.

The story of the adoption of progressive teaching practices in England offers a timeline somewhat different than that in the United States and an adoption framework that included support from the national government through official policy. The government's publication of the Hadow Report in 1931 had highlighted the importance of primary schools' recognizing the needs of individual children and had initiated support for the efforts of local schools and teachers to experiment and innovate (Central Advisory Council for Education, 1967). The 1967 Plowden Report, published by the Central Advisory Council for Education, investigated the status of primary education in England in order to make curricular recommendations and thereby provided the framework for official policy supporting child-centered, experiential primary education. Such national policy did not produce uniform progressive teaching practices across England, but it did legitimize efforts by teachers and whole schools to develop and implement curriculum and pedagogy in the progressive tradition. The fourth woman included in this discussion of progressive educators,

Sybil Marshall, represents those who had experimented with progressive practices in the years following Hadow and thus those whose work subsequently influenced Plowden and provided guidance to others who desired to heed Plowden's call for changes in practice.

FOUR WOMEN PROGRESSIVE EDUCATORS

Marrietta Pierce Johnson

Of the women selected for this discussion, the first to contribute to the development of progressive teaching practices chronologically was Marietta Pierce Johnson (1864-1938). She was one of several women who founded progressive schools that recognized children's growth and development and included their interests and experiences as starting points for the learning process (Zilversmit, 1993). Johnson's school served as a kind of laboratory, an experiment, where ideas could be tried out and where innovative pedagogy could demonstrate to others that such pedagogy actually was beneficial and possible to put into action (Newman, 1999).

Johnson established her school in Fairhope, Alabama, where it was linked to the political beliefs of its utopian community. Johnson herself was a Midwestern socialist whose school served all classes of children of all ability levels (Newman, 2002). Departing from her early traditional practices as a teacher and teacher educator, she opened the Organic School in 1907 after a period of intense self-education through reading the emerging literature in developmental psychology and pedagogy, including the work of John Dewey. From its beginnings as the public elementary school for the Fairhope community, the Organic School grew in size to include boarding students, a campus of 10 buildings and a high school. Numerous visitors to the school included John Dewey, who noted the breadth of its curriculum, the positive attitudes of the students, and the efforts of the staff to put into practice what other educators only talked of doing. As a school leader, Johnson focused on the importance of relationships and community, both within the school and with the town itself. Local children attended the school free of charge. She organized the groupings of children around stages in child development, stressed the role of experience in learning, and encouraged both teachers and students to satisfy their own needs for learning and growth rather than compete with each other. She included manual arts, gardening, and dance in the curriculum, and used the out-of-doors as a site for student activities.

Her national reputation developed through the reports of visitors to the school, parents who sent their children to the Organic School for a progressive education, and sponsors who became impressed with her work to reform schooling and who anticipated that this experimental school might influence changes in public schooling (Newman, 2002). Johnson's influence expanded in the second and third decades of the 1900s when she advised others who opened similar schools across the United States, as a founding member of the Progressive Education Association, and as she became involved in European support for progressive education.

However, the impact of the Great Depression on the survival of the Organic School was dramatic. Even though the school exists today and acknowledges its founder, it is now a private institution departing significantly from the educational principles that Marietta Johnson labored to realize (Newman, 2002). Her legacy through writing is also difficult to detect today. Johnson's first book, *Youth in a World of Men: The Child, the Parent and the Teacher* (1929), provided her perspectives on her work at the school; however, Newman (2002) noted that it failed to capture the "essence" of her beliefs and practice (p. 31). And, her capstone account, *Thirty Years With an Idea* (Johnson, 1974), only appeared after her death and in an educational context faced with the challenges of desegregation, increased national involvement in curriculum development, the influence of behaviorism on pedagogy, and increased public awareness of student achievement gaps. Although Johnson's influence as a teacher and school founder gained national recognition from her contemporaries and curriculum historians (Cremin, 1961; Kliebard, 1987) acknowledged her substantial impact, knowledge of her role in shaping progressive pedagogy and curriculum practices in the world of teaching and learning is rare today.

Laura Zirbes

The influence of Laura Zirbes (1884-1967) arose from progressive pedagogy in her own teaching, from her commitment to teacher education around values associated with progressive curricula, and through the establishment of a progressive school as a laboratory for practice that led to the inclusion of an elementary school within the University School at Ohio State University (Reid, 1993). Her practice and her writing reflected the need for a pragmatic interpretation of progressivism, for teachers to adapt principles to their situations, and for teachers themselves to innovate and hone their own thinking. At Ohio State, she linked formal teacher education with the work of its nationally recognized University School. From her position as director of research in the University School, Zirbes influenced teachers' reflections and research on progressivism in action (Scheirer, 2010). She encouraged teachers to develop their own philosophical perspectives to guide their efforts. Hundreds of speeches and workshops, over 200 publications, work in both demonstration schools and local public schools, and leadership in numerous professional organizations led to national recognition for her work in promoting teachers' professional growth. After her retirement, Zirbes reflected on her practice in a talk at the 1957 Association for Childhood Education International Study Conference and then later expanded her perspective in a capstone publication, *Spurs to Creative Teaching* (1959). She encouraged teachers to grow in their thinking and to adopt a creative stance as they enacted progressive principles.

As a result of these efforts, Zirbes influenced generations of teachers and thus helped to move the traditional, mainstream elementary education curriculum in the United States to developmentally appropriate practices that focused on the child (Scheirer, 2010). However, when I arrived at Ohio State in 1968, only 1 year after the close of the University School, Zirbes's influence on progressive education was sadly only a "sidebar" in classroom discussion. Nonetheless, in 1996, her student and colleague, Paul Klohr, poignantly and vividly recalled her impact on practice—locally, nationally, and through her students. In his contribution to a text celebrating teachers and mentors, Klohr identified four themes in her work—the necessity of "a democratic school setting" for an effective curriculum, the recognition that the process of curriculum planning itself generates new goals and purposes, the value of both cognition and the arts in problem solving, and the importance of the "developmental tasks of children and youth" as a focus within curriculum development (Klohr, 1996, pp. 144-145). And, in 1988, the journal of the Association for Childhood Education International, *Childhood Education*, reminded members of her views on children with the reprinting of her article on children's rights (Zirbes, 1988).

In Zirbes's case, influence in the curriculum field included her extensive work with teachers, her capstone writing, and the recollections of those who knew her and continued her work. Thus, her legacy took on an organic character. And, with the passage of time, close study of Zirbes's career provided others who were not contemporaries a perspective that connected her support for teachers as empowered professionals to subsequent trends in education (Reid, 1991).

Margaret Willis

The career of Margaret Willis (1899-1987) provides compelling evidence that the life of a classroom teacher, committed to ongoing professional and personal growth, can influence not only the students one teaches but also the work of colleagues (Kridel, 2002). Indeed, Willis's commitments championed the importance of teachers' ongoing education if progressive education were to flourish with their students. Her indirect leadership—much in evidence during her many years at the Ohio State University School—embodied modeling intellectual pursuits, both for her students and with colleagues, and writing for the school community so that the faculty could clarify their practice, hone their efforts, and thus promote the growth of the school itself. Her writing also captured for others' benefit the essence of the history of the school, its deliberations about practice, its growth in conceptualizing progressive education over time, and its struggles to maintain its progressive identity. She fostered experimentation as a way of professional living, collaboration with students and colleagues, and deliberation about complex curricular issues that shaped the school's culture of democratic community. Her energy and intellect allowed her to challenge those who pushed to close the school and thus to assume a political stance in support of pedagogical beliefs.

Willis was the consummate process person, dedicated to democratic engagement with other educators to enable the democratic learning of their students. When she wrote about important issues and challenges in progressive teaching, she wrote to spur her colleagues' thinking and decision making from the vantage point of the teacher. Even in her own scholarship, Willis served the needs of the educational community. She published a follow-up study of the students she had taught during the 1930s, though she credited the idea for the book to the students who in 1938 had written about their own secondary-school experiences in *Were We Guinea Pigs?* (Kridel, 2002). A final example of her writing was her history of the University School—a record of the efforts of a highly regarded progressive school focused on democratic community, written upon its closing.

Willis's focus was always on promoting the quality of curriculum deliberation within a democratic community. Indeed, she could be cast as playing the role of that individual in a curriculum-development team who would be responsible for insuring that the deliberative processes would occur democratically (Schwab, 1983).

Sybil Marshall

The fourth woman who contributed to the development of progressive teaching practice emerged as influential in the 1950s when progressivism was waning in the United States but becoming more widespread in England. Sybil Marshall (1914-2005) worked in near isolation in the Fens of England with 26 poor, rural primary children in a one-room schoolhouse from the early 1940s until 1962 (Lamont, 2005). Her practice was shaped by the challenges of meeting such diverse academic needs while conceptualizing her work as opening up possibilities for her students that extended well beyond the strictly academic to honor the local culture, environment, and way of life the children experienced. Previous experience as an uncertificated teacher had allowed her to experiment with art activities, with "only a fumbling sort of instinct to guide [her]" (Marshall, 1963, p. 10). As the only teacher in the Cambridgeshire school, she had the opportunity to experiment with the role of art in the learning process. Over time, as she developed her curricular approach, art became a central component of her students' experiences from which she made connections to the other subject areas. Her work with the children in integrating the arts and the core subject areas gained recognition, first locally and then nationally.

When she left education to pursue a writing career, she also published an account of her work in this unique setting, tellingly entitled, *An Experiment in Education* (1963). The rich narrative not only provided examples of her students' work but also offered detailed descriptions of the procedures and materials she used and insight into her own pedagogical thinking that set the context for that work. In addition, she then recounted one culmination of her efforts to integrate curricular content areas—an extensive project centered on Beethoven's Pastoral Symphony but extending into activities in nature that led to dance, poetry, prose, and history. For teachers in England, her vivid descriptions became a source for their own thinking and child-centered, experientially based practice. Even though the text was published by Cambridge University Press and likely influenced the Plowden Report of 1967, supported its subsequent implementation as educational policy for England, and contributed to acceptance by the public at large of progressive practices (Lamont, 2005), by the mid-1970s, the text and her work did not appear in the mainstream literature of progressive education in either the United States or England.

Lamont's 2005 obituary for Marshall in *The Guardian* recalled the extent of her influence on teaching practice through not only her writing but also her lectures for teachers across England and her faculty positions in primary education. And, her influence remains notable in that her teaching, on the ground, reflectively captured in a capstone publication, can be linked to shaping enlightened educational policy.

LEGACIES—LOST AND FOUND

The progressivism of Johnson, Zirbes, Willis, and Marshall was not a sentimental celebration of children's interests and the provision of enjoyable experiences. It was a pragmatic progressivism, with structure but without rigidity. Indeed, they recognized the complexities of progressive curricular and pedagogical practices that engaged learners in authentic work across all areas of human endeavor while nurturing the intellect and championing inquiry toward democratic ends. Their nurturing of others—whether their students or their colleagues—was vigorous, thoughtful, intellectual, and directed toward robust deliberation toward new understandings. Willis, in particular, exemplified this form of curricular enactment (Kridel, 2002). And, throughout their lives, they were learners themselves who took risks, experimented, innovated, analyzed their work, and grew professionally.

These women assumed a quiet, on-the-ground approach to promoting progressive curricula through their own modeling and communication with others. They lived their professional lives focused on practice. All experimented in their teaching, reflected on their efforts, honed their practice, and then shared their insights regarding these experiences with others. Practice shaped their theoretical views that, in turn, shaped their own and others' practice. They shared their perspectives with many colleagues in many forms—capstone books, articles, working papers, school documents, lectures, workshops, demonstrations, and classroom modeling. They eschewed simplistic recipe approaches to practice and shared their insights with a heuristic view, thereby engaging others but not didactically directing them.

Their career-long deep engagement with practice, reflection on practice, and questioning of practice are characteristics of the reflective practitioner (Schön, 1983). They developed a particular and essential form of knowledge necessary for enhancing thoughtful pedagogy. They exhibited in their daily pedagogical lives what may be called "the practical," that is, "the resolution of puzzles arising from states of affairs … or a practical dilemma" (Reid, 1999, p. 212). But they also used in those resolutions a "theoretical" perspective in that they engaged "states of mind" in consideration of "intellectual puzzles" (p. 211) arising from practice conceived as multidimensional, holistic, and interactive. When they looked to others' theoretical views, it was always to inform their own practice. And, they provided those who pursued "the theoretic" the necessary insights from practice to make theory robust. In this way, they embodied the integration of practice and theory as they grew in their professional identities, but always with a clear eye on the need to engage theory to move practice forward.

When these women shared their perspectives on their practice in progressive curricular settings, they did so after they had developed deep knowledge of both the work and its challenges. And, they did so in a variety of ways. Johnson founded a school within which she then modeled her practice and through which she demonstrated her commitment to serving children from all economic strata. She hoped that the Organic School as a "quasi-public institution ... would provide a model for reforming public education" (Newman, 2002, p. 29). Zirbes honed her practice in elementary classrooms and then took her pedagogical insights into a career in teacher education during which she also founded a local preschool. Willis demonstrated her curricular leadership as a teacher within an experimental school dedicated to democratic relationships among students and faculty alike. She moved the school's practice forward through her open exploration of ideas with colleagues and her critical intellect. And Marshall's contributions, wrought from years experimenting on her own, centered on describing the role of the arts in integrating the primary curriculum. These educators shared their reflections on their own practice, not to have others become their followers but rather to promote others' unique efforts to enact progressive education. In their writings, they exemplified what teachers aspire to do with their students—to guide but not to direct, to provide the conceptual tools and principles that support others' thinking and thereby their enlightened practice.

What the profession has lost by overlooking the contributions of these women to curricular thinking is the vantage point of practice. They developed their practice within the complexities of teaching. In their reflection on those experiences, they contributed to theory to guide further practice. Their knowledge was intended to facilitate the work of others that, in turn, could lead to further knowledge. They shared their perspectives on meeting the complex challenges of progressive pedagogy—much that can continue to inform those who would today support such approaches as alternatives to current standardized curricula. They also demonstrated that while such pedagogy demanded much of the teacher, the challenges could be met for the benefit of children. This perspective of honoring the contributions of practice to curricular thinking is notably rare in current curricular conversations. It is this loss that is most troubling.

That the curricular work of these women is relatively unknown today deserves serious analysis. Part of the reason recalls the adage associated with political histories; that is, those who win the wars write the histories. The curricular approaches they nurtured, developed, shared, and advocated became disfavored in the United States, first during the Cold War and later when the popular metaphor of a "Nation at Risk" became the dominant policy with progressive views denigrated. England, too, developed its National Curriculum and assessment policies in the 1980s to stress content-area achievement and to assure professional accountability. On both sides of the Atlantic, the progressive agenda of educating the whole child for life as a citizen in a democracy became passé.

A second reason lies in the nature of the contributions of these women. Their work of modeling practice and influencing others as mentors and supporters cannot be easily traced and studied by others. They achieved their leadership in curriculum and pedagogy through their practice to which others responded. Their work, on the ground, in the lived experiences of schools—teaching and learning with others—does not leave behind the kind of books and articles associated with academic efforts expected of the professoriate. And, when these women did write, their audience was the world of practice and the world of those who shared their philosophical views regarding the role of the school in fostering holistic child development within a democratic society.

And, not at all as a postscript, their work may be overlooked because of gendered expectations for influencing schools beyond the local level. This explanation (Sadovnik & Semel, 2002) recognizes that the dominant advocates of progressive education were men in the academy, and women as practitioners had less involvement with the academy. As a consequence, their work has received less attention from subsequent generations of those in the academy. Such an explanation also links women's marginalization to their focus on practice within schools, efforts that carry lower status than the theoretical work of those in the academy.

The work of these women—based so heavily on practice—provides our current generation with food for thought. First, it challenges those who champion school reform to consider the role of experienced educators' deep reflection on enlightened practice in shaping enlightened policy. Because these sources of perspectives may not be easily available in quick reviews of the literature or from more theoretical treatises or recommendations for practice, those who advocate reform must find ways to seek out this critical knowledge.

Reformers themselves might be encouraged to recognize that different forms of influence may be productive in promoting curricular change. Growth as the sine qua non of enlightened teaching practice occurs in many venues—through reading seminal texts, of course, but more likely through work with reflective colleagues, careful observation of others' practice, and the sharing of perspectives with knowledgeable others. The professional lives of these women demonstrated how such efforts could bring about enlightened practice.

In addition, the published work of these women provides exemplars for the development of a curriculum literature for our era that would neither reside exclusively in the theoretic nor reside in the realm of critical analysis of others' practices. Rather, such literature would explain the underpinnings of enlightened practice and describe implementation—but without succumbing to reductionist, preset guidelines or cookbooks. Within the current context of demands for reform, this curriculum literature would invite empowered professionals to examine their own practice, analyze options available to them, and chart their own ways forward to engage students for democratic growth and development. Those in the fields of "curriculum and pedagogy," both those within classrooms and those who support complex practice within those environments, might do well to pursue such an agenda so that the wisdom of practice might enhance both theory and policy.

REFERENCES

Central Advisory Council for Education. (1967). *Children and their primary schools: A report of the Central Advisory Council for Education* (Vols. 1-2) (The Plowden Report). London, England: Her Majesty's Stationery Office.

Cremin, L. A. (1961). *The transformation of the school: Progressivism in American education, 1876-1957.* New York, NY: Alfred A. Knopf.

Johnson, M. L. P. (1929). *Youth in a world of men: The child, the parent and the teacher.* New York, NY: John Day.

Johnson, M. (1974). *Thirty years with an idea.* Tuscaloosa, AL: University of Alabama Press.

Kliebard, H. M. (1987). *The struggle for the American curriculum, 1893-1958.* New York, NY: Routledge & Kegan Paul.

Klohr, P. R. (1996). Laura Zirbes: A teacher of teachers. In C. Kridel, R. V. Bullough, & P. Shaker (Eds.), *Teachers and mentors: Profiles of distinguished twentieth-century professors of education* (pp. 139-145). New York, NY: Garland.

Kridel, C. (2002). And gladly would she learn: Margaret Willis and the Ohio State University School. In A. R. Sadovnik & S. F. Semel (Eds.), *Founding mothers and others: Women educational leaders during the Progressive Era* (pp. 217-235). New York, NY: Palgrave.

Lamont, W. (2005, August 31). Sybil Marshall: A great educationist, her career spanned a one-room school, universities and best-selling novels. *The Guardian.* Retrieved from http://www.guardian.co.uk/news/2005/aug/31/guardianobituaries.schools

Marshall, S. (1963). *An experiment in education.* London, England: Cambridge University Press.

Newman, J. W. (1999). Experimental school, experimental community: The Marietta Johnson School of Organic Education in Fairhope, Alabama. In S. F. Semel & A. R. Sadovnik (Eds.), *"Schools of tomorrow," schools of today* (pp. 67-101). New York, NY: Peter Lang.

Newman, J. W. (2002). Marietta Johnson and the Organic School. In A. R. Sadovnik & S. F. Semel (Eds.), *Founding mothers and others: Women educational leaders during the Progressive Era* (pp. 19-36). New York, NY: Palgrave.

Reid, T. (1991). Laura Zirbes: Forerunner of restructuring. *Childhood Education, 68,* 98-102.

Reid, T. (1993). *Towards creative teaching: The life and career of Laura Zirbes, 1884-1967* (Unpublished doctoral dissertation). University of South Carolina, Columbia, SC.

Reid, W. A. (1999). *Curriculum as institution and practice: Essays in the deliberative tradition.* Mahwah, NJ: Erlbaum.

Sadovnik, A. R., & Semel, S. F. (2002). Conclusion. In A. R. Sadovnik & S. F. Semel (Eds.), *Founding mothers and others: Women educational leaders during the Progressive Era* (pp. 253-261). New York, NY: Palgrave.

Scheirer, E. A. (2010). Laura Zirbes. In C. Kridel (Ed.), *Encyclopedia of curriculum studies.* Thousand Oaks, CA: SAGE.

Schön, D. A. (1983). *The reflective practitioner: How professionals think in action.* New York, NY: Basic Books.

Schwab, J. J. (1983). The practical 4: Something for curriculum professors to do. *Curriculum Inquiry, 13*(3), 239-265.

Zilversmit, A. (1993). *Changing schools: Progressive education theory and practice, 1930-1960.* Chicago, IL: University of Chicago Press.

Zirbes, L. (1959). *Spurs to creative teaching.* New York, NY: G. P. Putnam's.

Zirbes, L. (1988). The inalienable rights of children. *Childhood Education, 65,* 24-26.

PART II

RE/TURNING TO PRAXIS

CHAPTER 11

PURPLE CRAYONS, WILD THINGS, AND DOTS

Getting Lost in Children's Literature and Curriculum

Chris Loeffler
Wilmington Friends School
Arcadia University

While the idea of getting lost in reading is known to many readers, the traditional writing structure that is privileged in academia may limit creativity and innovation. Traditional structures of a classroom can have similar effects. Elementary students frequently read the same types of chapter and picture books over and over again. As a third-grade teacher, I find it a joy to see the look on a child's face when she is presented with an atypical piece of writing.

Curriculum and classroom teaching methods can fall into this same realm of uniformity, which can be both frustrating and disengaging to teachers and students. This piece hopes to provide a nonconforming arrangement of text that might allow the reader to wander through its ideas with an open mind toward the benefit of diversity, in both curriculum and writing.

Although the multiple-column approach is not unique—see Patricia Lather and Chris Smithies' *Troubling the Angels: Women Living With HIV/*

Excursions and Recursions Through Power, Privilege, and Praxis
pp. 145–162
Copyright © 2012 by Information Age Publishing
All rights of reproduction in any form reserved.

AIDS (1997)—it is meant to develop the idea that learning is a simultaneous interaction of theory and narrative. Learners all at once connect their personal experiences with the prior knowledge gained from formal and informal education.

The left column in this piece develops the ways in which children's literature embodies an imaginative view of curriculum, specifically through a discussion of Maurice Sendak's *Where the Wild Things Are* (1988), Crockett Johnson's *Harold and the Purple Crayon* (1955), and Peter H. Reynold's *The Dot* (2003). The right column focuses on the theoretical connections with these children's books.

While it is possible to read this text with multiple approaches, it is helpful to have a familiarity with the children's literature mentioned above before considering their theoretical connections. Thus, it is suggested to start by reading the left column first and then read alternately between columns. The reader may consider the purposefully placed connections and alignments, but, as this piece points out, the reader will bring their own ideas and find many more connections than were originally intended.

* * *

"Imagination is the beginning of creation. You imagine what you desire, you will what you imagine and at last you create what you will."

—George Bernard Shaw (n.d.)

Children's literature has an innate way of connecting its reader to his or her childhood. The sound and rhythm of words, the energy of a character, and the vivid images created through the words and pictures draw us in to a story, helping one become lost in the text and illustrations that create worlds of realistic fantasy.

Theodore Seuss Geisel, a.k.a. Dr. Seuss, wrote with a style and

"Curriculum has to do with the life of meaning, with ambiguities, and with relationships. And, yes, it has to do with transformations and with fluidity, with change."

—Maxine Greene (1991, p.107)

rhythm that captured the imagination of children and adults through words and pictures. He stretched a reader's mind to a point where completely impossible situations seemed somehow connected to one's life.

The greatest children's books balance our dreams and realities so that we may endeavor one day to reach our lofty goals. Curriculum should take this same approach.

One of the greatest feelings of reading is the sense of being lost in a story. A reader becomes a part of the story; he wanders through scenes of emotion and conflict; she develops relationships with and learns lessons from the characters.

One of the greatest feelings of learning is to be lost in a journey for knowledge. Given the chance to explore, imagine, and create often generates the most promising ideas. Curriculum in any classroom should allow for exploration, creativity, and imagination. The same manner in which children's authors harness the energy of children to get lost in their worlds, we, as educators, must create curricula (or let children create curricula) that develop the inherently inventive nature of youth.

* * *

Curriculum theory takes a hopeful perspective of education; it is critical, often disapproving, and forward-thinking. There is an ever-present recognition of the what-is, while searching for the what-is-not-yet (Greene, 1984) as theorists attempt to improve upon preexisting curricular work.

Children's literature has a similarly hopeful, yet critical view of the world. Authors demonstrate an appreciation for the ambiguities, the relationships, transformations and fluidity of childhood. Children's literature can offer insight into the learning styles of children, and the reader should heed the underlying message of these narratives. If she can resist being completely swept up in the fantastical nature of the stories long enough to consider its curricular relevance, they will notice the light being shed on education that expands beyond the classroom and allows students to connect fields of ideas (Jardine, Friesen, & Clifford, 2003).

Three picture books offer such an opportunity. *The Dot*, by Peter H. Reynolds, *Harold and the Purple Crayon* by Crockett Johnson, and

From the classroom to the out-doors to the land of make believe, from a dot, to a line, to a multidimensional world, learners must use their imagination to connect ideas. Connecting dots can be seen as a simple metaphor for education and curriculum, but it appropriately describes the fixed curriculum that most students encounter in school. A student must connect ideas, but if students are simply given the points and the lines to connect them, then we, as educators, are failing in our attempt to develop independent, critical thinkers. Ideas reside in a multidimensional field and the path to understanding is not always a straight line. Peter H. Reynolds, Crockett Johnson, and Maurice Sendak illustrate this point in books that were written not only for children, but also for all of those who wish to understand learning and childhood.

In *The Dot*, Vashti, the main character, encounters a typical challenge—the blank sheet of paper problem. With the support of a teacher and through her own motivation and creativity, she explores a world of dots, discover-

Where the Wild Things Are by Maurice Sendak, help us see learning through a child's eyes. Each journey allows the child to not only make sense of everyday challenges, but also comprehend her own perspectives on and relationships to this world that she inhabits.

In these stories, it is not only the difficulty of childhood that becomes evident, but also the importance of these difficulties as learning experiences. We often recognize childhood challenges as an important element of growing up outside of school, but it is also a critical element of classroom education. Designing curricula that predetermines every step of a student's education leads to an oversimplification of knowledge, which inhibits students from making essential connections to personal experiences that will allow them to internalize understandings. It imposes limitations on a student's ability to improvise, or use prior perceptions and variations of knowledge to cultivate new understandings.

In his connection of John Coltrane's improvisational skills to curriculum, Jose Rosario cites a conversation between Coltrane and Miles Davis. "Why you play so long, man?" Miles would ask. "It took that long to get it all in," Coltrane would answer. What if education were treated with such "veneration, a sacred act whose enactment truly depends on the ability to improvise free of imposi-

ing not only the never-ending possibilities of this geometric shape, but also the never-ending promise of her own potential. This story may be the most realistic of the three, and it may also be the most frustrating due to the simple truth it reveals: given slight encouragement, an independently chosen objective, and the opportunity to delve deeply into an area of interest, any student can astonish with their capabilities.

Harold takes his Purple Crayon on an exploration during a simple walk by the light of the moon. Of course, we do not have the luxury of a magic crayon to bring our imaginings to life, but through the eyes of a young child, this story is not far from the truth. We each have hopes and dreams that, in our own way, we create. At times, these grand plans of ours get us into a difficult situation and we are left to our own devices to find a way out. Our success is reliant on our ability to improvise and problem solve utilizing prior knowledge, creativity and the support of others. Harold explores a world of his own creation, but it is the ideas of others that support his thinking, permitting him to make the world his own.

Max, the heir apparent to the throne of the Wild Thing Kingdom, is scolded, or redirected, by his mother to go to his room—to take a break from his wildness. His imagination runs even wilder, however, leading him to confront

tion and constraint" (Rosario, 1991, p. 180)? Creative exploration should be revered, as an opportunity for illumination, an investigation of current and developing understandings, and a method of education that fosters the growth of knowledge and innovation.

Educators must recognize the need for improvisation, through which students can examine and cultivate knowledge. "It is imperative that educators not become mesmerized by simulacra or seduced by the power of efficiency and control. Rather, they need to seek deeper levels of self-reflection and meaning making and the nurturing of a humanistic social vision" (Ferneding, 2002, p.62). Each student has a learning story that relates the student's personal experiences to the field of ideas that they occupy. Curriculum should promote the exploration of these experiences and ideas so that teachers can guide students to tell their own learning story, full of improvisation, determination, self-reflection and self-propelled discovery.

*   *   *

the very nature of unruliness, conquer it, and move forward. We can infer that Max most likely has similar struggles in the classroom, and we can only imagine his feelings about the often-monotonous tone of a school day. It is also not enough for us to consider Max as an aberration. Everyone has a bit of Max in himself or herself, and until we acknowledge this, it is unlikely that we will initiate a curriculum for the Wild Thing in each of us.

In each of these books, the main character is an independent learner with a goal in mind and, more importantly, the time, space and resources needed to explore his or her aspirations.

Beginning with *The Dot*, a singular point, we can visualize the possibility for imagination in a school setting, or making a dot come to life. Correspondingly, Harold's purple crayon brings life to lines, starting straight before swerves, bends and other changes of direction lead him off course and then back to his starting point again. Max takes us well beyond the realm of the classroom and reality, but demonstrates the multidimensional potential for education, and the extremes to which children can go to develop their ideas.

*   *   *

Peter H. Reynold's *The Dot* contrasts a traditional school problem with a nontraditional solution. The goal at the start of the story and lesson is clear enough—draw a picture. Though seemingly simple and straightforward, we have all encountered this challenge—how to overcome the blank sheet of paper. Vashti's initial solution comes only at the behest of her teacher. With the slamming down of a pencil, she reaches her goal with little inspiration, full of frustration and no wisdom gained.

The teacher's decision to frame and display Vashti's work is not only encouragement, but also the inspiration to go above and beyond one simple sheet of paper. It provides the perspective that Vashti lacked the day before. She could look critically at her work and decide on a path forward. Many students may have decided to simply move on to a new project that played to her or his strengths. Vashti's choice, however, leads to greater self-fulfillment and self-confidence, along with the realization that embarking on new challenges can develop a wide array of skills and attitudes.

Vashti takes days, weeks even, to examine dots; dots may be a simple geometric shape, but, from Vashti's newfound perspective, they possess infinite possibilities. Along the way, she gains insight into color, patterns, positive and negative space, media, and self-efficacy. This interdisci-

"We say, we are what we know. As well, we are what we do not know."

—William Pinar
(1992, p. 232)

That which we do not know is what inspires us; it is what leads us to dream beyond what has been known before. When we dream, we are in control of a story that can lead anywhere.

A learning story is an active, continuously transformative attempt to understand our surroundings and accomplish our hopes and dreams. And, while each person's story is autobiographical, it is deeply affected by others. Our story is guided by the generations of past learners as well as our present day friends, family and colleagues:

> that we live and grow in an interpretive, or meaning making community; that stories help us find our place in the world; and that caring, respectful dialogue among those engaged in educational settings—students, teachers, administrators—serve as the crucible for coming to understand ourselves, others and the possibilities life holds for us. (Pinar, Reynolds, Taubman, & Slattery, 2006, p. 548)

It is from this world and community of learners that we shape our knowledge and develop our purpose. We write the stories we wish to be told (Calkins, 2006), and we live the stories we wish to be lived;

plinary, teacher-initiated and student-led curriculum may have been circuitous, but Vashti's ability to veer from the traditional study of a geometric shape allowed her to gain knowledge that rarely would have entered the realm of a typical school room curriculum.

Although the author's true intentions are not definite, Vashti's Dot quite literally represents the starting point to her journey. The fact that the story ends with Vashti passing along her encouragement by helping a young boy draw his own path, literally a squiggly line that might lead anywhere, demonstrates the interconnectedness of learning that constantly occurs. It is a learning story that weaves hope and reality, experience and imagination. It allows students, like Vashti, to return to previous experiences with new and more sophisticated perspectives, as well as an ability to accept previously unseen learning and teaching opportunities.

* * *

either because they have already been lived and inspire us, or because they have not been lived yet, which motivates us to be the first; it is a stay with tradition or a break from it; it is our choice to make.

Max, Harold, and Vashti occupy these communities in different ways, yet each character crosses learning boundaries that enhance their learning story. Max escapes to a world completely of his own creation to test the rule of chaos. Harold's world is similarly imagined, but contains realistic settings and solutions among the fantastic. Vashti finds her place within a world of dots that combines home and school work into something transcendent. The authors—Sendak, Johnson, and Reynolds—each acknowledge the imaginary world within the realm of reality, for it is the intersection between these dimensions that allow children to make sense of the ideas that they encounter each day.

Contemporary education is a learning story, but it is a learning story written almost entirely by the adults within the education system. Predetermined curriculum does not allow the learner any voice or choice in their story. "Intelligence is made more narrow, and thus undermined, when it is reduced to answers to other people's questions, when it is only a means to achieve a preordained goal" (Pinar, 1992, p. 232). While most curriculum designers

A couple of years ago, as I was teaching my third graders to write fiction, the course of study for this unit was, of course, planned out well ahead of time with a little room for improvisation. We invited a recently published author to speak to the class about his method, his approach to each writing project.

The most important idea I took away was his description of the story as a living thing. While there may be a plan at the beginning, sometimes characters choose to do something completely different than what was originally intended.

Using *Harold and the Purple Crayon* as an example, our visitor described the fact that, often, he does not know where his characters will end up, which makes writing such an exciting adventure in and of itself. As he helped students imagine and develop their own fictional character's personality, I contemplated the fact that this published author uses an approach that almost completely opposed my previous teaching method of planning each step of the story prior to writing the scenes. His method required that writers get lost, along with their characters throughout the writing process—

attempt to create a learning path that is simple, linear and easily connected, this oversimplification limits opportunities for students to incorporate their own experiences.

Pinar's *currere* depicts an active process (Pinar et al., 2006); this activity allows the learner to be in control of the movement between the *what-is* and the *what-is-not-yet* (Greene, 1984). As in these children's stories, curriculum needs to be dynamic and stimulating, through which the learner's dreams are cultivated. The choice and voice provided for the learner in the telling of his or her learning story gives value to each student's experiences and growth. The learning story is a metaphor for what our education is and should be—a unique story, imagined in our own time and fashion, shaped by everyone and everything around us. In our learning story, we must choose our paths, take action and develop our ideas both independently and with others.

*   *   *

to deviate actively from the original plan.

Harold and the Purple Crayon became our inspiration. Crockett Johnson's book is a learning story of a young boy who gets himself in and out of trouble with a crayon, choosing and meeting challenges, solving problems and, ultimately, reaching a goal—the comfort of his bed after a long walk. His dreamlike world allows him to explore his interests, using his tools—his brain and his crayon—to surmount each challenge.

The action of writing or telling one's learning story is empowering. By "bringing the structure of experience to awareness, one enhances the ability to direct one's own development." (Pinar, Reynolds, Taubman, & Slattery, 2006, p. 522) Harold's direct interaction in telling, drawing, and acting out his journey is the truly educational element of his learning story. His experience of and active role in the story itself is an essential quality in the education of a critical thinker. Harold's magic crayon allows him to embody a narrative that far exceeds our expectations for experiencing a story.

In curricular terms, there are a few insights that we might gain from Harold's expedition:

- *Curriculum is generated by both learners and teachers.*

Curriculum—*n.* 1. The aggregate of course of study given in a school, college or university; 2. the regular or a particular course of study in a school, college or university

Origin: 1625-1635; < latin—action of running, course of action, race, chariot, equivalent to *curr* (ere) to run + -*i*- + -*culum,* -cule (suffix forming nouns)   (Dictionary.com unabridged)

While curriculum, the noun form, may represent a set of courses studied by an individual, the set of courses play a much lesser role in an individual's education than the running of the course, the *currere*. In education, as in competition, we expect to reach specific goals. When we reach that goal it will look, at the same time, distinctly similar and different than the expectations at the start of the race. This difference represents the learning experienced from the running of the course, the true learning.

There are at least two types of learning courses or stories. One is the repetitive course, conjuring up the image of a traditional oval-

- *The curriculum can, and should, change according to the student's experiences.*
- *A student-driven curriculum leads to greater insights into familiar experiences.*

We each have a learning story like Harold's—an independent adventure that is supported by generations past and colleagues present. Our story begins with a chosen path, with distinct goals in mind. Along this course, we choose actions that will lead the story in various directions—often ending in a different place than originally intended. Curriculum should give students the opportunity to dream their learning story into existence.

* * *

shaped dirt track, chariots or runners. The start and finish line, often the same, are demarcated by a line drawn in the sand, or possibly an expanse of string for the racers to break as they cross the finish line. The goal is clear from the outset: to cross the finish line. In most races, competition places greater emphasis on the order of finishing the race. Education has taken a similar perspective, while it should emphasize the way in which the course was run. The journey to the finish line, not simply the crossing of that line, plays the greatest role in the education of the racer. The racer will surely look at the finish line differently upon arrival than the moment in which they began.

The second type of course is similar metaphorically to the path of a casual runner. The route most likely meanders through a varied landscape, with or without a premeditated goal. The course may have a clear endpoint, or the objective may be based on the time or quality of the run. The challenge of the race is determined by the runner's imagination, not a stopwatch or competitor. Both courses offer a challenge and opportunities for growth, and it is up to the runner to determine how they may, or may not, learn from their pursuit.

Educationally, teachers might guide the learner along either route, providing small objectives along the way. The more casual course can give the student more options to find the best method to achieve these goals. The student might also, in a broader landscape, decide to change their target along the way to achieve more desirable aspirations. While a strong dose of focused effort can be helpful at times, the perspective at the start and finish is the essential element. There are two critical elements to this metaphor. First, a diverse set of courses must be available to a diverse set of learners. Secondly, the running of the race is more important than where a runner finishes.

A willingness to run the race, navigate the course and return to previous experiences epitomizes Pinar's *currere* (Pinar et al., 2006). From this independent exploration, the learner will arrive with a distinctly different perspective than one could have expected at the start of the course of study.

*   *   *

"If we provide enough room for restlessness so that it might function within the space, then the energy ceases to be restless because it can trust itself fundamentally. Meditation is giving a huge, luscious meadow to a restless cow. The cow might be restless for a while in its huge meadow, but at some stage, because there is so much space, the restlessness becomes irrelevant."

—Chögyam Trungpa
(Jardine, Friesen, & Clifford,
2006, p. 85)

Within a field of ideas, learners may be restless at first, but eventually they will gain focus and concentrate their energy in a given direction. It is our role as educators to allow students to use space as a mechanism for learning. With guidance and encouragement, like Vashti, students will find a path that fits their desires and follow it to exhaustion. The route may be short or long in time and distance, but it will provide a new perspective that was previously unknown.

Max, the wild thing, the image of restlessness, is asked by his mother to take a break from everyday expectations—the expectation to behave, the expectation to listen to his mother, the expectation to be nice to his sister —in the comfort of his room.

Given the time (*"through the night and day, in and out of weeks and almost over a year"*), space (a room seemingly without borders) and resources (unusual looking creatures that give instant feedback to their new fearless leader), Max is able to uncover his emotions ("Max, king of all the wild things, was lonely and wanted to be where someone loved him best of all") and develop an appreciation for the challenge of wildness.

Max's unbridled energy and zeal are seen as an impediment to his growth. For many students,

"Play, *Spiel,* is not a chaotic, unbounded space, but is full of character, full of characters. It is an open wisdom and open way in the world" (Jardine et al., 2006, p. 59). *Spiel,* or play, is the life force of learning. It is within this *Spiel,* this time for play, that a learner can become motivated to ascertain greater knowledge. "Elementary school students have shown us, over and over again, how invigorated they become in knowing that this *spiel* that they have come upon is real" (Jardine et al., 2006, p. 59). *Spiel* is not just real in its appearance to young children, but, more importantly, it is a real method for seeking wisdom. *Spiel* may feel joyful and exuberant while being viewed as lighthearted, but the passion with which one plays, the ambition one brings to *spiel* is the difference

the routines of school and everyday life are a challenge. In a typical classroom environment, Max would be redirected, reminded, and reproached until he changed his behavior. Every teacher has had a Max; a child who embodies the frustration of reminders and redirection that goes ostensibly unheard and unused. In many ways, teachers, including myself, often try to solve this *problem* by implementing greater levels of control. Max's journey to the land of wild things suggests that this strategy may be futile. Instead of trying to direct every step of that student's learning story, we need to allow our classroom's Max to explore the chaos independently. That being said ...

It would be common to hear a classroom teacher explain to her students that, "We all learn differently." Yet, the challenge of twenty to thirty students that learn completely in their own time and fashion is a logistical nightmare. The first step is recognizing the need for certain students to take a break from the daily routines that seem to stifle their natural creativity and imagination.

During Max's break from the uniformity of home and school, he is capable of exploring his wild side in a manner that is completely his own and open to personal interpretation. This learning story represents a *Veni Vidi Vici*-like story arc; Max came, Max saw, Max conquered. But between fun and rewarding experiences.

The passion that is brought to any given situation is what will permit a student to continue through the challenges met along the way, for they are sure to come. There is no doubt that every journey taken will lead to some learning, but when challenges are overcome, a student is able to return to their original field of ideas with a deeper understanding and awareness of their surroundings.

* * *

"The beginning of love is to let those we love be perfectly themselves, and not to twist them to fit our own image. Otherwise we love only the reflection of ourselves we find in them" (Thomas Merton, n.d.). Love and imagination are essential to teaching—how can we say we truly love our students when we only let them travel the road most traveled? If we agree that imagination is an essential ingredient in education, then, because of our love for children, we must allow them to imagine the path they wish to travel and guide them from a comfortable distance.

* * *

Contemporary public education and curricula is increasingly less likely to provide open-ended opportunities to our students. In essence, each student's learning

there is also one last piece of this story that is a fundamental element of an independent learning story—the reflection. To learn from a story is to experience the events and actions metacognitively, to make connections between one's actions and prior knowledge. From this metacognition, the main character of the learning story is capable of reaching new depths of knowledge.

After Max conquers his wild side and the wild things, he realizes that, while being wild is exhilarating, a balance between chaos and control is vital. Complete chaos engenders a sense of expectation, which can be both hopeful and distressing. Even Max felt the need to put a stop to his wild rumpus. Of course, the perfectly mirrored reaction between Max and his mother and Max and the wild things may be unlikely, but Sendak surely sheds light on the possibilities of a self-guided curriculum.

The exploration of his real-life problem in a fictional setting allows Max to make a connection between his current and prior actions. It is in this moment of realization that Max understands his mother's love and idea of home. He returns as a more perceptive learner, capable of empathizing with his mother and appreciating his own learning style.

Sendak explained that this learning story, along with *In the Night Kitchen* and *Outside over* story is predetermined by someone else.

> Curriculum as traditionally conceived, and as practiced in the vast majority of schools, is organized about the rationality of order, of linearity, and of diachrony. It is the path we follow to the goal of knowledge. It is the clearly marked passage on which we are always visible. (Block, 1998, p. 333)

Learners and educators, in different capacities, occupy this path toward knowledge. At times, we all find safety and comfort in this predetermined path, but it provides limited growth for its learners—in particular learners from non-dominant cultures (Block, 1998).

Part of every great learning story is the opportunity to be lost. We can become lost in understanding—so inspired and engrossed by some basic grasp of knowledge in a given topic that we forget all other matters for the time being. Or, we can become lost in confusion—so puzzled by a given topic that we challenge ourselves to find the answers that seem just out of our grasp.

When a learning story is told for you, instead of by you, there is a sense of your livelihood, your hope, being taken away (Fielding, 2007). The implementation of No Child Left Behind and other teacher accountability reforms have created a more homogeneous curriculum that leaves teachers with little room for

There, are "all variations on the same theme: how children master various feelings—danger, boredom, fear, frustration, jealousy—and manage to come to grips with the realities of their lives" (Lehmann-Haupt, 1981). Curriculum deals with exactly this, mastering the realities of life.

Our varied realities and diverse paths to grasp these realities highlight the necessity for a more varied curriculum that will support the unique characters that occupy our classrooms.

improvisation (Frelin & Grannas, 2010). This movement toward homogeneity can also be seen in cultural curriculum such as consumerism and sexism (Kenway & Bullen, 2010). These developments create an almost subconscious narrative that takes learning away from students. It is as if the curriculum is being determined without our participation in the design of these experiences, without our explicit knowing of its existence. We lose control over, or choice in, these elements of our narrative.

It is education's role to take back control of this narrative. Curriculum needs to be more like the *currere* that Pinar and Grumet describe (Pinar et al., 2006), an active story that allows for its author to make choices along the way. It must be a story with many layers: experiences in and out of school, experiences that cross generations, and experiences that are deeply rooted in the events that surround our lives at that very moment, but also project toward the future. Our job as educators is to help our students to weave these experiences together to create a unique complexity of knowledge and purpose.

Education, like life itself, is only truly living when it is consistently recreated. It is the events in our lives that enhance the academic learning we experience in the classroom, and vice versa. Children enjoy the experience of learning because it is this very balance of experienced knowledge with established knowledge that helps them understand the world around them. It is a story with a hopeful ending, one that has not been determined and can be exactly what we want it to be.

Curriculum should lead to this hopeful ending. Curriculum should support a learning story that connects student's lived experiences with their dreams.

REFERENCES

Block, A. (1998). Curriculum as affichiste: Popular culture and identity. In W. Pinar. (Ed.), *Curriculum: Toward new identities* (pp. 325-341). New York, NY: Garland.

Calkins, L., & Cruz, C. (2006). *Writing fiction: Big dreams, tall ambitions*. Portsmouth, NH: Heinemann.

Curriculum. (2012). *Dictionary.com Unabridged*. Retrieved from http://dictionary .reference.com/browse/curriculum

Ferneding, K. (2002). Stepping through the looking glass: Education within the space between modernity and postmodernity—The lifeworld, the body, and technology. *Journal of Curriculum Theorizing, 18*(3), 53-64.

Fielding, M. (2007). The human cost and intellectual poverty of high performance schooling: Radical philosophy, John McMurray and the remaking of person-centred education. *Journal of Education Policy, 22*(4), 384-409.

Frelin, A., & Grannäs, J. (2010). Negotiations left behind: in-between spaces of teacher-student negotiation and their significance for education. *Journal of Curriculum Studies, 42*(3), 353-369.

Greene, M. (1991). Blue guitars and the search for curriculum. In G. Willis & W. H. Schubert (Eds.), *Reflections from the heart of educational inquiry: Understanding curriculum and teaching through the arts* (pp. 107-122). Albany, NY: State University of New York Press.

Greene, M. (1984). The art of being present: Education for aesthetic encounters. *Journal of Education, 166*(2), 123-135.

Jardine, D. W., Friesen, S., & Clifford, P. (2003). *Back to the basics of teaching and learning: Thinking the world together.* Mahwah, NJ: Erlbaum.

Jardine, D. W., Friesen, S., & Clifford, P. (2006). *Curriculum in abundance.* Mahwah, NJ: Erlbaum.

Johnson, C. (1955). *Harold and the purple crayon.* New York, NY: HarperCollins.

Kenway, J., & Bullen, E. (2010). Consuming skin: Dermographies of female subjection and abjection. In J. Sandlin & P. McLaren (Eds.), *Critical pedagogies of consumption: Living and learning in the shadow of the "shopocalyse"* (pp. 157-168). New York, NY: Routledge.

Lather, P. A., & Smithies, C. (1997). *Troubling the angels: Women living with HIV/AIDS.* Boulder, CO: Westview Press.

Lehmann-Haupt. (1981, June 1). Book of the times. *The New York Times.* Retrieved from   http://www.nytimes.com/1981/06/01/books/books-of-the-times-139237.html

Merton, T. (n.d.). BrainyQuote.com. Retrieved from http://www.brainyquote.com/quotes/quotes/t/thomasmert121801.html

Pinar, W. F. (1992). "Dreamt into existence by others": Curriculum theory and school reform. *Theory into Practice, 31*(3), 228-235.

Pinar, W. F., Reynolds, W. M., Taubman, P. M., & Slattery, P. (2006). *Understanding curriculum.* New York, NY: Peter Lang.

Reynolds, P. H. (2003). *The dot.* Cambridge, MA: Candlewick Press.

Rosario, J. R. (1991). On thinking as a sacred act, Coltrane jazz, the inaccessible, and curriculum. In G. Willis & W. H. Schubert (Eds.), *Reflections from the heart of educational inquiry: Understanding curriculum and teaching through the arts* (pp. 174-181). Albany, NY: State University of New York Press.

Sendak, M. (1988). *Where the wild things are.* New York, NY: Harper Collins.

Shaw, G. B. (n.d.). BrainyQuote.com. Retrieved from http://www.brainyquote.com/quotes/quotes/g/georgebern113045.html

CHAPTER 12

TROUBLING TEACHING

Learning From Social Media

Susan L. M. Bartow
Miami University

Toward the end of the 19th century, school—our society's broad spectrum response to the need in a democracy for an educated citizenry—took the format similar to what was being developed in industries. It was designed to efficiently manage large numbers of students learning different subjects in buildings composed of isolated classrooms led by individual teachers (Tyack & Tobin, 1994). Since that time, school as an institution has expanded dramatically as attendance became compulsory, the population increased significantly, schools extended their services to older and more diverse groups of children, and teaching became a licensed profession. In the last 40 years, educational reform has been dominated by an increasing emphasis on standardization, accountability, and academic achievement. The discourse of school focuses on job preparation and global competition. Missing in teaching and learning is a focus on the relational (Bingham & Sidhorkin, 2004) and the relevant, the social processes and connections to people and ideas that are central to educative experience and the evolution of democracy (Dewey, 1966). With intermittent success over more than a century, progressive critics have sought to reexamine and restore or rejuvenate the connection between education and democracy.

Excursions and Recursions Through Power, Privilege, and Praxis
pp. 163–178
Copyright © 2012 by Information Age Publishing
163

For over a century progressive educators have struggled to pursue participatory and democratic ideals and are currently caught in a totalizing discourse of wide dimensions. Discursive practices produce constructions of social systems and organizations, shaping who can speak and what can be spoken about. Power makes subjects possible but is also "taken up and reiterated in the subject's 'own' acting ... the subject eclipses the conditions of its own emergence" (Sondergaard, 2002, p. 189). Today we are presented with economic, educational, and ethical challenges to a deeply embedded educational status quo. What is it that we cannot see or speak about school? How can we, subjects deeply enmeshed in but also producing the system, increase what is visible and create space for genuine democratic possibility?

Social media challenge our prevailing constructions of school, of teachers and students, and of teaching and learning, potentially opening discursive possibilities for those involved in education to re-create these systems and the roles and relationships within them in more egalitarian, progressive ways. They also deliver increasing avenues of surveillance and manipulation. The global spread of digital technologies, most recently and particularly interactive social media, has had pervasive influence on the ways we interact, communicate, and learn. Social media affect relationships between people and between people and ideas. Digital technologies have had a powerful effect on all aspects of life and are reconstructing our conceptions of the public, property, politics, authorship, authority, and knowledge production and consumption. The impact of digital technologies on education, especially social media is complex. However, in brick and mortar schools the use of digital media is still limited as information and communication technologies are marginalized to administrative functions and social media use is often restricted or forbidden. In this chapter, I explore the idea that educators are lost by considering what is missing in education for life in a democratic society and explore insights from some discourse-destabilizing lenses. These lenses unlock the possibility of a transgressive conversation about radically different constructions of public education and allow us to deliberate more openly about where we might go.

This chapter presents a study of normalization, an examination of a totalizing discourse, the power/knowledge constructing teachers and students as subjects in education. It is a search for counter discourse, a call for educators to recognize and consider the values and challenges of what is happening online today. First, I discuss the vital relationship between democracy and education and the failure of today's model of education to support that relationship. Second, I ask how we can see education differently and propose making school look strange from several vantage points. Third, I introduce the challenges and opportunities presented by the kinds of learning and engagement happening in online spaces. Lastly, I argue that we use these vantage points to destabilize our common sense regarding education so that we can free ourselves from constraints we are complicit in producing. Social media carry the potential of increasing the relational and the democratic but also the constraining and the commercial. It is our responsibility to address some of the concerns raised in social media use and to learn from its offerings. Can we use them to construct discourse about education that is more democratic, egalitarian, participatory, and just? Social media point out what we need to consider and demand that we be involved.

DEMOCRACY AND EDUCATION

The challenge for a democratic society is to develop the means by which the society can maintain a diverse range of shared undertakings and experiences and free and equitable relations that enable continuous readjustment. This interest, Dewey (1966) argues, makes a democratic society more interested than others in a system of education, a deliberate system of education that cannot be harnessed to either economic reproduction or the ends of the state.

Educational relations are unique because they exist to include learners in broadening relations. Dewey (1997) finds traditional education incongruous in a democracy and argues for more democratic and humane relations that contribute to a better quality of experience. Experience is social, involving contact and communication; educative experiences are those that lead to growth, growth in the direction of more experience. Dewey's (1966) belief in growth is a moral position placing the highest value on educative social interactions that foster ongoing powers to participate and share effectively in democratic life.

The nature of the work done in a democracy is social; authentic relational learning in education prepares us for that work. To learn we need to interact. We meet to learn, and we learn to meet (Bingham & Sidhorkin, 2004). Education for a democratic life entails collaborative work on common social issues and concerns confronting the students and the larger society (Beane, 1997). Education not connected with and conducted in social life is isolated school knowledge, differently applicable to life and not fulfilling its role in a democracy.

For at least 2 centuries, leaders in education, communities, and government have overtly and deliberately sought and developed a comprehensive organized response to a democracy's need for an educated citizenry. The response has taken a generalized form, the school, with very familiar and consistent characteristics. Over that period, bureaucratic institutions and associations evolved with the intention of providing and supporting that form of education for young people. Layers of structure and procedure were built, and policies were implemented. Markets grew up around institutions, meeting the needs of the institutions and creating ongoing interest in their own products or programs. An influential set of traditions and rituals, cultural norms, and a larger discourse has developed, one that circumscribes and prescribes our conceptions of education (Ball, 1990). Over that period, there has consistently been discussion, often contentious, and struggle among reformers about what should be learned in schools, who decides, who has access, what the best methods are, and how we will know what was learned (Kliebard, 2004). "But our schools, how we teach, where we teach, who we teach, who teaches, who administers, and who services, have changed mostly around the edges" (Davidson & Goldberg, 2009, p. 8).

Thanks in part to the climate and culture of testing in the U.S., formal school settings are places of reduced choices in learning at a time when technology is offering a widening range of choices. This climate and its restricted and restrictive market-based No Child Left Behind discourse has brought to the foreground the disparate achievement among minority groups but has also has drawn human resources away from other facets of life in schools, including those that contribute to consequential human relations. "Our institutions of learning have changed far more slowly than the modes of inventive, collaborative, participatory learning offered by the Internet" (Davidson & Goldberg, 2009, p. 9).

With our ongoing reliance on an increasingly irrelevant system and without the acknowledgement that pedagogies of relation are central to communication, to meaning and sense making, school relies on habitual or obfuscating discourses. The goal of education in a living democracy is to provide the means by which diverse people experience and seek continuing growth (Noddings, 2009). Recognition of the central importance of a relational nature of teaching and learning can drive the transformation of school as the prevailing model for education (Noddings, 2004). Changes in school as a model of universal education have the potential to regenerate our understandings of public education in contemporary democratic society.

Today's schools serve other masters. On the horizon may be "the mechanization of teaching" (Barseghian, 2012) and learning. How can we see school differently? How can we begin scratching the surface of the taken for granted, to begin seeing the masked coalition of social forces locking schools into their widely reproductive roles? How is resistance being limited and tamed by responding within a discourse developed by a neoliberal rationality? If we "apply a Foucauldian-like suspicion to our own actions and regimes of truth" (Smith, 2004, p. 238) what might we see?

MAKING SCHOOL STRANGE

The rules and regularities that undergird our current era's understanding of knowledge, children, education, and schooling don't just affect what we know. They affect what *teaching practices* we understand to be possible and legitimate, as well as what *"studenting" practices*, so to speak, we can legitimately expect. (Jardine, 2005, p. 91, emphasis in original)

History Makes School Look Strange

Two 20th century thinkers help us look at school through an alienating lens. As he analyzes the ways certain ideas become normative, Foucault's influential approach to understanding society helps us see school as strange. Foucault suspends the naturalness of certain accepted systems in order to make possible the perception and definition of others (Foucault, 1990). A Foucauldian look at education encompasses the dissemination of disciplinary practices but goes beyond, hinting at the role of education in creating subjects even more susceptible to modern power. Educational practices such as the examination, classification, and the training of teachers naturalized the industrial order and have had, through the broadening impact of mass education, a role in the increasing professionalization and bureaucratization of Western society (Jones, 1990).

Modern societies equate learning with a special place called a school, a separate place with a distinct appearance and structure that became foundational to school during the 19th century. In their concurrent move toward professionalization, educators claimed the territory of the school and allied it with closer supervision of students and specialization of instruction. The turn of the 20th century became a time of increasing bureaucratization as the effects of professionalization, inspection, and standardization—forces for safety and quality but also for embedding power—took hold and increasingly institutionalized learning (Cutler, 1989). Did we abdicate our responsibilities, trading them and authenticity away for security and convenience?

Illich (2002) makes school look strange when he asks us how we came to believe that teaching equals learning and posits that school teaches compliance with the other institutions of our society. In his 1971 polemic *Deschooling Society,* Illich (2002) argued the institutions of a technological and rational society have come to dominate social reality, defining learnedness, well-being, and safety by the standards of a dominant consumptive worldview. His attack is broad but Illich identifies school as the false public utility that "schools" us to accept others, the modern institution with the express purpose of shaping reality. Schools teach us that simple needs are answered institutionally, that individual action is unreliable, irresponsible, aggressive, and subversive. Schools manage options and futures, teaching us that learning is the result of teaching, that the value of learning can be measured and documented, that failure at schooling should be addressed by more schooling. Schools train the professionals that perpetuate school. Schools foster misleading faith in progress, production, and consumption. Illich finds social institutions such as school to be counterproductive, developing effects counter to their expressed aims as their size and scope increase. Ritual keeps the spells intact, intensifying as needed to hide dissonance. With remarkable prescience, 40 years ago, Illich decried our educational funnels and encouraged us to deinstitutionalize learning and allow learning webs to form. His descriptions uncannily foreshadow today's participatory use of the internet.

School appears "strange" from many lookouts—its history, the buildings, the schedule, the distinct structure of the curriculum and its relationship to disciplines or fields of knowledge, the ratio of students to teachers, the reliance on tracking people by age. Overall, history helps us see that modern education is preparation for an industrial society and "minimal citizenship in a passive representative democracy" (Kellner, 2006, p. 242).

Social Media Makes School Look Strange

In today's society, the ubiquity and engagement of social media as a form of communication and knowledge consumption and production make school look strange. More than ever people of all ages learn and share knowledge in social relations that are virtual. Virtual spaces and relationships open approaches that transgress dominant discourses through troubling and paradoxical narrations of learning and education. Before investigating these alienating discourses, what are considered social media and who is using them? Wikipedia defines social media as "the use of web-based and mobile technologies to turn communication into an interactive dialogue … Internet-based applications that build on the ideological and technological foundations of Web 2.0, and that allow the creation and exchange of user-generated content" (Social Media, 2011).

Two widely cited sources offer descriptions of today's students as users of social media. Michael Wesch (2007) and his undergraduate students collaborated on a compelling digital ethnography exploring the impact of digital technology and social media on young adults. Their work puts into sharp focus the incongruity of students' roles in a lecture hall furnished with chairs bolted to the floor versus their roles when encouraged to access their cell phones to find, share, and produce information. Over the last decade the Pew Research Center has operated the Pew Internet & American Life Project and conducted over 100 surveys studying the social impact of the internet. All their surveys are available for free on their website at http://pewinternet.org/. In a 2010 report the following data on social media use were compiled (Lenhart, Purcell, Smith, & Zickuhr). The sections on social media use by young people indicate that:

- Internet use is nearly ubiquitous as 93% of teens go online;
- The average teen owns 3.5 electronic gadgets (cell phones, iPods, computers, game consoles, hand-held gaming devices);
- four out of five teens own gaming devices—both wired and portable;
- three quarters of wired teens use social networking sites;
- thirty-eight percent participate in online content creating activity (photos, videos, artwork, stories);
- ninety-seven percent of teens play computer, portable, or console based video games spanning a wide variety of genres (music, puzzle, sports, shooters, massively multiplayer online game).

CHALLENGES, OPPORTUNITIES, AND CONCERNS WITH SOCIAL MEDIA

Social media have something to teach us. From impacting how certain courses are taught to questioning the design of the entire system of school itself, there are straightforward educational, ethical, and organizational/structural reasons for educators to pay attention to the lessons of social media.

Educational Reasons to Pay Attention

As we consider the educational reasons to listen, challenges for educators come from several education-related fields. To begin, we must look at who else is teaching young people today: YouTube, Facebook, Wikipedia, Minecraft, Words with Friends, Tumblr, Reddit, StumbleUpon, Habbo, and countless others. And who else is teaching? There are a plethora of success stories in free education and the open source movement ranging from courses at prominent and not so prominent institutions to encyclopedias, organizations, collections, operating systems, software, browsers, apps, tools—open source software and materials created by individuals working to support an open internet by developing and sharing online materials for free. Often the only condition for modifying them is that modifications are also freely available. The work is transparent, ongoing, and difficult to associate with an owner, exemplifying a community versus brand orientation. Creative Commons licenses are an alternative developed in the "copyleft" movement, issued by a nonprofit organization seeking to enhance the public domain while helping authors variably negotiate rights of ownership and rights waved for the benefit of sharing and growing knowledge.

Outside of school, young people are actively involved in participatory cultures, a term that "cuts across educational practices, creative processes, community life, and democratic citizenship" (Jenkins, Purashotma, Weigel, Clinton, & Robison, 2009, p. 9). A participatory culture is described as one with low barriers to civic engagement and creative expression with strong support for sharing creative work and a ready informal system of mentorship whereby more experienced members pass on knowledge to novices. In contrast to the experiences of too many in schools, members of participatory cultures feel connected and that their contributions matter. Inherent in these cultures is shared and interactive learning.

Schools have been slow to react to these compelling participatory spaces as technology has been historically marginalized. We have not been able to genuinely rethink the structures of knowledge, the modes of organization, or the relationships between students, teachers, and subject matter. The paradigm of school is at odds with contemporary culture (Jenkins et al., 2009, p. 9). What is foundational about the kinds of learning happening outside of schools is the facilitation of modes of learning that don't fit the tradition, power, and bureaucracy-bound learning institutions of the last century and a half. Learning in many online settings features process (Davidson & Goldberg, 2009). The interaction between technology, creator, and audience is not passive or unidirectional. It blurs lines of authorship and authority, flattening access to information and challenging the nature of expertise. Pedagogy is decentered, altered when self and peer enhanced learning is enabled in an environment of endless information and endless ways to contribute. We must be asking if our institutional structures can "shift from the weighty to the light, from the assertive to the enabling" (Davidson & Goldberg, 2009, p. 34).

Discussions of learning ecologies (Siemens, 2003) offer important insights. *Learning ecologies* refer to and acknowledge the nearly boundless dimensions of learning, the "set of contexts found in physical or virtual spaces that provide opportunities for learning" (Barron, 2006, p. 195). A learning ecology perspective is useful in conceptualizing learning and teaching across Web 2.0 spaces of home, school, work, and community (Greenhow, Robelia, & Hughes, 2009). Proponents argue developing models of learning must embrace the wide range of learning opportunities and different modes of social and cognitive development occurring outside institutionalized structures of bounded classrooms and hierarchies of information and content. Researchers articulate changing teacher capacities, learner dispositions, and conditions, describing new conceptions of teachers as content experts, facilitators, consultants, mentors, and improvisationists (Spires, Wiebe, Young, Hollenbrands, & Lee, 2009).

Learning sciences "researchers have gained a richer understanding of human learning as it happens in situated contexts of social participation and collaboration" (Robinson, 2010, pp. 192-193). Linguist and games scholar James Gee (2004) has studied learning for decades. In the last decade, he has focused on videogaming, searching for what gamers and game designers can teach us about making schools more motivating, authentic, and equitable. Gee argues educators need to recognize that young people are mastering complex specialist languages to play games, tenaciously and voluntarily pursuing lengthy and difficult challenges. Learning in a game setting is contextual. Social learning is facilitated. Skills are integrated. Learning, Gee (2004) continues, is involved with action and identity and situated in learners' material and social world. Learning in games is multimodal, redundant and just in time. In contrast, learning in school settings is generally removed from active practice and peers. Gee finds it ironic that educators often advocate multicultural education but ignore these rich lessons from out-of-school "low culture" learning spaces.

School teaches hyperindividuality and relies on monotextual linear reading. Recognition of multimodal means of communication challenge narrow, printed text based, linear literacy. We need to move beyond "chalk and talk pedagogy" (Luke, 2006, p. 272) to mix traditional and newly blended genres and cultural frames of reference. What might cyber pedagogy look like? Connectivity and access are breaking the tyranny of time, distance, and the one-directional flow of information. Carmen Luke has researched multimedia literacies and new media and developed prototypes for helping teachers integrate old and new media and critical media proclivities. She finds that relationships in information, knowledge, learning, communication, time, and space are shaped in "rhizomatic" (Luke, 2006, p. 272) rather than linear or checkerboard mental maps.

> There is a new sense of spatiality that defies the sorts of modernist under-
> standings of knowledge, of place, of sociality that is so foundational to our
> own schooling experience and the normative social science and teacher
> training most of us underwent at some time in the last several decades.
> (Luke, 2006, p. 272)

Rather than forecasting the end of the teacher, she sees teachers' roles as
indispensable, as mediators and mentors, "craft experts with specialized
expertise who induct new learners into communities of practice" (Luke,
2006, p. 274). In this view, teachers must increasingly be experts at creating innovative hybrids in the spaces between *new* and *must do*.

Ethical Reasons to Pay Attention

As educators and as members of a society we have compelling ethical
obligations to pay attention to social media. What questions do we have
about the nature of learning in online spaces? Everyone is aware that with
open access and fluid interactivity come abuse, exposure, violation,
manipulation, and obfuscation as well as egalitarian potential. In the participatory spaces of fandom, for example, lie both a creative and emanci-
pating shift of producer and consumer roles with implications for
interactions with economic and political fields of power and cleverly concealed manipulation and mass deception (Shefrin, 2004). A plethora of
war games mobilize rhetoric and naturalize U.S. roles and responses in
global settings for young people (Stahl, 2006). Embracing these changes
means recognizing an even greater need for critical media literacy and
the ability to critically evaluate the rhetoric behind its use.

What concerns do we have about unequal access to technology and
unequal mentorship in its use? How do we address the digital divides and
wide variations in learning ecologies that exist in both home and school
settings? What we think of as a "digital divide" is not singular and one-
dimensional. There are divides in access, autonomy, social support, skill,
and types of use—differences in what people do online, in their abilities,
and in their purposes in both content production and consumption (Hargittai, 2004). Technical skills vary according to household income. People
from different socioeconomic backgrounds exhibit different forms of use
leading to different outcomes (Zillien & Hargittai, 2009). "Access and use
of new media is embedded in various social processes and does not evolve
in isolation from existing social institutions" (Hargittai, 2004, p. 138). We
should not buy into the myth of the digital native. Hargittai's (2010)
research indicates higher levels of web use skill are associated with higher

levels of parental education, with being male, and with being White or Asian American.

Echoing a recurrent and often problematic drive in the history of American education to address health issues, we hear contemporary calls for curricula that teach healthy digital behavior and the development of responsible digital citizenship. We cannot ignore new versions of perpetual concerns over cheating and bullying that call for educators to work with others in embedding elemental ethical curricula to address recurring problems in new spaces. And what are our obligations to address rising concerns with privacy, with defining "professional" behavior, or the compilation and manipulation of data by dominant social networking sites such as Facebook?

Organizational and Structural Reasons to Pay Attention

The biggest questions and deepest challenges to traditional models of education constitute the most radical reasons to pay attention—those that challenge the entire system itself. Social media teach us that factory schools as a paradigm for education no longer fit and demand that we look forward to a transformation. Collins and Halverson (2009) argue the changes we see represent a great transformation in schooling reflective of the transformations sweeping other social and cultural institutions. The transitions from apprenticeship to compulsory universal schooling brought changes in the location of, the responsibility for, the purpose and content of, the instructional and assessment strategies, and the relationship between teachers and learners. Today, Collins and Halverson contend that earlier computer-based instructional models and instructional technologies had little impact on school and have never come close to the power of peer-to-peer, socially constructed inquiry facilitated by participatory social media. They characterize the shifts from apprenticeship to mass schooling to lifelong learning like this:

- responsibility for education—shifting from families/the master to the state and back to family or individual;
- expectations for education—shifting from social reproduction to success for all to choice;
- content of education—shifting from practical skills to disciplinary to learning how to learn;
- pedagogy—shifting from apprenticeship to didacticism to interaction;

- assessment—shifting from observation and one-on-one interaction to testing to embedded;
- location—from home to school to anywhere;
- culture—from centering on adult culture to peer culture to mixed-age culture; and
- relationships—from personal bonds to authority figures to computer-mediated interaction (Collins & Halverson, 2009).

Critiquing on a very broad scale, Waks (2010) contributes an extensive analysis of the shortcomings of the factory school system as an organizational paradigm. Exercising a deep commitment to social justice, Waks lays out the need, a vision, and practical steps toward a more just and complete transformation of the existing paradigm of education. Justice demands more than universality and efficiency. Education, not necessarily school, is what every citizen needs. Education has to work well, he says, for everyone, especially those in less advantaged positions. He details how modifying school to incorporate the web (virtual schools, Classroom 2.0, etc.) essentially fails to make the leap, fails to match the possibilities for collaboration, exchange, collective action, user-generation of content inherent online. First order results of education—knowledge and skills—can be obtained today outside the factory school system. Waks develops the distinction between retrofitting the internet to school and what is necessitated in revolutionary institutional change—breaking the reliance on a hierarchical, one size fits all model that serves as both the gatekeeper to further education and the social and economic status and privilege it affords. He argues social transformation is taking place now as economic, cultural, political, and technical changes are transforming other institutions. Waks encourages educational leaders to innovate, creating more adaptive organizational models that enable open learning experiences and new ways and new drivers for assembling them into much more varied avenues of learning. Like Foucault's historical one, his lens shifts perspectives in irreversible ways.

Despite the development of Web 2.0 technologies and students' habits outside school, educators are caught in the historically discipline-based perspective and use the internet to augment "information retrieval rather than supplanting traditional resources and activities" (Greenhow et al., 2009, p. 248). Far too often teachers are the successful products of a system dominated by market-based discourses of effectiveness, outcomes, and accountability. Possibly blind to the deep, camouflaged productions of the classroom and its limiting relationships, our imaginations are confined. We are one of the barriers to bridging the gaps between the kinds of learning happening inside and outside school, one of the barriers to transformative change. Can we explore new subjectivities that engender more egalitarian and participatory relations?

CONCLUSION

Educators have a role in exploring the dialectic between corporate and democratic interests and potential in online spaces. When looking at schools Kellner (2006) sees the technical and economic pressure for change making possible the radical social and educational reform that Dewey (1966), Illich (2002), and Freire (2007) sought. The important question is the nature of the reconstruction of education. This revolution "poses tremendous challenges to educators to rethink their basic tenets, to deploy the new technologies in creative and productive ways, and to restructure schooling to respond constructively and progressively to the technological and social changes currently underway" (Kellner, 2006, p. 241). First we must see clearly and be involved. Will education continue to reflect market interests or can conceptions of teachers, students, and learning, the traditional transmission-style pedagogies, and the cramped social relations of school be restructured in the service of democracy and the cause of social justice?

Social media present critical educational, ethical, and organization/ structural challenges to schools. Most of the conversation regarding the impact and potential of social media originates outside the discourse of education and comes from fields such as the learning sciences, communication and mass media studies, new literacy studies, or educational technology. Formal educators have been curiously silent. Schools are beginning to address these issues with extreme caution, taking tentative steps into policy, administration, and curriculum discussions that surround these initiatives. Here and there, teachers, central to any lasting reform (Cuban, 1993) are experimenting with using social media as a part of their teaching. These teachers take risks and become facile at bricolage pedagogy (Luke, 2006, p. 275). They transgress traditional student/ teacher categories but struggle with the confines of the system. They may make abnormal the ubiquitous "furniture" of school and the material realities of the classroom. Do social media practices enable us to listen to subjugated and disqualified knowledges? Do they enable us to look at the same things in different ways, to see new things, to find what surrounds us strange? Will we step outside?

Those whose interests are now being served will not carry out a revolution (Freire, 2007). If we have the imagination, now is the moment to take part in reshaping the discourse. We must be present to the opportunities *and* the risks and not be afraid. Will social media be grafted onto the existing system, enhancing surveillance and management aspects with features like the mobile app for classroom management (Watters, 2011) or sets of mobile devices ready to boost test scores (Brainchild, 2011)? Or will we allow them to expand what can be thought and spoken, expanding the discursive categories of student, teacher, knowledge, pedagogy, and even school in ways that promote more engaging, more relevant, more fluid, and more egalitarian relationships and the senses of agency vital to democratic living? We are not talking enough yet. Those interested in education have a great deal to think about as vast movements for change sweep the societal organizations that have been responsible for education for over a century. Those involved in education, recognizing the possibility inherent in various discursive formations, can swim against the stream of what is taken for granted and consider an expanded horizon for where their efforts might lie.

REFERENCES

Ball, S. (Ed.). (1990). Introduction. In *Foucault and education: Disciplines and knowledge*. New York, NY: Routledge.

Barron, B. (2006). Interest and self-sustained learning as catalysts of development: A learningecology perspective. *Human Development, 49*, 193-224.

Barseghian, T. (2012, March 30). Amidst a mobile revolution in schools, will old teaching tactics work? Retrieved from http://blogs.kqed.org/mindshift/2012/03/amidst-a-mobile-revolution-in-schools-will-old-teaching-tactics-prevail/

Beane, J. (1997). *Curriculum integration: Designing the core of democratic education*. New York, NY: Teachers College Press.

Bingham, C., & Sidorkin, A. (Eds.). (2004). *No education without relation*. New York, NY: Peter Lang.

Brainchild Corp. (2011). Match the device to your goals. Retrieved from http://www.brainchild.com/mobile-learning/

Collins, A., & Halverson, R. (2009). *Rethinking education in the age of technology: The digitalrevolution and schooling in America*. New York, NY: Teachers College Press.

Cuban, L. (1993). *How teachers taught: Constancy and change in American classrooms 1880-1990* (2nd ed.). New York, NY: Teachers College Press.

Cutler, W. (1989). Cathedral of culture: The schoolhouse in American educational thought andpractice since 1820. *History of Education Quarterly, 29*(1), 1-40.

Davidson, C. N., & Goldberg, D. T. (2009). *The future of learning institutions in a digital age.*Cambridge, MA: MIT Press.

Dewey, J. (1966). *Democracy and education*. Toronto, Ontario, Canada: Collier Macmillan.

Dewey, J. (1997). *Experience and education*. New York, NY: Touchstone Books.

Foucault, M. (1990). *The history of sexuality—Volume 1: An introduction*. New York, NY: RandomHouse.

Freire, P. (2007). *Pedagogy of the oppressed.* New York, NY: Continuum.

Gee, J. P. (2004). *Situated language and learning: A critique of traditional schooling.* New York, NY: Routledge.

Greenhow, C., Robelia, B., & Hughes, J. (2009). Web 2.0 and classroom research: What pathsshould we take now? *Educational Researcher, 38*(4), 246-259.

Hargittai, E. (2004). Internet access and use in context. *New Media & Society, 6*(1), 137-143.

Hargittai, E. (2010). Digital na(t)ives? Variations in internet skills and uses among members of the "net generation." *Sociological Inquiry, 80*(1), 92-112.

Illich, I. (2002). *Deschooling society.* London, England: Marion Boyars.

Jardine, G. (2005). *Foucault and education.* New York, NY: Peter Lang.

Jenkins, H., Purushotma, R., Weigel, M., Clinton, K., & Robinson, A. (2009). *Confronting thechallenges of participatory media: Media education for the 21st century.* Cambridge, MA: MIT Press.

Jones, R. (1990). Educational practices and scientific knowledge: A genealogical reinterpretation the emergence of physiology in post-Revolutionary France. In S. Ball (Ed.), *Foucault and education: Disciplines and knowledge.* New York, NY: Routledge.

Kellner, D. (2006). Technological transformation, multiple literacies, and the re-visioning of education. In J. Weiss, J. Nolan, & J. Hunsinger (Eds.), *The international handbook ofvirtuallearning environments* (pp. 241-268). Amsterdam, The Netherlands: Springer.

Kliebard, H. M. (2004). *The struggle for the American curriculum* (3rd ed.). New York, NY: Routledge.

Lenhart, A., Purcell, K., Smith, A., & Zickuhr, K. (2010). Teens and social media. Retrieved from http://www.pewinternet.org/Reports/2010/Social-Media-and-Young-Adults.aspx

Luke, C. (2006). Cyberpedagogy. In J. Weiss, J. Nolan, & J. Hunsinger (Eds.), *The international handbook of virtual learning environments* (pp. 269-277). Dordrecht, The Netherlands: Springer.

Noddings, N. (2004). Foreword. In C. Bingham & A. Sidorkin, (Eds.), *No education withoutrelation* (pp. vii-viii). New York, NY: Peter Lang.

Noddings, N. (2009). Caring, caring for ideas. In T. E. Lewis, J. G. A. Grinberg, & M. Laverty (Eds.), *Philosophy of education: Modern and contemporary ideas of education* (pp. 503-544). Dubuque, IA: Kendall Hunt.

Robison, A. (2010). New media literacies by design: The game school. In K. Tyner (Ed.), *Media literacy: New agendas in communication* (pp. 192-208). New York, NY: Routledge.

Shefrin, E. (2004). Lord of the Rings, Star Wars, and participatory fandom: Mapping newcongruencies between the Internet and media entertainment culture. *Critical Studies in Media Communication, 21*(3), 261-281.

Siemens, G. (2003). Learning ecology, communities, and networks: Extending the classroom. Retrieved from http://www.elearnspace.org/Articles/learning_communities.htm

Smith, S. (2004). School choice through a Foucauldian lens: Disrupting the left's oppositional stance. In E. Rofes & L. Stulberg (Eds.), *The emancipatory promise of charter schools: Toward a progressive politics of school choice* (pp. 219-244). Albany, NY: State University of New York Press.

Social Media. (2011). In *Wikipedia*. Retrieved fromhttp://en.wikipedia.org/wiki/ Social_media

Sondergaard, D. M., (2002). Poststructuralist approaches to empirical analysis. *QualitativeStudies in Education, 15*(2), 187-204.

Spires, H., Wiebe, E., Young, C., Hollenbrands, K., & Lee, J. (2009). Toward a new learningecology: Teaching and learning in 1:1 environments. Retrieved from http://scholar.googleusercontent.com/scholar?q=cache:D34nxjHxSIYJ :scholar.google.com/+Toward+a+new+learning+ecology:+teaching+ and+learning+in+1:1+environments&hl=en&as_sdt=0,36

Stahl, R. (2006). Have you played the war on terror? *Critical Studies in Media Communication, 23*(2), 112-130.

Tyack, D., & Tobin, W. (1994). The "grammar" of schooling: Why has it been so hard to change? *American Educational Research Journal, 31*(3), 453-479.

Waks, L. J. (2010). Learningweb revolution proposal. Retrieved from http:// www.stevehargadon.com/2010/05/leonard-waks-on-web-20-educational.html

Watters, A. (2011, Sept. 7). Can mobile phones help teachers manage classroom behavior? Retrieved from http://mindshift.kqed.org/2011/09/can-mobile-phones-help-teachersmanage-classroom-behavior/

Wesch, M., (2007). A vision of students today. Retrieved from http://www .youtube.com/watch?v=dGCJ46vyR9o

Zillien, N., & Hargittai, E. (2009). Digital distinctions: Status-specific types of Internet usage. *Social Science Quarterly, 90*(2), 274-291.

CHAPTER 13

RECEPTIVE PRAXIS

Laura Rychly
Georgia Southern University

In some ways, the model of public education we have in place at present is failing many, if not most, children and young adults. Erikson et al. (2008) describe a continuum of toxicity, ranging from "increasingly toxic," to "manageably toxic," to "relatively positive" to qualify students' experiences of school. Ken Robinson (2008) explains the high numbers of children taking prescription drugs for attention deficit disorders as being necessary because students require anesthesia in order to make it through long days of passively sitting that are counter to their other experiences in the world. Many scholars have directed their attention toward contributing ideas about how schools can be places where children awaken to themselves, recognize themselves as powerful thinkers and problem solvers, and learn to participate as necessary members of our nation's democracy.

One particularly important body of scholarship about how schools can be places where all children experience success and growth is that of culturally responsive pedagogy. It is common to hear talk about traditionally marginalized populations in schools, usually "children of color": African American, Hispanic, and Native American students, and about what can be done to "close the achievement gap" between them and White students (Gay, 2000). The paradigm of culturally responsive teaching is one approach designed to correct the reality that "too many students of color have not been achieving in school as well as they should (and can) for far too long" (Gay, 2000, p. 1). While I embrace the idea of responsiveness, I

Excursions and Recursions Through Power, Privilege, and Praxis
pp. 179–189
Copyright © 2012 by Information Age Publishing
All rights of reproduction in any form reserved.

recognize that Gay's (2000) intentions are mostly for the marginalized populations named above. But, given the recognition that schooling today fails to meet the needs of many children, regardless of culture, there is room to expand the responsibility for responsiveness beyond the boundaries of culture. Additionally, the concept of "cultural responsiveness" is becoming institutionalized and appropriated by schools and school people; I worry this might usurp its good intentions and replace its potential with more oppressive expectations. It will get woven into curriculum revisions as just something else for teachers to do; so it will become an act and will be put upon teachers and students. By "put upon" I mean imagining something like culturally responsive pedagogy, something that should be dynamic and present in the space between teachers and learners, being extracted out of this space and fixed into a "thing" that can be laid upon them as an expected, observable, measureable way of being.

This is one way of thinking about what has happened over time with the IQ test. Alfred Binet originally developed the test as a tool to identify children who would benefit from extra educational services when regular methods were not fully effective; it was never meant to be used as a way to label children (Gould, 1996). Our system of public education, however, has used IQ tests to measure a perceived fixed level of intelligence, and students' scores have been used to sort them according to a perceived inherited, measurable amount of intellectual potential (Gould, 1996). An example related to culturally responsive pedagogy is that the teacher assessment system used in my state looks for teachers to maintain a "culturally responsive classroom." Under this heading is the following requirement: "Incorporates multicultural information, resources, and materials in all of the subjects and skills routinely taught in schools" (Georgia Department of Education, 2008, p. 50). A teacher's cultural responsiveness is being extracted out of the relationship she shares with her students in measureable bits such as this. One problem with this particular defined element of a culturally responsive classroom is that multiculturalism and cultural responsiveness are not typically thought to be the same thing. Multiculturalism is about the inclusion of curricular materials that reflect the variety of cultures inhabiting a classroom but may stop short of altering teachers' orientations to diverse students and actual instructional practices (Gay, 2000). Culturally responsive pedagogy is more holistic and calls for diverse cultural characteristics to be the reasons for changes made to classroom practices (Gay, 2000). Another problem is that this seems to be an "add on" that some reject as a solution to a one-size-fits-all classroom and curriculum (Dimitriadis & McCarthy, 2001). I am not saying it is always only superficial, but, because it is a box to be checked on a rubric, it has become potentially only a surface-level modification to classroom practice instead of being a way that teachers are with students. The rubric is troubling because while the box will be checked if genuine cultural responsiveness has been woven into teaching, the converse is not necessarily true, that just because the box is checked we can be sure the teaching is culturally responsive. There is a two-sided nature to an assessment such as this: a checked box could be evidence of the presence of, or a mask for the absence of, culturally responsive pedagogy. My point is to caution against a complacency that could stifle the benefits of an orientation to teaching and to learners that culturally responsive pedagogy calls for.

My suggestion for a way to protect a dynamic between teachers and learners that would make school a more satisfying place for both to inhabit is for a receptive praxis to exist prior to our responses to students. This prior moment would apply to all students, the "universal other." Receptive praxis is a way that we suspend our understanding of another, withhold our knowing, silence our certainty, so that whomever emerges before us enters a space that expects them to just be exactly as they are and not as who they are plus who they *should* be. Such a praxis adheres to Freire's (1993) explanation of transformative human activity as being action and reflection, theory and practice, happening together. We can learn to pause our impulses to know and name. When we receive students in this way, we re-open our expectations of them, which gives them back all of their possibilities for being. We do respond to them, but we do so keeping in mind that our response is based on *our* perceptions of our students' language, behavior, appearance, and achievement. Students have their own perceptions of themselves, and receiving students means we remember not to privilege our perception above theirs.

PERSONAL AND PHILOSOPHICAL GROUNDS FOR *RECEIVING*

Personal

My first lesson on receiving, though I could never have known I was learning it at the time, was taught to me by my husband. It was one of the first times that I knew what an amazing person I had fallen into the company of. We had just begun dating, and I was riding in the passenger seat in his truck while he drove. I can remember being wrapped up in that fabulous feeling that someone else in the world was excited about me, and being equally excited about him. I do not remember where we were going, but we were driving on one of the busier roads in our town when suddenly he was cut off by a car that switched lanes aggressively in front of him. I tensed, ready for the thing people do when they are cut off in traffic— curse or complain or accuse the other driver of being unsafe. He did not say a word. I looked at him, and it was as if nothing had happened. It seemed to have gone right over him. A few years later, when I was sharing with my dad all the reasons that I wanted to marry this man, I recalled this story. I told my dad it was like he just figured the other driver had to be wherever he was going faster than he did. He had no need to judge the other person or be "right" over him or her, no need to take it on. Even if he felt indignant, he did not believe his own perception to be the only right perception. In his response he remembered to invite the other's perception as being as equally valid as his own.

My second lesson on receiving came from documentary filmmaker Trinh T. Minh-ha (Bourdier & Mihn-ha, 1982) in her film *Re-assemblage: From the Firelight to the Screen*. The film, set in Senegal, Africa, shows images of villagers doing their daily work. Music accompanies the images but occasionally stops abruptly. The images continue in silence. The experience of the silences is fascinating because the viewer does not know when to expect them, and they are contrasted with lively snippets of drumming and voices. It occurred to me while I watched the film that Minh-ha might have included the silences to model what we should hear in our own heads while viewing the images of African villager-as-other doing his or her regular life. She might have anticipated the noise in viewers' minds, buzzing with commentary and explanation for that which we cannot hope to understand, as we are "wholly other." If we can practice such a silence, then we can create a receiving space for our students to come into. Receiving would be when we suspend our understanding of another, withhold our knowing, silence our certainty, so that whomever emerges before us enters a space that expects them to be. Believing ourselves to be incapable of a precise, knowing judgment makes it so that our understanding of another is interrupted.

Philosophy

Philosophy about our responsibilities to the other, such as is found in the work of Martin Buber and Jacques Derrida, legitimizes a possibility and a necessity of receiving. When we do not own up to how little we can ever really know each other is when, according to Martin Buber (1970), we damage a potential relationship between two people. Buber (1970) referred to this potential as a "relation," and contrasted it with the way that we "experience" each other. The latter is when I think I know someone. When I experience another I objectify him into some*thing* that I can know. Buber (1970) called this an I/It relationship. This is not a relation. A relation, by contrast, is an encounter between two people that requires no objectification. Buber (1970) called this an I/You or I/Thou relationship. The difference between I/It and I/You relationships is that the former limits our being and the latter extends it:

The human being to whom I say You I do not experience. But I stand in relation to him,

> in the sacred basic word. Only when I step out of this do I experience him again. Experience is remoteness from You … You is more than It knows. You does more, and more happens to it, than It knows. No deception reaches this far: here is the cradle of actual life. (Buber, 1970, p. 60)

We do not want to experience our students because this limits them (and us), but we want to be in relation to them, or "encounter" them (Buber, 1970, p. 62). Buber (1970) explained that relations, or encounters, are "passive" and reciprocal (p. 62). The only way for me to genuinely be with another, for a teacher to be with a student, is to passively and reciprocally encounter him. This is what happens to a first-grader named George when he interjects that he does not think studying farm and zoo animals will be cool and that he would rather study amphibians (Rymes, 2009). Despite George's reputation for being a troublemaker, his teacher gives him a space to interact beyond the limits his label would generally afford him by not punishing "him for rudely rejecting her unit plans and the school's standard curriculum" (Rymes, 2009, p. 13). When we interact with a student's label instead of the student himself, we objectify him into an "it." The word "receiving" captures Buber's (1970) intentions about how teachers can be with students in a way that wholly validates the students' being. George's teacher received George instead of making his interruption mean something about her classroom management or his behavioral deficits.

Poststructural thinking about "the other" shows how there is necessary and inevitable distance between any two of us. In a roundtable conversation held at Villanova University in 1994 Jacques Derrida said about the other: "The structure of my relation to the other is … a relation in which the other remains absolutely transcendent. I cannot reach the other. I cannot know the other from the inside and so on" (quoted in Caputo, 1997, p. 14). Derrida's conception of "the other" illustrates a possible way of thinking about the relationship that exists between a teacher and her students. Face to face with each other's otherness within classroom walls, teachers and students can only approach what it would be to actually know one another, because we are always only approaching a possibility of knowing (Caputo, 1997; Deutscher, 2005; Miller, 2001). Avital Ronnell, a subject interviewed for the documentary film *Examined Life*, said about the other:

> The other is so in excess of anything you can understand or grasp, or reduce, this in itself creates an ethical relatedness, a relation without rela-

tion because you don't know, you can't presume to know or grasp the other. The minute you think you know the other, you're ready to kill them ... if you don't know, you don't understand this alterity, it's so other that you can't violate it with your sense of understanding then ... you have to let it live, in a sense. (Imperial & Taylor, 2008)

Letting it live is the first step toward receiving. I recognize this way of being in both my husband's response to the driver who cut him off and in the silences in *Re-Assemblage*. In both cases the other is allowed to live, unknown, exactly as they are.

Though teachers and students may not be able to completely know each other, what is also true is that we require each other for our own being: "I always require the other for identity. I am always lost and waiting to be found, and the discovery by the other ensures my existence" (Block, 2009, p. 74). So while there is an inevitable distance between members of a classroom community, in that they are all others, there is also dependence on this distance. It is in this space where a teacher and her students cannot fully know each other, but depend on each other for their own being, that we can learn to receive one another. While I understand that I cannot ever receive, if receive means know, or recognize, or understand, another, I believe it is possible to: "let the other come, and the other comes or does not come, unpredictably" (Miller, 2001, p. 273). Receive, in this way, means that we create an opening for students to come into, "an opening for the coming of the other," but we do not have an expectation of what students will be, or who they will reveal themselves as (Caputo, 1997, p. 42). We also are not waiting with guns drawn, ready to fire off a judgment when our students do reveal themselves. This kind of receiving exists as

> Respect, on this account, is not about treating the other as another rational subject like myself, but about *responding* to her specificity in a way that secures her right to be other. That is, as hospitality faces the other as other, she is welcomed without limits and without conditions. (Todd, 2009, p. 111)

This use of *responding* aligns with my above description of the difference between receiving and responding to another. Receiving is the moment prior to a response in which, in Todd's (2009) words, the other's "right to be other" is secured. Abandoning "limits and conditions" is another way to say what I mean by suspending understanding. Abandoning and suspending our need to know, or be "right," grants others a quiet clearing in which they are allowed to just be.

Here is another personal understanding of what it means to receive another, and the possibility and necessity of such an orientation to our work as educators. We have a very ritualized bedtime routine in my home.

After the bath and jammies and teeth are brushed, after we have all read stories together in our big bed, each of my little girls goes into her own room and waits for me or my husband to come in and snuggle and sing a few sleepy songs. I always lie down beside them, try not to fall asleep myself, and rub their little bodies to help them relax. I love the feel of my hand on their backs, and on their tummies, and how my hand can still stretch over their sweet heads. I play with their hair, and try to be present to this, not think about the reading, or writing, or dishwashing, or drying clothes, that wait for me. At some point I remember to slow the pace of my touch, so that it is for them, and not based on me. It comes from me, and though I cannot be under their skin, sensing my own touch from their side, I have to remember to imagine what it feels like to them, and to remain humble about believing in the primacy of my perception:

> The man whose calling it is to influence the being of persons that can be determined, must experience this action of his ... ever anew from the other side. Without the action of his spirit being in any way weakened he must at the same time be over there, on the surface of that other spirit which is being acted upon—and not of some conceptual, contrived spirit, but all the time the wholly concrete spirit of this individual and unique being who is living and confronting him.... The educator who practices the experience of the other side and stands firm in it, experiences two things together, first that he is limited by otherness, and second that he receives grace by being bound to the other. (Buber, 1947, p. 118)

I am not lessened or reduced by orienting myself toward my children in a way that is "them first." I am more fully someone when I let them come into me: "we cannot decline this double challenge if we are to become 'ourselves' in the fullest sense of the world" (Halliwell & Mousley, 2003). To think of myself at all as a parent or as a teacher means believing in this way of being with others, which to me feels like receiving them.

COLONIALISM: A METAPHOR

Applying a metaphor of colonialism to modern public schools illustrates how they are places where students' and teachers' hearts, minds, and bodies are not received. We are colonized because we have been purposed; we are being exploited for our measureable yield. This yield is ultimately adequately trained producers and consumers to enter into and sustain our economic machine (Robinson, 2008; Weaver, 2010). Colonialism prevents any sort of receiving of the other, because its very nature is to identify or construct differences between two groups in order that one dominates and the other is dominated: "the themes of discovery, conquest, possession, and dominion are about ways of knowing the world, of bringing it to order, of surveying, mapping, and classifying it in an endless theorizing of identity and difference" (Willinsky, 1998, p. 85). Historically, as Western imperialism spread, education-in-the-name-of-colonization looked like

> fostering a science of geography of race; renaming a good part of the world in homage to its adventurers' homesick sense of place; and imposing languages and literatures on the colonized in an effort to teach them why they were subservient to a born-to-rule civilization. (Willinsky, 1998, p. 4)

This naming and renaming of the world canceled other ways of knowing, and "is about the power to place-name against those who previously named it and have lived on it for centuries" (Willinsky, 1998, p. 36). And this is how a metaphor of colonization can be applied to our public schools. In our institutions we forget that students come to school as those who best know and have already named themselves and their worlds. They are experts of their lives. If schools were receiving places, then their expertise would be honored and built upon, instead of replaced or ignored, instead of appropriated and misused in the name of higher test scores or economic growth (Weaver, 2010).

HOW RECEPTIVE PRAXIS HELPS US BE RESPONSIVE

Earlier I mentioned the frustrating possibility that a powerful paradigm such as culturally responsive pedagogy might, as it becomes institutionalized, find itself divided up into measureable or observable bits that can then be put upon teachers and students, hindering both from being present in the relationships they share. Because receptive praxis is grounded in philosophy and curriculum theory that resists the "techno-scientific" model (Jardine, 1992) which permits this sort of putting upon, I am enthusiastic about its potential for extending a paradigm such as culturally responsive pedagogy. This extension is both into the future, as culturally responsive pedagogy is strengthened against urges to define it and assess it, and also into deeper relationships shared between teachers and learners.

I find it interesting to ask, "What is it that I am responding to?" when thinking about making my teaching and the content responsive in the ways that Gay (2000) and others suggest. I ask the question as a gentle critique of this scholarship. The literature often says to both attend to characteristics of common difference between mainstream and other cultures and be careful not to essentialize. This dualism is well illustrated in the following two thoughts taken from the same article. First: "teachers must be able to construct pedagogical practices that have relevance and meaning to students' social and cultural realities" (Howard, 2003, p. 195). Second: "while there may be central tendencies shown within groups, teachers should develop individual profiles of students based on students' own thoughts and behaviors" (Howard, 2003, p. 201). These are of course two necessary ways for teachers to be with students, but it has been my experience that the literature describes the "students' social and cultural realities" to which I should respond as "central tendencies" that I am to avoid. This has been one path to the idea of "receiving." In advance of being able to respond to each of my students' "own thoughts and behaviors," I have to know what those are. I have to be with their thoughts and behaviors without in the same moment judging them as being "right" or "wrong" or "appropriate" or "annoying." A praxis that receives students is this first moment, a moment prior to our proceeding with a response to what we have perceived. It is a way to reclaim the possibility of responding to students and not students-as-they-are-labeled.

CONCLUSION

A praxis which guides us to receive students precisely as they are without judgment for who they should be creates an opening for them to come into. In this opening there is light: "The other is not an object that must be interpreted and illumined by my alien light. He shines forth with his own light, and speaks for himself " (Wild, 1961, p. 14). Students shining forth with their own light seems like infinite potential for them to be transformed by learning experiences that are newly available in the open space. Buber (1947) contributes that for teachers who are present to each child's uniqueness, "in the manifold variety of the children the variety of creation is placed before him" (p. 112). The "variety of creation!" This is not a plan for anyone's specific potential. It is just the potential that belongs to each of us, granted to each of us simply because we are here.

It is my view that a receptive praxis resists the kind of definition or explanation that would facilitate its evaluation. This is in light of the idea that responsive pedagogy might be becoming institutionalized by our wanting to evaluate it, and this may be leading to a surface-level presence that is not the same, not as powerful, as what might exist invisibly between teachers and learners. Receptive praxis is an orientation to students. To conclude with any suggestions for future definition or evaluation would feel like hypocrisy, going back against my complaint about what happens when we pull out artifacts as proof of our genius. I do think that teachers can embody this idea of learning to quiet ourselves when our students present themselves to us. We can begin to hear ourselves describe students as labels: underprivileged, at-risk, Autistic, disruptive, gifted, etc. We can hear these sounds and then choose to free students from them, even if only for a moment, so that our students' automatic natures can be okay and welcome in our presence. This possibility is well-said by Maxine Greene (2001): "I believe that opening windows and doors for persons, releasing them to use their imaginations and their minds and their perceptual capacities, may save lives as well as change them" (p. 47). Saving lives, building lives, opening students to their own possibilities, should be the business of schooling. While this is in many places not the case currently, it is possible to reimagine the relationship between teachers and students into one that creates this kind of opening.

REFERENCES

Block, A. A. (2009). *Ethics and teaching: A religious perspective on revitalizing education.* New York, NY: Palgrave Macmillan.

Bourdier, J. P. (Producer), & Mihn-ha, T. T. (Director). (1983). *Re-assemblage: From the firelight to the screen* [Motion picture]. United States: Women Make Movies.

Buber, M. (1947). *Between man and man.* New York, NY: Routledge.

Buber, M. (1970). *I and thou.* New York, NY: Charles Scribner's Sons.

Caputo, J. D. (1997). *Deconstruction in a nutshell: A conversation with Jacques Derrida.* New York, NY: Fordham University Press.

Deutscher, P. (2005). *How to read Derrida.* New York, NY: W. W. Norton & Company.

Dimitriadis, G., & McCarthy, C. (2001). *Reading & teaching the postcolonial.* New York, NY: Teachers College Press.

Erickson, F., Bagrodia, R., Cook-Sather, A., Espinoza, M., Jurow, S., Shultz, J. J., & Spencer, J. (2008). Students' experience of school curriculum: The everyday circumstances of granting and withholding assent to learn. In F. M. Connelly, M. F. He, & J. Phillion (Eds.), *The SAGE handbook of curriculum and instruction* (pp. 198-218). Thousand Oaks, CA: SAGE.

Freire, P. (1993). *Pedagogy of the oppressed.* New York, NY: Continuum.

Gay, G. (2000). *Culturally responsive teaching.* New York, NY: Teachers College Press.

Georgia Department of Education. (2008). CLASS Keys: Classroom Analysis of State Standards: Georgia Teacher Evaluation System.

Gould, S. J. (1996). *The mismeasure of man.* New York, NY: W. W. Norton & Company.

Greene, M. (2001). *Variations on a blue guitar: The Lincoln Center Institute lectures on aesthetic education.* New York: Teachers College Press.

Halliwell, M., & Mousley, A. (2003). *Critical humanisms: Humanist/Anti-humanist dialogues.* Edinburgh, GB: Edinburgh University Press.

Howard, T. C. (2003). Culturally relevant pedagogy: Ingredients for critical teacher reflection. *Theory into Practice, 42*(3), 195-202.

Imperial, B. (Producer), & Taylor, A. (Director). (2008). *Examined life* [Motion picture]. Canada: Sphinx Productions.

Jardine, D. W. (1992). Reflections on education, hermeneutics, and ambiguity: Hermeneutics as a restoring of life to its original difficulty. In W. F. Pinar & W. M. Reynolds (Eds.), *Understanding curriculum as phenomenological and deconstructed text* (pp. 116-127). New York, NY: Teachers College Press.

Miller, J. H. (2001). *Others*. Princeton, NJ: Princeton University Press.

Robinson, K. (2008). RSA animate: Changing education paradigms. Retrieved from http://www.youtube.com/watch?v=zDZFcDGpL4U

Rymes, B. (2009). *Classroom discourse analysis: A tool for critical reflection*. Cresskill, NJ: Hampton Press.

Todd, S. (2009). *Toward an imperfect education: Facing humanity, rethinking cosmopolitanism*. Boulder, CO: Paradigm.

Weaver, J. A. (2010). *Educating the posthuman: Biosciences, fiction, and curriculum studies*. Rotterdam, The Netherlands: Sense.

Wild, J. (1969). Introduction. In E. Levinas (Au.), *Totality and Infinity: An essay on exteriority* (pp. 11-20). Pittsburgh, PA: Duquesne University Press.

Willinsky, J. (1998). *Learning to divide the world: Education at empire's end*. Minneapolis, MN: University of Minnesota Press.

CHAPTER 14

AGENCY AND CHOICE IN TWO SECOND-GRADE CLASSROOMS

Katrina F. Cook
The Ohio State University

In re/turning to the classroom with an eye toward social justice and a commitment to praxis, the concepts of *agency* and choice naturally arise. A classroom that values teacher and student agency is one that includes the voices of all classroom participants, respects their backgrounds and experiences, and encourages them to make changes that will affect their environment. Many schools and classrooms in today's society, however, are not designed for social change, as students and teachers are often placed in adversarial relationships (R. Smith, 2009). District leaders expect teachers to "control" their students and pass on a specific set of knowledge; both student and teacher freedoms are encroached upon. In contrast, when teachers and students respect each other as individuals with the rights to make their own choices, classroom participants have control of their teaching and learning.

A person with a strong sense of personal agency is one who feels she has the right and the opportunity to take action to benefit her own life (Alexander, 2005). When teachers feel a strong sense of agency, they are able to structure their classroom and make choices in such a way as to benefit their own professional goals and aid their students' development. Students who

Excursions and Recursions Through Power, Privilege, and Praxis
pp. 191–207

feel a strong sense of personal agency have the freedom to make choices in classroom events that will further their interests and help them feel a sense of belonging as classroom participants (R. Brown, 2009).

In the following chapter, I discuss opportunities for and constraints to teachers and students exercising their own agency. I address how the two teachers, Donna and Susan,[1] are not only in a position to be agents of themselves but also agents of change for others (Moore, 2008). Drawing on my research into teacher and student agency in two second-grade classrooms, I address how agency was enacted in the classrooms, both in teacher and student actions and in the curriculum.

I begin by presenting the theoretical assumptions that guided my research and a description of the participants and research methods. Following that, I describe Donna and Susan's sense of personal agency in the classroom and how they both encouraged or discouraged student agency. The final sections address students' personal sense of agency and whether or not they saw themselves as agents of others. Finally, I conclude with a discussion of what groups are hindering agency in students' and teachers' lives and how teachers in particular can encourage agency in their classrooms.

THEORETICAL ASSUMPTIONS

New Literacy Studies

I began this study with certain theoretical assumptions and based my research on a new literacy studies framework, with an additional focus on the concept of hidden curriculum. From a new literacy studies (NLS) perspective, literacy is a culturally defined construct and is situated within contexts (Purcell-Gates, Jacobson, & Degener, 2004). Instead of treating literacy as a neutral, universal concept, I focused on understanding classroom literacy practices, which were the cultural ways of using reading and writing within the classroom and were based on the values and beliefs held by those engaged in reading and writing (Street, 1995). Although literacy practices are based on participant beliefs, these values are not always equal, particularly in classrooms, where various power structures are at play. Some participants' values are not always included or considered equally, and students frequently end up at the bottom of the hierarchy (Purcell-Gates et. al, 2004).

Hidden Curriculum

Similar to the NLS framework is the theory of the hidden curriculum, which is based on the assumption that texts and curricular structures are not neutral. Instead, texts and structures represent values and beliefs that district leaders and curriculum writers expect classroom participants to accept and internalize (Apple, 2004). The hidden curriculum is in contrast to the overt intentions of schooling and the curriculum, and may or may not be deliberate. Although the express purpose of the curriculum assigned from participants Donna and Susan was to help students become better readers and writers, the curriculum contained other expectations as well, including messages of obedience to authority and conformity to specific lifestyles. When these messages are included in the curriculum, they sometimes counteract any agency teachers and students might feel and discourage classroom participants from developing as independent thinkers.

Agency

Agency has been defined in various ways; at its most basic, it is the ability to act decisively and deliberately to achieve one's own desires. When teachers have a strong enough sense of personal agency, they recognize they have the right to structure their classrooms according to their own personal teaching styles and preferences (Gutstein, 2007). When they exercise their personal agency, they are making choices that will improve their own lives and help them reach their goals. When classroom participants have a sense of agency, they are aware that their own actions affect the environment around them, and they have the ability to use available resources to meet their needs (Johnston, 2004; Moore, 2008). It is a deliberate choice made with the expectation that one will effect change.

Moore (2008) represents agency as "the conscious role we choose to play in helping people bring about social change" (p. 591). This definition neglects a significant aspect of agency development. Rather than present social change as a part of the basic definition of agency, other researchers represent agency as the sense of having the ability to use available resources to achieve one's own desires (Johnston, 2004). It is most useful to discuss agency as two distinct concepts: agents of self and agents of change. When one is acting as an agent of self, the focus is inward, on personal benefit and advancement. An agent of change is focused outward, on helping others develop and advance, even helping them develop their own sense of agency. This focus can either be on encouraging change in individuals or society.

Learning environments are fundamentally social, so when teachers or students make choices, the results of their choices affect those around them. Rather than focus on individuals' isolated actions, researchers recognize that people's actions influence others and agency research must reflect that (Johnston, 2004). Particularly in classrooms, where teachers' actions are designed to affect change in their students, both students and teachers' actions have significant influence on other classroom participants. These choices may either hinder or encourage others' personal sense of agency. As such, classroom members may not merely act as agents of themselves, but also as agents of others.

Often, becoming an agent of change occurs naturally as people become agents of themselves. When people develop their own sense of agency and change their circumstances, they act to deliberately influence their surroundings. Ahearn (2004) observed that as women in Nepal exerted their agency in developing literacy practices, they used the texts they created to change the cultural practices of their society.

Constraints on Agency

Agency is not limitless, especially in schools, and some classroom practices are often dictated by district and curriculum expectations. Researchers have found that teachers frequently feel constrained by administrative expectations and the structure of the curriculum (Fowler, 2008; Gutstein, 2007; Mills, 2007). Student agency is often limited by dominant power structures that come from not only district policies but also teachers and how teachers use curricular texts (Gutstein, 2007; Mills, 2007). Their perspectives and desires are devalued in favor of those held by people in positions of power (R. Smith, 2009).

Teachers' sense of agency has sometimes been described as "surface autonomy"—although they have some freedom and limited sense of agency, much of the structures and texts of their classrooms are controlled by outside forces (Gutstein, 2007; Hamilton, 2009). Teachers are often limited by budgets, available curricular resources, and required high-stakes testing (Gutstein, 2007; Mills, 2007). When they are expected to follow a set curriculum and have limited resources available to them, it can be difficult for them to use those resources to exercise change.

METHODS

Participants

This study took place in two second-grade classrooms in the same school in the middle of a medium-sized Midwestern city. The students at Clayton Elementary mostly came from working-class homes, although some families struggled with poverty and homelessness. Violence and drugs were commonplace in some students' homes and unheard of in others. Eighty-two percent of Clayton's 305 students qualified for free or reduced lunch. Being almost 50% White and 50% Black, all of Clayton's students spoke English as their primary language.

Teachers. Donna had been teaching for over 30 years when I entered her classroom. Having started out as a special education teacher at a time when there was no special education curriculum, Donna had learned the importance of finding her own classroom resources and often used her own resources in the classroom.

Donna preferred to see herself as a "not done product," always learning, so she tried to express to her students that she was not necessarily the absolute authority in the classroom and in fact enjoyed learning new things from her students. Donna saw learning and reading as inherently social and frequently encouraged students to help one another. Over three decades, Donna has seen a lot of change go through the school system, and experienced some curricula that greatly constrained teachers and others that gave a lot of freedom. At the time of my research, Donna saw herself as a professional trying to teach her students and give them what they needed but constrained by testing requirements and students' disadvantaged backgrounds.

Susan had been teaching for 13 years, initially in middle school before she moved to teach first and second grade. As she came from an affluent area of the city, her students' lives were something of a surprise to her and she struggled at times to know how to best meet their needs. She described her childhood as "apparently spoiled" because "I just thought life was great. Everybody has a wonderful family, everybody wants to go to school, everybody's going to college."

Susan's teacher education program focused mostly on teaching phonics and following the assigned teacher's manual. Small group instruction was encouraged by her professors, "but I remember it was a lot of emphasis on just, whatever our district is doing, that's what you have to try." Despite wanting to help every student become successful, Susan often felt that she lacked the resources and had to sacrifice her philosophy of teaching to every student's needs along with certain curricular expectations because of time constraints and students' achievement levels. Her first experiences teaching were "shocking" because she felt unprepared for dealing with the experiences her students had and how different they were from her own. Susan struggled with knowing how to address the poverty and hunger some of her students experienced and felt her best choice was to "try to treat 'em like normal children and teach 'em what I think they should know."

Students. Most of the year, Donna and Susan have between 20 and 22 students in their classrooms. In order to gain a clearer understanding of students' perspectives, I selected four focal students from each class, two

White, two Black, including two boys and two girls. I tried to get a mix of achievement levels as well. I selected these students after I had observed them in the classroom for three months. A few were chosen because I had developed a rapport with them; others were chosen because they were the only students available, due to some parents not signing consent forms.

In focusing my interviews and much of my attention on these students, I was able to develop a picture of the variability of students' lives and perspectives. Some of them came from financially stable homes, while a few had to worry about homelessness. For some, their parents were able to be heavily involved in school activities, but other students' parents were either unwilling or unable to become involved in classroom activities. During one interview, I asked each focal student to look through their story anthology, which was the collection of stories the reading curriculum focused on, using one main story a week. Each student was asked which story they thought was most like them, but few of them felt connected to the characters or their home lives.

Research Procedures

The data presented in this article arose from a larger case study, in which I examined the cultural underpinnings of the reading and writing instructional time in two second-grade classrooms. Based on an ethnographic perspective, my goal was not to evaluate classroom practices, but rather to understand them (Green, Dixon, & Zaharlick, 2003), particularly the values embedded within second-grade literacy instruction and curriculum and involved observation, interviews and document collection. Researching with an ethnographic perspective is about presenting an understanding of reality from the participants' perspectives (Hammersley & Atkinson, 2006; Lillis, 2008). I took detailed field notes of my direct observations of the reading and writing block in both classrooms. Through the course of six months, I observed both classrooms for two days a week, sometimes staying in the background and other times taking part as an unofficial aide or teaching a brief lesson. Donna and Susan, the classroom teachers, welcomed me into their rooms and encouraged me to help and talk with the students as needed. They also aided me in selecting four focal students for each class, chosen to represent the racial and academic make up of both classes.

DATA ANALYSIS

The process of data collection and analysis was a recursive one, in which analysis began almost as soon as data collection (Purcell-Gates et al., 2004). Analysis of my research involved identifying literacy events and common patterns and themes within these events. A significant aspect of a new literacy studies theoretical framework is the concept that the use of text and social interaction are intertwined in identifiable literacy events. My use of the literacy event as a unit of analysis was based on the notion that literacy and the social world it is in are coconstructed through interpersonal interaction (Bruna, 2007; Purcell-Gates et al., 2004). As people create and use texts, they are drawing on cultural rules for the texts. The texts do not exist by themselves, but rather are part of the situation.

My primary data sources were copies of the curriculum texts, handwritten field notes, and student and teacher interviews. Data analysis began with an analysis of the curriculum materials, in which I looked for common patterns in how teachers and students were to behave and common themes in stories and other classroom texts. I used the concept of literacy events, defined as specific social interactions involving texts, to understand what values were present in the district-imposed curriculum, and looked for patterns of behavior and text (Brandt & Clinton, 2002). They were not actual events that I had observed but rather those being described as potential literacy events.

I immediately began analyzing and looking for patterns, trying to discover the cultural meaning behind what I had observed, so it could further inform my observations and questions (Purcell-Gates et al., 2004). As I began analysis, I frequently reviewed my field notes and coding for the next day's observations. As I observed, I kept a mental list of emerging codes, and paid careful attention to any confirming and disconfirming occasions that expanded my understanding. This process of analysis led to continual coding and recoding of field notes, sifting through and grouping interactions in order to find common themes and patterns.

Theme #1: Teacher Agency

Teachers as Agents of Self.   Studies of agency that are focused on students tend to portray teachers as powerful participants reinforcing dominant culture (e.g., Fowler, 2008). Despite the fact that teachers are often portrayed as those in power, they do not always feel empowered to make their own decisions. They may feel a constrained sense of agency or no agency at all because of the many power structures controlling classroom practices (Mills, 2007; Moore, 2008). Agency is not solely freedom or power; teachers frequently have some freedoms in their classrooms, but whether these freedoms allow teachers to enact significant changes in their classrooms is questionable. Both Donna and Susan had some freedom in their classrooms, but the official freedoms were often superficial and sometimes ambiguous. According to Donna, whether or not they had the freedom to alter the curriculum "depends on who you ask" and Susan could only say she "thought" they were allowed to make changes. The distinction between freedom and agency came in the question of whether or not teachers recognized the freedoms and power they had and believed they had the right to act on those freedoms.

When teachers feel a sense of personal agency, they feel empowered to make choices and use resources that will benefit their teaching and professional development. Donna had been teaching for several years and had developed a strong sense of agency through her experiences. She frequently made changes to texts, activities and class structure according to her own teaching and learning preferences and what she believed her students would need and prefer. District policy was that teachers were occasionally allowed to make changes, but there were still some district leaders who insisted teachers closely follow both content and lessons in the curriculum. Donna understood that if teachers wanted to make changes, they had to take the initiative and ask, or, as Donna occasionally did, make changes without asking permission. Susan, on the other hand, occasionally made changes to curricular activities but did so hesitantly and rarely altered the content or class structure. She believed the curriculum and district held authority over her, and felt a limited sense of power in her teaching.

Despite the fact that both teachers in my study were required to follow the same curriculum and were given the same resources, they had differing levels of agency and employed different levels of change in their classrooms. Susan had been taught to teach according to whatever curriculum was provided and admitted she did not know what else to do to. The few occasions she did add lessons and activities to the curriculum, she did so hesitantly. On one occasion, students had to write a report on an animal they chose, and Susan, borrowing an idea from her daughter's teacher, decided to have them structure the reports onto lift-up flaps, rather than traditional essay-style. This was a detailed process and took several days, most of which were somewhat chaotic. Some students struggled to understand what they were to do, in part because it was so unfamiliar in comparison to the typical work Susan assigned. Midway through the project, Susan turned to me and said, "I don't know how other teachers do stuff like this all the time." She did not feel prepared to structure her class to facilitate projects or detailed, personal student work.

Donna, on the other hand, had several lessons and activities in her repertoire she had collected over the years. While admitting she probably changed the curriculum more than she was supposed to, she did so because they were the activities she preferred that allowed her to structure her class the way she wanted. While most of the time she followed the curriculum content, during holidays she included several activities, including having students use candy conversation hearts as parts of sentences during Valentine's Day. In doing this, Donna demonstrated she had a measure of control over her classroom.

Teachers as Agents of Others.   When teachers feel empowered to exercise agency for themselves, this agency can translate into them becoming agents of change for others to benefit their students and better enable them to learn and grow (MacCleod, 2004). Unfortunately, the unequal power relationships students and teachers are in can make it difficult for teachers to create spaces that encourage students to challenge existing power structures and exercise their own agency (Gutstein, 2007). Encouraging students to recognize and exercise their own agency can be difficult because teachers are responsible for maintaining order in classrooms and thus are viewed by students as adversaries (Gutstein, 2007). It is often expected that they will "control" their students rather than empower them. This adversarial relationship does not only limit students' freedoms, but also teachers' freedoms, as they feel they do not have the opportunity or ability to create more democratic classrooms. Susan often felt this way, as she preferred quiet and order over the busyness and chaos that sometimes ensued with more boisterous projects. As such, her classroom was very teacher centered and students were given few choices regarding their work.

Another hindrance to teachers encouraging student agency was that the teachers, particularly Susan, often saw students as passive recipients of instruction and teachers' actions (Fowler, 2008). In treating children this way, Susan denied the very existence of student agency and did not see students as active meaning-makers in the classroom community. To recognize students as participants and full-fledge citizens in the classroom, teachers first need to understand children's cultural values and where they are coming from (MacCleod, 2004). Susan had become very overwhelmed with the backgrounds and home lives of her students and confessed to me that she only wanted to teach the subject matter. As Susan was already set up as the sole power broker in her classroom, this denied students the opportunities to bring their home lives and cultures into the classroom. Several scholars have identified teachers' successful attempts at helping students feel more empowered in the classroom by changing curriculum structures, inviting community members into the classrooms, and altering social interactions (Gutstein, 2007; MacCleod, 2004; Moore, 2008).

My observations provided a distinct contrast between the two teachers, as Donna, who felt some personal agency, worked to encourage her students to become agents of themselves, while Susan, who had a limited sense of personal agency, did not believe her students had many choices.

In fact, in response to an interview question regarding what choices students had in the classroom, she stated plainly, "They don't really have any choices; they're here to do the work and learn how to read and write and that's, you know, their job." Of course, this was not entirely true, as students could choose to comply or disobey, do their work or not, pay attention or distract themselves, but the overall message was that Susan was in charge of their learning and the classroom and students' only option was to follow orders.

This message of passive compliance to authority was prevalent in Susan's classroom but was contradicted by Susan's emphasis that students were responsible for their successes or failures. When the midterm grades came out, Susan told her students that many of them would not be happy with their progress and that if they wanted to be ready for third grade, they needed to work harder and learn. The narrative that they were in control of their learning was in direct contrast to how Susan structured her class. Susan gave the impression of her students being in charge of their learning, but instead, they were expected to passively accept whatever work and directions they were given.

While Susan's classroom practices hindered student agency, Donna worked to make power structures visible to her students and even encouraged them to challenge those structures to further their own learning and desires. Both Donna and Susan felt their agency was constrained by district power structures, but Donna made these constraints visible to her students and placed herself with her students as under the thumb of higher authorities. In doing this, she tried to help students see the reason for the expectations placed on them. "A lot of them see it as a drudgery, as a job, as a chore and so we talk sometimes about, you know, why in creation would they make us sit here and read this stupid thing, and we come up with our own brainstorming ideas. So I try to do that as a way to make it more personal to them." In helping her students see the relevance assigned work had in their lives, she was presenting the message that classroom events were directly related to their lives and thereby encouraged her students to recognize how their actions could benefit or hinder their lives.

Donna also subtly encouraged her students to have more active roles in taking control of their learning by challenging power structures and texts. She initially did this by modeling these behaviors. During the morning instructional time, Donna would sit in a chair with the students seated on an area rug in front of her. Due to the scripted and detailed nature of the curriculum, both teachers frequently needed to keep the lesson book on their laps at all times. On occasion, Donna would flip through the lesson book, commenting, "I don't want to do that, it's boring. No, I don't want to do that either." Although Donna had already chosen what lessons she would and would not include in the day's activities, she was giving the impression that she was at that moment rejecting the expectations placed on her. This was a deliberate attempt to send a message to her students that it was possible and permissible to sometimes reject the expectations placed upon them, thereby encouraging them to feel the freedom to control what expectations to accept and reject.

This freedom was carried over in students' work assignments. In both classes there was a strong message that students were under the authority not only of teachers but also of the texts they interacted with, but Donna presented a message that this authority could be challenged, not just by her but also by her students. On one occasion, Donna had assigned a proofreading worksheet in which students were to read a paragraph and identify errors. While going over it as a class, Donna projected an image of the worksheet on the wall with her document camera. The capital "I" confused her students because of its font and students thought it was either a one or a lowercase "l." Donna explained, "That I is a capital letter on a computer. They don't tell you that, but if you want you can put the extra lines in." A few minutes later, students commented on Donna changing something that wasn't an error and she told them, "I'm fixing [the "I"] because you guys don't like it." This change was rather superficial, but it demonstrated to the students that they had the right to make changes to texts. In contrast, Susan would insist on following the answers of the book and making sure students were aware the answers must always match with the stories they had read and not deviate from the assigned texts. Challenging her authority, or those from the curriculum or texts, was not allowed.

In seeing texts as fallible, Donna encouraged her students to take control of their learning and challenge texts from time to time. On occasion, worksheets would have typographical or content errors in them, and students would point it out to Donna. Over time, because of Donna's efforts, students felt the freedom to go further in challenging texts and would present alternate answers than the ones provided. These alternatives always had to be cleared through Donna, so their freedom was still limited, but Donna had set up a classroom climate that encouraged her students to recognize their agency and exercise it in limited ways.

Theme #2: Student Agency

Understanding student agency in classrooms was tricky at times because students were frequently in the position of being under the control of adults in positions of power (R. Smith, 2009). Student agency is often limited and their perspectives devalued by teachers and outside authorities, in part because they are seen as "just children," with limited abilities to make decisions (K. Smith, 2008; R. Smith, 2009). Teachers are sometimes afraid of encouraging students to take control of their learning and make decisions because of the fear that their decisions will be incorrect (Smith, K. 2008). When children are denied the opportunity to become agents of themselves and take actions that will benefit and change their situations, they are denied the opportunity of learning ownership and responsibility for their actions (R. Smith, 2009).

When students do attempt to exert their agency in classrooms, sometimes these attempts are thwarted by teachers due to teachers misinterpreting their actions. Susan's students encountered this a few times. One day, while they were engaged in independent work, the four students in the back row, with their desks touching each other in a line, set up their books and pencil boxes as barriers, isolating each desk. One student turned to me and said, "Look, we got our own office," pretending another book was a computer. Once the students had set these up, they went back to work, having created their own personal spaces, pretending they were working in cubicles in an office building. Susan, upon seeing them a few minutes later, said, "What is with the books? Put 'em in your desk. No one is going to copy you. Everyone's doing a different report." Susan was assuming one meaning and not allowing for the possibility that the students had a different purpose in mind. These students were not simply pretending to be in an office, but were enacting a scenario in which they were adults and in charge of their work. Susan rejected their meaning and in doing so, took away their opportunities for becoming more agentive and actually taking control of their work.

As second graders, the participants in my study were still developing their sense of personal agency and working to understand how to exert it and make changes in their lives. Once students feel a strong sense of agency, they may feel empowered to exert their agency even in situations where they feel it is constrained, and often in any way they can. Fowler's study (2008) demonstrated that when students felt their freedoms were being limited, they would push back in any way they could. When the students in this study had their freedoms taken away, they struggled to find ways to exert their agency, and often in ways teachers considered inappropriate (R. Smith, 2009). Despite the fact that Donna believed she gave her students ample choices in her classroom, none of the focal students in either class felt much freedom. During interviews, I asked each student if they had choices in their class, and with each of the 8 focal students, the answer was an immediate "no." Although they knew they had the choice to comply or disobey, work hard or not, they recognized that these choices were not true agency; instead, they were merely the only options they had for reacting to the power structures around them.

Student Power Versus Being Agents of Change.   Although students did not feel a sense of agency, many of them recognized that they, too, held a certain amount of power over their environment despite not believing they had the freedom or right to control their own lives. They knew they could influence the lives of those around them. Most of the time, this power resulted in how they behaved toward fellow students. They had the freedom to help or hinder their classmates, both in academic and social situations. At times, this caused them some confusion, because they struggled to understand (and the teachers struggled to explain to them) the difference between helping someone understand their work and doing the work for them. Frequently Donna and I would remind students that "telling is not helping," in order to encourage struggling students to learn to do the work on their own, or at least with minimal help.

Students also recognized they had the power to negatively affect their classmates. Although this did not happen often in my observations, there were a few times that students exercised this power. In the instance below, Matthew was looking at a book that was of interest to several students. Lucy, who was somewhat socially awkward, had been asking him to share it, but he refused, choosing instead to share it with Becca.

> Lucy: Matthew, when you're done reading the Pokemon book, can I read it?
> Matthew: I'm reading it.

Matthew sat and held the book up to his face so Lucy couldn't see the pictures.

> Matthew: (to Becca, sitting on his other side) just ask me "can I see the Pokemon book" and you can get it out of my desk.
> Lucy: can I see the Pokemon book?
> Matthew: let me alone!

In denying Lucy access to his book and going so far as to provide another classmate access, Matthew was using his book to exert dominance over Lucy. Similar power struggles happened on occasion in both classrooms, with students choosing to help or refusing to help certain classmates. These decisions did not always relate to personal disputes, but rather were a means of exerting power in the one way they knew how, against the only people they could.

Theme #3: Representations of Agency in the Curriculum

The initial phase of my study included an analysis of Harcourt's *Story-Town* curriculum, a nationally recognized commercial literacy program that included teacher lesson books, student textbooks, worksheets, leveled readers, and practice workbooks. Content dealt with comprehension strategies, phonics, spelling, vocabulary, listening skills and writing. Teachers were provided with materials and detailed descriptions of lessons that were partially scripted, including what to say, what questions to ask and what students' answers should be.

The messages and structure of the curriculum were not designed to encourage student or teacher agency. Events were scripted with specific words teachers were to say and responses students were to give. The rigid nature of the lessons and tightly controlled schedule in the curriculum as a whole left Donna and Susan feeling as though they had few choices and as if their teaching skills were undervalued. Teachers were expected to follow the same schedule each day, addressing the same content and activities and asking students the same questions in lessons. This expectation of strict conformity is the antithesis of encouraging teacher agency and the curriculum structure and texts went even further in discouraging student agency.

Most lessons in the curriculum were designed to be whole-group, with all students participating in the activities. There were some allowances made for placing students in supplementary ability groups, but in some ways this served only to further pigeonhole the children. Students placed in the "advanced" group were expected to participate in the same lesson, despite the fact that some of the students in Donna and Susan's classes were slightly higher than grade level, whereas others were two grade levels higher. Similarly, students who were placed in the "below-level" group were all given the same work. Some found this even more of a struggle, because those activities were still too difficult for them. According to Donna:

> They have the three levels supposedly but they're not low enough and they're not high enough. It hits the middle kids real good. It hits the low of the middle and it hits the high of the middle. It doesn't hit the truly high kids and it doesn't hit the truly low kids. The low kids cannot read the low books. They're not low enough.

IMPLICATIONS

Encouraging Student Agency

When people feel a limited sense of agency and do not feel empowered to act on their own accord, they interpret successes and failures as the effects of outside forces (Johnston, 2004). Children whose agency has been limited and discouraged may develop a passive interpretation of events and will not believe their actions affect the world around them. When they succeed, they will interpret their success as "this is good because the teacher helped me" (Johnston, 2004, p. 30).

As my research revealed, teachers are not powerless but rather wield a great deal of influence in the classroom and they have the choice to use that influence to either encourage or discourage student agency (Gutstein, 2007). Susan tightly controlled classroom structure, making sure all students participated in literacy events in the same way and determining what meaning was acceptable and what was not. Donna's classroom literacy events were less rigid, and she demonstrated to her students that authority and texts could be challenged at times. Although at this time, her students did not feel a personal sense of agency, had Donna continued to encourage these challenges and provided students with more choices, there is some hope they would eventually develop agency.

The development of student agency cannot happen by accident. It must be encouraged and nurtured by teachers and they must encounter messages of encouragement in classroom texts and structures (R. Brown, 2009). If teachers want to create a democratic classroom, they need to create a space where children's beliefs and backgrounds are respected, working to understand those beliefs and how to incorporate them into the classroom. Writing is a useful tool for encouraging students to feel agency by allowing them to make their voices heard. Donna attempted to do this at times by having students keep personal writer's workshop folders where they could write anything they wanted, but there was little focus on these and they were treated more as extra work for students to do once the "real" work was finished.

Encouraging Teacher Agency

Before they can help students feel a sense of agency, teachers need to first recognize their own agency and the power they hold in their classrooms. According to Donna, there was a significant amount of contradiction among district administrators regarding their freedoms in the classroom. "It depends who you ask" to know whether or not they were required to follow the curriculum exactly. This sentiment led the teachers to understand that their freedoms were controlled by outside forces and gave the feeling that agency was not their own—instead, it had to be granted to them from above. Having seen many changes in education during her 30 years of teaching, Donna recognized and sometimes pushed back against these forces, occasionally altering classroom structure, literacy events and content. Susan, on the other hand, did not feel confident to make choices or even question the curriculum or district leaders.

Curriculum developers and district leaders need to consider how classroom curricula are structured and give teachers the freedom to change or challenge the materials they are given. Respecting teachers enough to allow them to have this control in their classrooms can lead to increased teacher agency. When teachers do feel a sense of agency, they recognize they have the choice to reinforce, challenge or ignore the messages in the curriculum, which can in turn lead to children who learn they too have the right and power to accept or reject the narrative they are being taught. The end result is classroom participants who all recognize they have the right and freedom to effect change in their lives and those of others.

NOTE

1.   Names of the school and all participants have been changed.

REFERENCES

Alexander, H. (2005). Human agency and the curriculum. *Theory and Pedagogy, 3*(3), 343-369.

Apple, M. W. (2004). *Ideology and curriculum*. New York, NY: Routledge.

Brandt, D., & Clinton, K. (2002). Limits of the local: Expanding perspectives on literacy as a social practice. *Journal of Literacy Research, 34*(3), 337-356.

Brown, P. U. (2005). The shadow curriculum. *Yearbook of the National Society for the Study of Education, 104*(1), 119-139.

Brown, R. (2009). Teaching for social justice: Exploring the development of student agency through participation in the literacy practices of a mathematics classroom. *Journal of Mathematics Teacher Education, 12*, 171-185.

Bruna, K. R. (2007). Traveling tags: The informal literacies of Mexican newcomers in and out of the classroom. *Linguistics and Education, 18*, 232-257.

Fowler, Z. (2008). Negotiating the textuality of further education: Issues of agency and participation. *Oxford Review of Education, 34*(4), 445-441.

Green, J. L., Dixon, C. N., & Zaharlick, A. (2003). Ethnography as a logic of inquiry. In J. Flood, J. M. Jensen, D. Lapp, & J. R. Squire (Eds.), *Handbook of research on teaching the English language arts* (pp. 201- 224). Mahwah, NJ: Erlbaum.

Gutstein, E. (2007). And that's just how it starts: Teaching mathematics and developing student agency. *Teachers College Record, 109*(2), 420-448.

Hamilton, M. (2009). Putting words in their mouths: The alignment of identities with system goals through the use of individual learning plans. *British Educational Research Journal, 35*(2), 221-242.

Hammersley, M., & Atkinson, P. (2007). *Ethnography: Principles in practice*. New York, NY: Routledge.

Johnston, P. H. (2004). *Choice words*. Portland, ME: Stenhouse.

Lillis, T. (2008). Ethnography as method, methodology and "deep theorizing." *Written Communication, 25*(3), 353-388.

MacCleod, F. (2004). Literacy identity and agency: Linking classrooms to communities. *Early Child Development and Care, 174*(3), 243-252.

Mills, K. A. (2007). Access to multiliteracies: A critical ethnography. *Ethnography and Education, 2*(3), 305-325.

Moore, F. M. (2008). Agency, identity, and social justice education: Preservice teachers' thoughts on becoming agents of change in urban elementary science classrooms. *Research in Science Education, 38*, 589-610.

Purcell-Gates, V., Jacobson, E., & Degener, S. (2004). *Print literacy development : Uniting cognitive and social practice theories*. Cambridge, MS: Harvard University Press.

Smith, K. (2008). Becoming an "honors student": The interplay of literacies and identities in a high-track class. *Journal of Curriculum Studies, 40*(4), 481-507.

Smith, R. (2009). Childhood, agency and youth justice. *Children & Society, 23*, 252-264.

StoryTown, Grade 2. (2007). Harcourt School Publishers. Orlando, FL: Houghton Mifflin Harcourt.

Street, B. V. (1995). *Social literacies*. New York, NY: Longman.

ABOUT THE EDITORS

Brandon Sams recently received his PhD in education from UNC-Chapel Hill and works as an assistant professor of English education at Auburn University. His research interests include reading and writing pedagogy, curriculum studies, creativity and arts-based research. His publications have appeared in *Curriculum Inquiry* and *Educational Studies*. In 2010, he was awarded the James T. Sears Award by the Curriculum and Pedagogy Group for his essay, "Reading, Writing, Performing with *Fugitive Pieces*." He is also in his fourth year as associate editor for *The High School Journal*, a UNC Press publication. He enjoys working closely with authors and reviewers on scholarship influenced by a variety of theoretical and critical traditions, yet firmly grounded in schools and curriculum.

Jennifer Job is a PhD candidate at the University of North Carolina. Her dissertation, under the direction of Lynda Stone, addresses the changing discourses of curriculum post-9/11 and how they affect policy of education. Her interests include international comparative analysis of curriculum, curriculum studies, and politics of curriculum. Her writing has appeared in *Educational Foundations*, *Gifted Child Today*, and *National Teacher Education Journal*. This is her second year as managing editor of *The High School Journal*. Jennifer is currently working to bring the textbook *Educating Exceptional Children* to the Internet, connecting the text of the book to online teaching resources. Recently, Jennifer was inducted into the Frank Porter Graham Honor Society for outstanding service to the academic community.

James C. Jupp works as an assistant professor of curriculum at Georgia Southern University and previously worked at Arkansas State University as an assistant professor of educational foundations. He worked in rural and inner-city Title I settings for 18 years before accepting a position training teachers and administrators at the university level. A veteran of teaching children of color in rural and inner-city Title I schools, one line of his research focuses on White teachers' understandings of race, diversity, and difference pedagogy. Drawing on his experiences as a teacher of Mexican immigrant, Mexican-American, and Latino students, and as administrator in Title I schools, he is the author of "Culturally Relevant Pedagogy: One Teacher's Journey Through Theory and Practice," a piece which adds to discussions on White teachers that has been anthologized several times. He has published more than 20 scholarly articles in a variety of journals including the *International Journal of Qualitative Research in Education*, *Curriculum Inquiry*, *Urban Education*, the *Journal of the American Association for the Advancement of Curriculum Studies*, the *Journal of Curriculum and Pedagogy*, the *English Journal*, and *Multicultural Review*. He is currently working on a book designed to capacitate preservice and professional teachers entitled *Becoming Teachers of Diverse Students: Professional Identifications of Committed White Male Teachers* that will be published by Sense Publishers in 2013.

ABOUT THE CONTRIBUTORS

Polly Attwood is a teacher educator and former high school teacher. Her commitment to antiracist, critical multicultural teacher preparation has been, and continues to be, shaped by the writings, conferences, and activism of multiracial feminists and by her Quaker practice and mentors. She is also a bicycle commuter and finds joy and rejuvenation walking in the New England woods with her partner and her dog.

Sue Bartow is a former kindergarten through eighth-grade science, health, wood shop, physical education teacher, and school administrator. She is currently a teaching assistant and PhD candidate in the PhD program in curriculum at Miami University in Oxford, Ohio. Her research interests are in alternative, democratic, progressive education; a critical view of school and the profession of teaching; and in the risks and opportunities of social media in formal and informal education. Her greatest joys have been raising four children, teaching and learning with young people, running, and traveling.

Bridget A. Bunten is an assistant professor of education at Washington College in Chestertown, Maryland. Within the education department, she is the coordinator of the elementary education program. She currently teaches language and literacy methods courses for preservice teachers and supervises interns in various public elementary schools. As a former bilingual and ESL educator in Massachusetts, she worked with elementary-aged students from all over the world and facilitated professional development seminars for K-12 public school teachers on language acquisition, cultural sensitivity, and second language literacy. Bridget's research interests include addressing the needs of English language learners within teacher education, understanding the language and literacy development of English language learners, and interpreting language policy and its impact on students, teachers, schools, and communities.

Katrina Cook recently graduated with her PhD in literacy from Ohio State University. Before entering graduate school, she spent 2 years teaching English in China. Her dissertation research focused on the literacy practices of two second-grade classrooms, with a focus on curriculum and cultural values.

Monique Cherry-McDaniel is a doctoral candidate in the Educational Leadership Department at Miami University and a language arts teacher at Miamisburg High School in Ohio. Her scholarly interests include interrogating the literature canon and creating a literature-based countercurriculum for African American women and girls.

Raygine C. DiAquoi is a fifth year doctoral student in culture, communities, and education at the Harvard Graduate School of Education. Her research interests include antiracist education and the applicability of anticolonial theory in schools. She has conducted research on the pedagogy of African American teachers in Afrocentric schools and on the experiences of students of color in elite educational settings. Her work on students of color at an elite boarding school has been published in the book *Educating Elites: Class Privilege and Educational Advantage* (Rowman & Littlefield, 2010). She is also coeditor of the book *Education for a Multicultural Society* (Harvard Educational Review, 2011). She holds an EdM in education from Harvard University and a BA in sociology from Columbia University.

Miryam Espinosa-Dulanto's writing departs from identifying herself as a woman of color, a Mestiza from the Borderlands, and a nonmainstream person in the United States. From that perspective, she explores the construction and transmission of knowledge. She has taught in urban and rural settings, worked in teacher professional development, and had poetry readings in Asia, Europe, Latin America, and the United States.

Chris Loeffler is currently in his seventh year as a third grade teacher at Wilmington Friends School in Wilmington, Delaware. He is also pursuing a master's degree in curriculum studies at Arcadia University.

Jennifer L. Milam is an assistant professor in early childhood/elementary curriculum at The University of Akron. Her primary areas of interest include curriculum and cultural studies, feminist theory, and qualitative research methodologies. She is particularly focused on the intersections of teacher education, autobiography, and critical curriculum studies.

Zahra Murad is a doctoral candidate in curriculum studies at the University of Toronto. She is interested in antiracist curriculum, Indigenous knowledges in education, decolonizing education, and critical race theory. She hates writing bios, but loves her cat.

Cole Reilly is an assistant professor of education at Towson University, where he teaches elementary methods courses to seniors as well as graduate-level, curricular coursework for practicing educators. His scholarly interests draw upon teacher inquiry, reflection, professional development, service learning, feminist pedagogies, and curricular (re)design as well as social constructivist meaning-making around notions of gender(ing), sexuality, race, and class.

Elva Reza-López is an assistant professor in the Bilingual Department at Boise State University where she teaches critical biliteracy classes and supervises preservice teachers in dual-language schools. A bilingual educator with more than 20 years of kindergarten through 12th-grade classroom experience, Dr. Reza-López advocates for teachers' as cultural workers and humanizing the educational system for a more just and democratic society.

William M. Reynolds teaches at Georgia Southern University and was a visiting professor at McGill University. He has authored, coedited and co-authored the books *Understanding Curriculum: An Introduction to the Study of Historical and Contemporary Curriculum Discourses* (1995), *Curriculum: A River Runs Through It* (2003), *Expanding Curriculum Theory: Dis/Positions and Lines of Flight* (2004) and *The Civic Gospel: A Political Cartography of Christianity* (2009). He is the series editor for *Cultural Studies: Toward Transformative Curriculum and Pedagogy*. His current interests are youth studies, critical pedagogy, cultural studies, political theory, and their connection to curriculum studies.

Laura Rychly is a doctoral candidate in the curriculum studies program at Georgia Southern University. Her dissertation research is on how students in schools develop a sense-of-self that is a result of language exchanges between themselves and their teachers. This includes the relationship between language and thinking and how each influences the other.

Elinor A. Scheirer is a professor in the Department of Leadership, School Counseling, and Sport Management at the University of North Florida in Jacksonville, Florida, where she teaches courses in curriculum, foundations of education, pedagogy in elementary education, and qualitative research methodology. She is also a member of the doctoral faculty in educational leadership. Her research and writing have focused on the promotion of progressive elementary and secondary education, the requirements for curriculum dialogue and deliberation, qualitative research methodologies, and support for teacher empowerment.

Boni Wozolek is a doctoral student at Kent State University. Her scholarly interests focus on the intersection of curriculum, gender, and embodied ways of knowing. In addition to her role as full time mother, she teaches high school Spanish at a suburban school in Northeast Ohio.